Protests, Land Rights and Riots

In memory of our grandson, Lachie Morris
A little life, much loved

Protests, Land Rights and Riots

Postcolonial Struggles in Australia in the 1980s

Barry Morris

berghahn
NEW YORK · OXFORD
www.berghahnbooks.com

Published by
Berghahn Books
www.berghahnbooks.com

This version
©2015 Berghahn Books

This version of *Protest, Land Rights and Riots* is published in arrangement with the
Australian Institute of Aboriginal and Torres Strait Islander Studies

©2013 Australian Institute of Aboriginal and Torres Strait Islander Studies

Not for sale in Australia or New Zealand.

Library of Congress Cataloging-in-Publication Data

Morris, Barry.
 [Protests, land rights and riots]
 Protests, land rights and riots : postcolonial struggles in Australia in the 1980s / Barry Morris.
  pages cm
 Previously published: Canberra : Aboriginal Studies Press, 2013.
 Includes bibliographical references and index.
 ISBN 978-1-78238-537-0 (hardback : alkaline paper) -- ISBN 978-1-78238-538-7 (ebook)
 1. Aboriginal Australians--Government relations--Australia--New South Wales--History--20th
century. 2. Aboriginal Australians, Treatment of--Australia--New South Wales--History--20th
century. 3. Aboriginal Australians--Land tenure--Australia--New South Wales--History--20th
century. 4. Aboriginal Australians--Civil rights--Australia--New South Wales--History--20th
century. 5. Protest movements--Australia--New South Wales--History--20th century. 6. Riots--
Australia--New South Wales--History--20th century. 7. Postcolonialism--Australia--New South
Wales--History--20th century. 8. Neoliberalism--Australia--New South Wales--History--20th
century. 9. New South Wales--Race relations--History--20th century. 10. New South Wales-
-Politics and government--20th century. I. Australian Institute of Aboriginal and Torres Strait
Islander Studies. II. Title.
 DU124.G68M67 2015
 333.3089'99150944--dc23

2014020320

British Library Cataloguing in Publication Data
A catalogue record for this book is available from the British Library

ISBN: 978-1-78238-537-0 hardback
ISBN: 978-1-78238-538-7 ebook

Contents

CONTENTS

Illustrations

Foreword

This book covers an important historical era for Koori people in New South Wales in that events such as Black Deaths in Custody and Land Rights impacted and burnt into the consciousness of political and public opinion. The ramifications were such that from an international perspective Australia had an 'image problem' as our country was being branded the 'new South Africa'.

In August of 1987, my then dear brother-in-law, Lloyd Boney was found dead in a police cell in Brewarrina, in far-western New South Wales. The Prime Minister, Mr Robert Hawke, immediately called for a Royal Commission Into Aboriginal Deaths in Custody (RCIADIC). This enquiry would uncover a 'mass social problem' in regards to the State, the judiciary and the policing procedures in communities across New South Wales, especially in highly populated Aboriginal areas. A week after the RCIADIC was announced the Brewarrina Riot occurred and lengthy court proceedings followed over a five-year period. As a central figure in the so-called Riot, I was so appalled and outraged by innocent men being put on trial, who were not even involved in any form or manner. I contacted Dr Barry Morris and Dr Tom Ernst to act as observers during the trial of the Brewarrina 17, as we became known.

I would argue that the book says a lot about the difficult relations between Aborigines and the police at the time, which were tense and involved acts of violent conflict. Despite the commendable recommendations of the RCIADIC and other inquiries, the troubles continue with further deaths in custody since 1987, overrepresentation of Kooris in gaols, be they male or female or juvenile, and 'no-go zones' unless in police numbers to quell disturbances in Koori communities.

How can our youth have faith in the future when old habits die hard and they are being subjected to racism in the education system and other public service agencies, the same as those before them experienced. This is not something new. In 2013, as it was in the 1970s and 1980s, the 'problem' has not been solved and with no end in sight it would seem to overcome it.

If this book achieves anything, it will show how things happened and will give a sense of life of Indigenous people at time that was filled with promise and struggle. Back then, it was not seen as false hope or pie-in-the-sky mentality to want to be treated as equal. We demanded it, as did those before us. I believe that these 'troubles' and the conflicts between Aborigines and the police, and, more importantly, between ourselves, can be overcome if we stop looking in the wrong direction for the right answers.

Yours in Unity,
Albert (Sonny) Bates

Acknowledgements

This book has been many years in the making. It has grown in fits and starts over this period. As a result, the intellectual influences and scholarly engagement and my personal gratitude have similarly grown for those who have supported this research in numerous ways.

My deepest gratitude goes to Sonny Bates, Arthur Murray and Arthur Orcher, who invited me, Tom Ernst and Kerry Zubrinich to a trial that, unbeknownst to me, would significantly alter my understandings of the world I live in. I am also grateful in particular to Colin 'Cody' Campbell and the members of Kempsey Regional Aboriginal Land Council, who, in 1990, supported my research at a time when the government was determining their fate. The world I observed, they actually lived through.

In particular, I would like to thank Sonny Bates, for without his support and encouragement this book would be significantly poorer. Similarly, I owe an intellectual debt to Andrew Lattas and Bruce Kapferer, who have always supported, challenged and nurtured my anthropological research. They have continually enlivened my enthusiasm for anthropology through their critical engagement with the discipline, as well as by being available for political discussions and the 'quiet drink', plied with wry humour. A major intellectual and personal debt is due to Gillian Cowlishaw, who saw the possibilities of this research from its earliest stages and has patiently and steadfastly fostered this project ever since. We have had countless exchanges and spent immeasurable time discussing this research in a field where she has continually made a significant contribution. Her knowledge and inputs have been indispensable. Jeremy Beckett has been instrumental in sparking a continuing interest through his excellent writings in this field of anthropological research. Like Gillian, Jeremy did research and writing that addressed issues in a manner and in a field that most Australian anthropologists preferred to ignore. In their research, Indigenous people were never the exclusive subjects of ethnographic analysis, but considered in terms of their interactions with and responses to a non-Indigenous world that encapsulated them. The research would not have begun without Tom Ernst and Kerry Zubrinich, who have always remained generously supportive. Chapter Five owes much to Kerry's insights. This circle of friends all graciously read chapters of this book and provided inspiration and invaluable feedback that shaped and improved the final version of this manuscript. The flaws, omissions and oversights are mine.

The path to a completed manuscript was not short and I have been fortunate to have institutional support from Charles Sturt University in the form of sabbatical leave, in the early 1990s, which aided the then new research in a major way. Institutional support in terms of research funding was also received from The University of Newcastle in the form of a new staff research grant in the mid-1990s. More recently, in 2008, the Centre for Asia Pacific Social Transformation Studies provided editorial assistance to a rough manuscript that was given clearer shape and clarity by the editing work of Maria Friej. During the development of this manuscript parts of some chapters have been previously published in the *Critique of Anthropology* in 2005 (Chapter 1), in the *Journal of Australian Studies* in 1995 (Chapter 3) and in *Oceania* in 2001 (Chapter 5).

I have also been fortunate to be well supported by the good company of family and friends. Ken Woodbine, Phil Mahoney and John Terrey know me well and have long been available to keep me on track travelling through some dark and difficult Australian terrain. And last, but not least, I thank my wife, Chris, who has shared this long journey with me right down to the inevitable reading of final proofs. My children, Dan, Nick and Evan, have grown up listening to the discussions of the events and the participants for what must seem to them time immemorial.

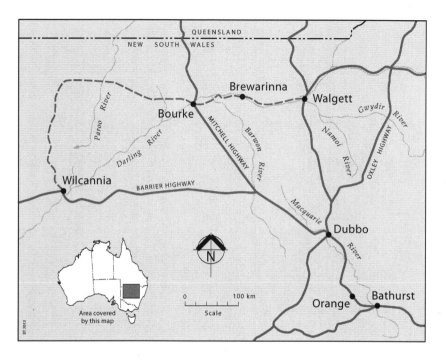

Map of mid NSW.

Introduction

The colonial system lives on as long as the contradictions it left behind are not truly surmounted ... (original emphasis, Bourdieu and Sayad 2004:470)

The legacy of colonialism casts a long shadow over the political landscape of many modern nations. This book considers the complex fate of Indigenous peoples in settler colonial states, where struggles for autonomy and recognition are politically convoluted and where legal and institutional integration pervades everyday life. Not only must Indigenous rights be achieved without the abject flight of the colonisers, but the historical trajectory of 'breakaway settler colonialism' (Byrd 2011) seeks no less than to transform its own subordinate colonial status into an autonomous, self-governing entity — a transformation 'primarily characterized by indigenous deter-ritorialisation accompanied by a sustained denial of any state-making capacity for indigenous peoples' (Veracini 2010:105). This 'sustained denial' takes many forms.

Even where the colonisers have been forcibly ejected (as in Algeria, referred to in the quote above), contradictions are never fully resolved. In the contemporary polity of settler colonial states, as Byrd (2011) argues, the act of colonial dispossession is displaced as irreversible.[1] In the United States, however, an unresolved tension continues between the original colonial dispossession and the settler colonial state's 'national construction of itself as an ever more perfect multicultural, multiracial democracy' (Byrd 2011:123). In Australia dispossession is erased and substituted by 'progressive' remedial discourses. Addressing social inequality and rejecting racism are the focal points for knowledge of the social and economic marginalisation of 'minority' groups. In Australia neoliberal policies invoked a variation on a populist form of historical erasure, whereby Indigenous rights threatened to divide postcolonial settler futures.[2] The contradiction that the prosperity and freedoms of the post-settler state rest upon the dispossession of its Indigenous peoples is neither effectively 'left behind' nor 'truly surmounted'.

Protests, Land Rights and Riots captures the contradictory forces that characterised the politics of Indigenous recognition in Australia from the 1970s onwards. This period marked a new era that may be defined as postcolonial — by which I do not mean *after colonialism*, but, as Bruyneel (2007:xviii) asserts, the 'consistencies, contingencies, and fissures in the practices of colonization and decolonization'. Bruyneel (2007:xviii) continues, 'the colonizer's impositions, be they cultural, economic, or structural, are never fully exhumed from the colonial context, and the so-called colonized are never fully without agency or independent identity'. This book explores the interplay between the cultural, economic and institutional forces that have developed in a postcolonial state. Social and political agency and the open possibility for change and recognition occurred for Indigenous peoples on a hitherto unparalleled scale. For a generation of Indigenous men and women, the period from the 1970s to the 1990s was one of unprecedented political agency and legislative change in their struggles for recognition of postcolonial rights.

This study provides a social analysis of the way such gains were recomposed in the ensuing political effects of neoliberal policy to conform to its own patterns of governance. It is less concerned with neoliberal economics than with the way neoliberal policy takes on a particular political emphasis when applied to post-settler colonial societies. The political processes occurred against a background of epochal economic change. Rural communities, where significant Aboriginal populations continue to live, experienced major structural changes to their social world, which led to social fragmentation and unparalleled unemployment. The period marked the emergence of neoliberal political ideology that reshaped the state's role in the economy and redefined government programs and services. New social forces were unleashed and clashed as a post-settler colonial state grappled with its past anew.

Neoliberal ideology is conspicuous for its belligerent free market approach to economic development and demands for trade liberalisation, privatisation of state industries, and deregulation of markets and wages. The thorough economic and political realignments set in train political changes that continued in the following decades. Economic development occurred at a national and local level and had significant consequences for working people in general. The automation of production, the casualisation of labour and the deregulation of wages combined to destroy much of the pre-existing patterns of work and the culture that surrounded it in rural communities. For Indigenous people, who typically engaged in non-unionised, low-waged seasonal work, changing rural conditions made life more difficult, tenuous and uncertain.

My analysis considers Indigenous relations in an era in which Indigenous status, cultural recognition and representation were a major locus of political support and contestation. The substantive research is situated in New South Wales, where quite dramatic changes in Indigenous recognition occurred in the 1980s. Subsequently, in the 1990s, these were undermined by an emerging new political orthodoxy that overlapped and contested previous Indigenous policy. Earlier policies of land rights, self-determination, anti-racism and affirmative action, and a revised history of Australia, had attempted to redress the growing demands of Indigenous peoples. Such developments were not uncontested; indeed, they generated considerable opposition as Australia moved towards a more inclusive post-settler colonial society.

This book studies several 'riots' and protests that punctuated Indigenous politics in New South Wales. The period became notorious for what were described as 'racial tensions' in rural towns as much as for experiments in Indigenous rights. References to racism, rather than self-determination and land rights, reflect aspects inherent to settler colonialism in Australia. Barsh (1988:97) accurately observed that 'It is difficult for a North American to escape the feeling that Aborigines suffer the combined fate of American Indians

and American blacks. That is an unusually heavy burden of alienation and discrimination for any people to bear.'

The term 'racism' is frequently used by Indigenous and non-
Indigenous commentators and institutions.[3] In an era of anti-racist
policies and revisions of colonial history in Australia, the explanatory
power of racism is less effective in analysing the Indigenous situation
as it is a focus for some of the cherished moral certainties of racism.
The shadow of racism has not disappeared, but the complexity of the
contemporary situation can be more fully understood by unravelling
the contradictions that underpin post-settler politics.

The study begins with the dramatic events in Brewarrina in
New South Wales and the events surrounding the 1986 'Brewarrina
riot' and the trials that followed. The event differed from other
disturbances between Aborigines and police in the 1980s because
a television crew recorded the confrontation — and it became a
major national media event. It led to an extensive criminal trial in
a regional court and became part of the deliberations of the Royal
Commission into Aboriginal Deaths in Custody (RCIADIC). As
Chapter 1 sets out, the Brewarrina riot acted as a switch point in
a political struggle over the nature and direction of government
policy in Indigenous affairs. This riot provided fertile grounds for
the reworking and reassertion of conservative polity that emerged
in New South Wales and later interventions of neoliberal policy in
relation to Indigenous affairs.

Such events have long been the subject of anthropological analysis.
It is the atypicality of these events (rather than their use as 'apt illus-
trations' for ethnographic generalisation) that provides significance
(see Kapferer 2010:1–27). The atypical event requires close attention
because it expresses conflicts that capture the social and political
tensions that are obscured in the orderly routine of ongoing social
practices. The focus on protests and riots is not so much on the
spectacle of violence itself, but on the structures of its existence.
Indeed, an analysis of spectacular violent acts might sometimes
obfuscate more indirect forms of structural violence.

What began with a trial opened into an exploration of the social
conditions of existence for Indigenous peoples in New South Wales
as a neoliberal epoch emerged. The impact of neoliberal economics is
well established in the literature. Evidence from the 1980s makes an

emphatic case for the period as one of major structural adjustment. In particular, the experience of fracture and social fragmentation in rural communities was intense and definitive in reshaping rural life. In 1985 a nationally organised protest rally took place in the nation's capital, Canberra. As an estimated 40,000 rural producers assembled on the lawns of Parliament House, the rural unrest produced by social adversity reached its climax (Lawrence 1987:12). Farmer militancy against foreclosures of bankrupt farms reached its high point in the same year as media attention focused on farmers rallying against the evictions of fellow farmers and their desperate plight (Lawrence 1987:1). In the previous 15 years, the Bureau of Agricultural Economics estimated that 19,000 farmers had left agriculture; the farm workforce declined by 32,000 and the total rural workforce by 100,000 (Lawrence 1987:13). The general decline in employment opportunities facilitated a corresponding decline and withdrawal of public services and facilities (transport, education, health, banking and small business) from rural areas and small towns. In 1947, according to Lawrence (1996:48–9), 31 per cent of Australia's population lived in rural communities, but by the mid-1980s only 12 per cent of the population lived in rural communities. Rural Australia in the late twentieth century was not a social world open to possibility, but one oriented towards the foreclosure of possibility.

Social adversity was evident across many rural communities. The rate of unemployment in rural areas was two to three times higher than the national average (Lawrence 1987:48).[4] By the early 1990s, 33 of the 37 poorest electorates in Australia were located in rural regions and 'the general health of rural people [was], by urban standards, very poor ... [with] above average rates of premature mortality and death through heart disease, cancer, suicide and tuberculosis' (Lawrence 1996:335). The social circumstance of many rural communities' most marginal populations, Indigenous Australians, was invariably worse. An unemployment survey of Indigenous people in New South Wales found only 17.7 per cent of males and 12.3 per cent of females were employed (Ross 1988:3). The survey consistently recorded all unemployment rates as above 70 per cent.[5] The impact of these astonishing rates of unemployment in rural communities on issues of poverty and inequality as part of the general decline in economic conditions remains unaddressed.

Such significant economic decline had a major impact upon Indigenous and non-Indigenous rural populations.[6] The period marked the collapse of small rural centres, the increase in migration to urban and regional cities, and the fragmentation and dispersal of working populations that had been reliant on local industry.[7] What was clearly left in the wake of the new economic order was that the most marginal populations carried the burden of the inequalities. In addition, the demands of new welfare measures on social welfare recipients rendered access to benefits more difficult and reduced their value. Both structural forces and government policies were involved. This political–economic transformation took place in less than a generation and has continued for following generations.

Policies implemented by neoliberal reforms do not address such profound structural adjustments, but celebrate them as the triumph of market forces. Political decisions and choices are translated into questions of economic accountability or how to maximise the efficient use of resources and are treated as if they are not social but economic choices. Neoliberal forms of governance are redirected to facilitate individual responsibility, choice and enterprise as part of the 'enabling state'. In neoliberal programs it is as if there is no such thing as involuntary or structural unemployment, but only voluntary unemployment. The economic decline in rural areas would seemingly be arrested by state-funded retraining in which individuals avail themselves of one or another program. This is not so much a with-drawal of the state, but its reregulation into new forms of intervention and monitoring of marginal and unemployed populations.

These social conditions derive in part from specific economic circumstances. However, they should not obscure the reregulation of the political conditions that facilitate the institutional scaffold-ing for such economic changes. As Wacquant (2012:68) succinctly says, neoliberal reforms involve 'the remaking and redeployment of the state as a core agency that actively fabricates subjectivities, social relations and collective representations suited to making the fiction of markets real and consequential'.

Neoliberal rationalities seek to transform prevailing subjectivi-ties. Welfare state interventions do not emancipate individuals from the shortcomings of unregulated market forces but imprison them in passive forms of dependency. Dependency, in these political discourses, is regarded as an 'incomplete state in life: normal in a child, abnormal in an adult' (Fraser and Gordon 1994:309). Poverty and inequality are reframed in terms of welfare dependency and the poor as victims of the welfare state. Indeed, the state's responsibility to those unemployed and in poverty is removed as policies based upon 'enabling' programs to facilitate individual 'self-actualisation' replace them. In such programs, unemployment ultimately reaffirms individual failure, incapacity and limited abilities. The low skilled face a future of poor wages, intermittent and casualised labour or unemployment, an endless search for jobs, compulsory training schemes and volunteer charity work.

In Australia public discourses explaining Indigenous disadvantage in terms of 'passive welfare' criticise previous policy as inducing 'passive dependency' (Pearson 2000; Sutton 2009). In effect, the issue of poverty and inequality is seen as a problem created by an overly generous welfare system that encourages individual indolence. Being welfare dependent, it is argued, inhibits Indigenous self-realisation. Similarly, self-determination programs have produced adverse effects not only for individuals but also for communities over recent generations. In part, such assertions conform to neoliberal ideology that welfare and dependence are in keeping with beliefs that government is the problem rather than the solution and that poverty is a problem *for* society rather than *of* society.

This book offers a counterview that emphasises the institutional and structural dimensions of social conflict and the economic and political interests fuelling such transformations. This analysis is influenced by the work of anthropologist Paul Farmer (2005), who emphasises 'structural violence' as the systemic component of marginalisation and social inequality. This conceptualisation rejects the neoliberal emphasis solely on individual actors and their actions: 'such suffering is "structured" by historically given (and often economically driven) processes that conspire — whether through routine, ritual, or, as is more commonly the case, the hard surfaces of life — to constrain agency' (Farmer 2005:40).

My focus on the structural context involves economics and politics in which new social tensions and social configurations emerge and their interrelations are played out. The study involves politicians, political campaigns, bureaucrats, parliamentary committees, legislation and judicial procedures. State institutions provide powerful mechanisms for the implementation of policy and create categories that reshape public and individual identity. In particular, I stress that governments that advocate neoliberal philosophy or polity have reframed the political choices, as well as economic imperatives.

In Chapters 2 and 3, I consider in more detail the implementation of neoliberal approaches to Indigenous policy and sustained political opposition to Indigenous rights in the context of the land rights movement of the 1980s. In championing the primacy of the individual against the claims of social collectives, the contrast between the imperatives that have driven neoliberal polity and the assumptions that underpinned land rights legislation could not have been starker. Yet the demand by the New South Wales government for repeal and reform of the 1980s recognition of Indigenous rights was itself subject to compromise. The new government's attempt to repeal the *Aboriginal Land Rights Act 1983* was not framed in terms of earlier opposition to treating Aborigines differently to other Australians; instead, opposition was set out in neoliberal terms of economic efficiencies and land rights as a gross misuse of financial resources. The significant new policy direction advocated the 'mainstreaming' of Indigenous affairs and sought reincorporation of specific Aboriginal services into existing state institutions. The prospect of land rights had potentially changed the relationship between Indigenous peoples by experimenting with a new form of citizenship that involved limited forms of recognition and new forms of Indigenous participation *within* the state.

Chapter 3 discusses the new forms of political governance. The ascendancy of neoliberal policies reregulated rather than deregulated the arenas of state interest and intervention and fell heavily on disadvantaged and marginal groups. The novel intertwining of neoliberal economics and conservative thought in Anglo-American countries became the new political, as well as economic, orthodoxy. Not only did the political reforms shift to more punitive obligations on welfare recipients but to a more punitive approach to criminal justice. The striking consequence of the advent of neoliberal politics in social justice is, as Michael Tonry (1994) argues, that 'disadvantaged visible minority groups' in Anglo-American countries are likely to be in correctional institutions. In the 1980s and 1990s the situation of Indigenous Australians proved no exception. In New South Wales Aborigines also became the focal point for a politics of fear and were subjected to law and order campaigns.

The historical context developed in the 1970s, when Indigenous populations in rural New South Wales were no longer legally confined to segregated spaces of managed reserves. They had progressively gained equal rights and access to public facilities — the school, the hospital, the streets, the hotel, and local parks and swimming pools — thus, all discriminatory legislation had been removed (see Morris 1989). Correspondingly, a massive increase occurred in the overrepresentation of Indigenous people in the criminal justice system. By 2007 Indigenous Australians made up 24 per cent of the total prisoner population, although they comprised 2.4 per cent of the national population (Wong 2008:3). RCIADIC figures released in 1991 showed that 14 per cent of the total prison population was Indigenous, which was regarded as outrageous at the time. Since the RCIADIC findings and recommendations, the proportion has nearly doubled. In the context of these troubling statistics, I explore the forms of governance used in the shifts and changes ushered in by the new political order. In the contemporary context, to what extent did the regulation, monitoring and control of the Indigenous population of rural towns become a function of policing, the courts, juvenile justice and the prisons? State regulation has not been withdrawn, but its arenas of interest have changed.

Lastly, this anthropological study investigates the interface through which interlocking practices and relations are organised in complex social fields. The content of our analysis of the social world is not exhausted in the details at the level of face-to-face interactions, which provide more description than analysis. In contrast, this study of social disadvantage and suffering concentrates on the historical, structural and institutional forms of violence. Asymmetrical power relations cannot be accounted for only by detailing the courses of action evidenced in the immediate conditions any more than violence can be understood solely in terms of individual actors and physical injury; they can, however, be accounted for more inclusively through the institutional relations that order and sustain them. As Wolfe (1999:163) reminds us, settler colonialism 'is a structure not an event'. Post-settler colonial contexts require an analysis of the broad social and economic configurations and systemic forms of governance that pattern interrelationships of marginalisation. The impact of structural processes is critical to understanding recent political interventions.

Neoliberal politics, in part, rejects a politics of recognition. Addressing historical and cultural injustice through recognition and Indigenous rights is seen as irrelevant and, at its most extreme, as a hindrance to Indigenous advancement.[8] The pervasiveness of this critique is such that self-determination is bundled together with the recognition of land rights and native title and the creation of decision-making Indigenous organisations, all of which are deemed to have failed.[9] The success of neoliberalism is to transform political and economic strategies into necessary and unavoidable interventions as if they occur without conflict. Bourdieu (1998:56–7) reminds us:

> What appears to us today as self-evident, as beneath consciousness and choice, has quite often been the stake of struggles and instituted only as a result of dogged confrontations between dominant and dominated groups. The major effect of historical evolution is to abolish history by relegating to the past, that is, to the unconscious, the lateral possibilities that it eliminated.

I argue in this book that there has never been a period when Indigenous political activism, dogged confrontations and struggles were more evident and sustained in contrast to current neoliberal-inspired critiques, which rendered Indigenous struggles indistinguishable from other forms of difference and inequality. These critiques of pre-existing Indigenous policies seek to rewrite the highly contested political arena in which self-determination emerged as passive compliance to Indigenous demands.

Ultimately, I seek to explore the complex ways a generation of Indigenous men and women advanced social and cultural recognition of postcolonial rights. The struggles and confrontations involved the alternative possibility and expectation that pervaded political aspirations. The book restores to the ledger an account of the political agency, and the struggles for visibility and for recognition of postcolonial rights. The convergence of the structural adjustments that neoliberalism unleashed in the economy was no less evident in the new state forms of governance applied to Indigenous issues of cultural recognition and representation. The politics of recognition did open up the potential for emancipatory change as a result of the instability engendered in terms of the pre-existing category of 'Aborigine', which created a space of new political possibilities. Such engagements with mainstream politics and the law served to make visible the erasure of histories of dispossession.

Chapter 1

Crisis of identity: Aboriginal politics, the media and the law

'Blood on the streets the night a town exploded' reported the front-page headlines of the *Sydney Morning Herald* (*SMH*) on 17 August 1987, framing the melee that become known as the 'Brewarrina riot' as a violent eruption between Aborigines and police in a small country town. Despite its characterisation as a riot, the civil disturbance was not an outbreak of frenzied communal violence, but a specific confrontation between state authority and the local Indigenous people of a small country town. The violence and anger were directed specifically at the police and the clients of one local hotel. For these reasons, it is more appropriate to refer to the disturbance as a melee rather than a riot. The civil disturbance in Brewarrina was one of a number of confrontations between police and Indigenous peoples in New South Wales in the 1980s. In the previous year, violence had taken place between police and the Indigenous people of nearby Bourke, where extensive and indiscriminate damage was suffered throughout the commercial sector of the town (cf. Cowlishaw 2004). Such violence matched more readily the mayhem of a riot, yet the reportage of the Bourke confrontations caused scarcely a ripple compared to the full-blown media treatment that the Brewarrina riot generated.

The initial national response to the Brewarrina riot was one of disbelief and disavowal of its significance. The disavowal of the event was evident in the use of the video footage of the riot a couple of years later in the Australian Broadcasting Commission (ABC) national television documentary program *One Nation* (1991). The program questioned whether Australia's growing cultural diversity would lead to violent division. Could we live as one nation now that a variety of identities were recognised? The voiceover framed the opening scene, incorporating the 'riot' footage, by stating that the scene was 'more reminiscent of Brixton or Johannesburg than Australia'. The comparison inflates the scale and the duration of the Brewarrina riot significantly, but provides a sense of its dramatic impact. The violence is seen as having no national precedent; similes are drawn from outside Australia. It is as if violence and disruption are neither part of Australian history nor part of the fabric of social life, but must be learned or imported from outside sources.

What separated the Brewarrina riot from other disturbances between Aborigines and police in the 1980s was that a television crew recorded the confrontation. According to evidence submitted in the trial that followed some years later, the filming was a fortuitous event. The television crew had been in Brewarrina to cover the funeral of Lloyd Boney earlier in the day. The crew members were relaxing in their motel rooms with a beer when they heard the sounds of yelling from the park across from the motel, where they knew friends and relatives of the deceased were holding a wake. Hastily gathering their equipment, they scrambled out of the rooms, into the street, and immediately began filming.

The so-called 'Brewarrina riot' became a major media event. It led to a criminal trial in a regional court and was part of the deliberations of a Royal Commission. The riot is recorded in three different registers, each with its own specific account for public consumption. The media reportage at the time constructed the riot out of a search for social causes and their effects. By contrast, the criminal trial sought to draw from the riot specific individual acts and match them to particular violent attacks on police; that is, as crimes. In the third register, the riot became an inseparable part of an inquiry into one death investigated by a Royal Commission, set up to inquire into Aboriginal deaths in police custody, and the possible involvement of police and policing practices in relation to these deaths. In each case, the riot contrasted markedly with preparations for the upcoming bicentennial celebrations (26 January 1988), commemorating

200 years of European settlement in Australia, which were occurring at the same time.

My analysis of the riot is part of a broader research interest in the shifts and changes of social and political processes of the Australian state that form such a critical part in the continual defining and redefining of Aboriginal identity. The Brewarrina riot occurred on the cusp of change, when political mobilisation was moving from a period characterised by welfare state reform towards a more neoliberal polity. The changing relationship between Aborigines and state institutions has been explored often: what is often ignored, however, is the conflictual political landscape in which those relations take shape and the way political discourse condenses around particular events.

Since Aborigines have been dispossessed and socially marginalised for the major part of settler colonial history, Indigenous insignificance within the nation has been the discursive norm. Forms of biological racism that rendered the Aborigine as irredeemable and doomed to extinction were replaced in the early decades of the twentieth century by policies that increasingly sought assimilation. Biological essentialism was replaced by the view that Aborigines were socially and culturally deficient products of their environment and to change them one needed to change their environment (see Morris 1989). Policies of assimilation were developed through Aboriginal confinement on reserves and the removal of many children to institutional environments to retrain and transform their identity and subjectivity.

The logic of settler colonial states has been to deny the legitimacy of the Indigenous population. The aim in the assimilation era was to transform Indigenous beliefs and morals, values, and behaviours to conform to the norms of mainstream society. The homogenising of the 'Aborigine' was a state invention as part of a universal application of policy towards the management of people to be dealt with under 'native affairs'. Officially, cultural inferiority replaced biological inferiority as the source of social difference. Yet the shift from biology to culture did not herald significant changes regarding racism and social exclusion at a local level. Institutional domination and the local social hierarchy gain expression through cultural inferiority and racism expressed in the unquestionable superiority of settler colonial society.

In the 1960s the Aborigine emerged as a new political subject and created tensions and new alignments in the Australian political landscape. Central to the new Indigenous polity was the increasing visibility of their struggles. In 1965 the Freedom Ride, led by Aboriginal activist Charles Perkins, travelled through a number of country towns in New South Wales and confronted the persistence of policies and practices of segregation in local towns.[1] The political campaign created a great deal of media attention and condemnation of rural exclusionary practices that were deemed racist in the national and international media. Much of the television footage covered local white communities in violent confrontations with the 'protesters' who sought Aboriginal entry into local swimming pools from which they were banned. The Freedom Ride symbolised the beginning of a more assertive Indigenous politics, but, more importantly, one to be carried out on a national stage.

Indigenous activism placed a national focus on local forms of rural discrimination against Aborigines and drew attention to the treatment they received on reserves managed by the Aborigines Welfare Board (AWB), which was abolished shortly afterwards in 1969.[2] The AWB's alleged function had been to retrain the Aboriginal population for its gradual assimilation into mainstream society. The segregation of housing, schooling and hospital care and the dismantling of local discriminatory practices — night curfews, segregated seating in cinemas, and the ban of Aborigines from swimming pools and drinking in hotels — were brought to an end. In effect, the granting of equal rights led to a realignment of both state and local social practices, which guaranteed Aborigines a great deal more social and political autonomy in rural towns. The AWB no longer determined where people could live, how they raised their families, where they travelled or who could visit them. Not only did people have greater personal autonomy, but potentially they could also move from their position at the bottom of the social hierarchy.

Importantly, public debate about Aborigines was no longer dominated by local rural attitudes and sentiments, but increasingly became defined as a national issue. In the new alignments that followed, local white-dominated rural communities in regional areas lost control of the agenda involving the management of Aborigines. The alignments were given expression in new government policies, and, in particular, the creation of Indigenous representative structures and specialised services. Such changes reflected a growing recognition of the rights of Aborigines, not just as equal rights, but as rights as Indigenous peoples. This emphasis created a new political landscape that moved beyond political agendas restricted to social and civil rights. The changes reflected the political dominance of metropolitan agendas. Indigenous struggles emerged in tandem with the urban-based political force of multiculturalism, as immigrant groups resisted assimilation policies that had hitherto characterised the expansion of the post-war welfare state. The metropolitan polity was increasingly receptive to revisions of welfare state policy that extended citizenship to incorporate within public culture the specific social demands of immigrant and Indigenous groups.

For many rural communities, this produced a crisis of identity. Metropolitan centres took the role of guardians of the rights of Aborigines, and, often, the failure of rural communities to embrace this new diversity saw them characterised as redneck and racist. Rural communities saw local control falling from their grasp, and they became subjects of the moral scrutiny of the metropolitan press.

Increasing tension between Aborigines and the police also became significant in this period (Morris 2001). The Aboriginal Legal Service was established in response to the inadequacies of existing legal services, but also (from the view of 'Aboriginal activists') because 'Aboriginal people were regularly arrested without cause' (Lyons 1984:137). Police/ Indigenous relations became a major national issue when Aboriginal deaths in police custody generated national media scrutiny. In 1981 an Aboriginal youth, Eddy Murray, died in police custody in the New South Wales town of Wee Waa, under circumstances many thought sinister (Muirhead 1989). The coroner recorded an open finding on his death. Throughout the 1980s the media reported a succession of Aboriginal deaths in custody, and Aboriginal groups and others inten-sified their demands for a public inquiry. Pressure mounted on the federal government to call a Royal Commission. In the week following the death of Lloyd Boney in police custody in Brewarrina, the Prime Minister announced that a Royal Commission would be held into Aboriginal deaths in police custody.

The major shifts in Indigenous polity of this period produced new fault lines, as well as new social and political alignments. The social and political tensions crystallised in the Brewarrina riot. Polarised positions emerged in an engagement between rural and urban polities in relation to Indigenous peoples. The interpretations of the images of the Brewarrina riot revealed a split between those who saw them as affirming the need to curb a threatening Indigenous autonomy that produced the eruption of violence and those who saw it as evidence of the continuance of local redneck attitudes and discrimination. The Brewarrina riot acted as a switch point, where both the conservative and liberal positions contested the conditions of Aboriginal autonomy and polity within the Australian state. The images of the riot provided fertile grounds for the reworking and reassertion of a conservative polity, which was ultimately to gather impetus in the shift from welfare state to neoliberal forms of governance and policy.

The Brewarrina riot: a summary

In 1987 Brewarrina was in the throes of economic decline, part of a regional decline, which resulted from the collapse of the pastoral industry.[3] The 'Brewarrina riot' or 'Brewarrina funeral riot' occurred on the evening of Saturday, 15 August 1987, and followed the funeral of Lloyd Boney, the young Aboriginal man who had been found hanged by a football sock in a police cell nine days earlier. A wake had commenced in a local park earlier in the week and proceeded without incident. The mourners rejoined it after the funeral and hostilities

Figure 1: Funeral of Lloyd Boney (Fairfax Photos)

developed between the white patrons of an adjacent hotel and some Aboriginal people in the park. At this stage, the police intervened and a confrontation ensued and spilled out from the park. The wake came to an abrupt end. During the melee, police and Indigenous people confronted each other on the streets of Brewarrina. Four policemen were injured.

Details of these events demonstrate how the police (mis)perceptions are crucial elements in explaining the escalation of the violence. The police strategy to end the hostilities was to break up the wake and drive the mourners out of the park. Eight police officers, most of whom were equipped with riot gear, were dispatched from the local police station to the park. The police arrived separately in two police cars and assembled in two groups on the two sides of the park closest to the hotel, then, moving forward into the dimly lit park and beating their batons on riot shields, yelled at the mourners to get out of the park. The mourners did not comply and confronted the police. In the melee that followed, the police were forced to retreat to the street. A street confrontation followed between a large number of angry Aboriginal people who swore and shouted abuse at, and challenged, police who were standing in a single line along the street, with aluminium batons and shields at the ready. Bottles were thrown and smashed against a parked police car. Ultimately, the police retreated from the scene in their vehicles, one officer in an ambulance. For a short period, Aboriginal swearing and abuse was redirected at an individual holding a gun on the balcony of the hotel and an Aboriginal man systematically smashed the windows of the hotel. The so-called 'Brewarrina riot' had run its course; the wake was terminated and the park was deserted as people disappeared into the night of their own accord. Two trials arose from this event, and the arrest of 17 Indigenous people in Brewarrina in the days following the riot led to a lengthy legal process (see Chapter 5).[4]

The media riot[5]

The initial treatment of the Brewarrina riot in the metropolitan media differed little from the coverage of ghetto riots — the urban uprisings that formed part of the visibility of a black modernity in both Britain and the United States. The melee was framed as a violent eruption. A police statement from Sydney, released to the press and picked up by metropolitan and regional papers, stated simply that 'missiles had been thrown at police and the hotel starting at 7.30 pm on Saturday night' and 'the police were hailed with missiles as they stepped from their van' (*Western Advocate* (Bathurst), 17 August 1987, p. 3; *Central Western Daily* (Orange), 17 August 1987, p. 2).[6] The regional papers also recorded comments from the local court clerk, the resident spokesman of the town.

One regional newspaper, the *Daily Liberal* (Dubbo), ran the story that provided the causal framework for the accepted interpretation of the event and the focus of media interest in the following week.[7] The headline read, 'Alcohol given to rioting Aborigines: Witness' (*Daily Liberal*, 17 August 1987, p. 1). The report detailed the claims of an 'Aboriginal woman' who said she had seen ABC television journalists supply Aborigines with alcohol shortly before the riot. The witness alleged that she saw two female journalists take alcohol into the park and give it to the Aborigines, and then provoke them to riot. The Channel 7 television news carried the same story, expressed in an interview with the local court clerk, on its evening news (17 August 1987) (Goodall n.d.:9). The shire president supported the court clerk with a call for an investigation into what happened and into the 'Sydney media involvement'. On the following day a member of the state opposition demanded a police investigation into the claims (*Age*, 18 August 1987, p. 3).

The themes developed in the newspapers, as Goodall (n.d.)[8] points out, were reproduced in the television news coverage. After the initial extended showing of the 'riot footage' on the ABC, shortened versions of the footage inverted the chronology and visually affirmed the Aboriginal people as the perpetrators of the violence. The extended initial coverage was aired on Sunday, 16 August 1987, and followed the chronology of the uncut version: (1) the police car and police are situated in the street near the bank; (2) a number of individual confrontations between Aborigines and police occur in front of the bank; (3) an injured policeman is placed in an ambulance; (4) Aboriginal people shout abuse and attack the Brewarrina Hotel, throwing stones and bottles, and a man smashing a number of windows with an iron bar is depicted; and (5) the father of the publican holds a gun, which rests on the balcony of the upstairs verandah of the hotel (see Goodall n.d.:5, 6).[9] The common editing practice of privileging the most dramatic images to grab audience attention inverted the temporal sequence of events so that the man smashing the windows came before the police arrived.

The Channel 7 coverage presented the shortened version of the ABC footage, combined with the visual interviews of its own reporter, who was sent to Brewarrina on the Sunday. Only non-Aborigines were interviewed and only their views of events were aired in the segment. Channel 7 used the video footage that opened with the scene of Aboriginal people shouting abuse and attacking the Brewarrina Hotel and the man smashing a number of windows (Goodall n.d.).[10] The voiceover of the reporter describes the event as 'a melee, involving 120 drunken Aborigines' (Goodall n.d.:9). Within this reordering, there is a linking of cause and effect. The temporal sequence is reversed to reveal the 'truth' of the event in accordance with a white worldview. The drama is resolved and everything explained in a well-worn image: the drunken Aborigine.

The rendering of Aborigines as inebriates is an artefact of domination with its own history. As Langton (1993) has shown, the image of 'drunken Aborigines' has a long and extensive settler colonial history in Australia. The 'drunken Aborigine' is not only a person who cannot hold his or her alcohol (Langton 1993:199), but a product of European colonial contempt. The notion encodes a version of the white man's burden. As Langton (1993:205) argues, the 'drunken Aborigine' is representative of 'living a fantasy of wanting to become like the white man, but unable to do so'. The Aborigine is defined not so much in terms of what he or she is not, but what he or she cannot be. An equivalent status is conceded only to be simultaneously withdrawn, because the Aborigines' attempt to be un-Aboriginal continually fails. The drunken Aborigine becomes the object of contempt, censure and reform.

In addition to the spectre of the drunken Aborigine, the television reportage, like the newspaper reports, injected a local register on the interpretation of the events. Local whites interviewed and quoted in the Channel 7 report constructed the history of the town as 'quite peaceful' and stated that the violence was caused by 'Aboriginal stirrers from out of town' (Goodall n.d.:9). The local accent is distinctive as it seeks to assert non-complicity in the events, seemingly to forestall the positioning of the town as racist and redneck by the 'Sydney media'. Town spokesmen conveyed the view that no problems or tensions existed within the town and displaced such problems as stemming from the actions of outsiders from the city. The Channel 7 coverage, in effect, was ordered in terms of the interpretive framework of the local whites. The temporally reordered footage and the voiceover statements confirm the actuality of white rural discourses of the riot. The ABC footage ultimately gave an empirical accent to such interpretive frameworks. The image of the drunken Aborigine provided a code for public consumption that made for a readily knowable explanation.

Local political representatives, who focused on the role of the television crew in the riot, led an assertive defence of the reputation of the rural town. In the following days, the sitting National Party member for Parkes, Michael Cobb, took the issue into the arena of federal politics. An article titled 'ABC lashed over riot coverage' reported that on 22 August 1987 in federal parliament Cobb claimed that he had received a number of allegations about ABC crew members supplying alcohol to Aborigines and added new evidence to substantiate the claims of ABC involvement (*SMH*, 23 September 1987, p. 9). He claimed that an ABC crew member had withdrawn $177 from an ABC account and put it into an account in her own name and then withdrawn $1000. The connection between the ABC and Aborigines involved in the riot was supported by the claim that later in the day Aborigines were seen with $100 notes. Cobb found further corroborating evidence of ABC involvement in the fact that after the film crew left Brewarrina they went on assignment to New Caledonia, where more racial riots occurred, and he suggested that this crew instigated both riots (*SMH*, 23 September 1987, p. 9). The New South Wales Police Association added its own weight to the claims by demanding the Commonwealth Ombudsman investigate the ABC.

The allegations that the ABC incited the riot had moved rapidly from the domain of local knowledge to the arena of national and international politics. On the following day, in an article, 'Riot drinks claims sparks bank inquiry', Cobb's allegations were rejected (*SMH*, 24 September 1987, p. 3). The article explained the circumstances of the withdrawal and rejected the connections inferred between (1) the withdrawal of money and Aborigines seen with $100 notes as circumstantial and unsubstantiated and (2) the film crew inciting riots in Brewarrina and New Caledonia. The news film crew in Brewarrina was not the same as the *Four Corners* film crew in New Caledonia. The *Four Corners* crew had been in Brewarrina, but had flown out the afternoon prior to the riot. For the politicians, the defence of their own local electoral constituency was given an added political edge as the focus on the ABC, a government-funded institution, carried with it a misuse of public money. Unlike the commercial channels, the ABC was seen as the prominent voice of left-liberal metropolitan concern on Indigenous issues.

Local white constructions, expressed through political representatives, dominated debate about the causes of the riot. The veracity of the local knowledge, sourced to an anonymous local newspaper informant and anonymous local constituents, and given currency through the local coroner, court clerk and federal member, dominated national media coverage and explanations. Two major themes remain consistent in this explanation: (1) outsiders meddling in the town's affairs incited the riot and (2) it was Aborigines in a state of drunkenness who rioted. The Indigenous people had been primed to act through the cynical manipulation of metropolitan journalists, outsiders to the town.

The shire president's criticism of a previously published article on race relations in the *Sydney Morning Herald* echoed the sentiment that outsiders who do not know the practical difficulties of managing Aborigines created problems. The article, 'Drinkers know their place in Bre' (*SMH*, 8 August 1987, p. 13), described racial discrimination and segregation in Brewarrina by using examples of the 'out of town fringe dwelling' and unhealthy 'shanty town' existence of Aborigines and the segregated nature of drinking in hotels. Non-Aborigines drank at one hotel and Aborigines at the other. In the local regional newspaper, the shire president said that the article was one-sided and caused unrest in the town and unwarranted outside intervention (*Daily Liberal*, 17 August 1987, p. 1). Minimising the existence of problems within the town was an overriding concern. The focus was shifted from the town to the ABC, the 'Sydney media', which allegedly incited the riot by, in the first account, directly supplying Aborigines with alcohol, or, in Cobb's revised version, via the withdrawal of $1000 and its distribution to Aborigines. In Cobb's account, it was the ABC film crew that brought disorder, regardless of location (that is, even in New Caledonia). The claim of cynical manipulation of the event by members of the city media preserves the interests of the rural or bush community, which set up a staunch defence of the town against counter claims that it was racist and redneck.

If the ABC film crew was constructed as the catalyst of the riot, this dovetailed with the second theme that the active participants were drunken Aborigines. The ABC crew exploited not the underlying social tensions, but an inherent Aboriginal weakness for alcohol and the loss of bodily and mental control that follows. The catalyst for such events was the outsider, but the agent of the riot was the intoxicated, and hence undisciplined, behaviour of Indigenous people. Their intoxicated behaviour was seen as the locus of the public disorder and an expression of irrational violence as opposed to the rational manipulation of them by the (white) ABC news team.

The images of the riot and the considerable coverage given to rural interpretation on a national scale provided impetus for a regrouping of a conservative polity. The advance of policies that enhanced Aboriginal autonomy had been opposed by a conservative politics. Representations of a drunken and violent Aboriginality repositioned the primacy of issues of law and order and directly challenged the direction and results of Aboriginal policy. Rural communities clawed back some of the moral high ground they had lost to a metropolitan polity as the riot was represented as a spectacle of the Aboriginal problem. At the local level, the reaffirmation of the Aboriginal problem relieved the moral crisis of white status in the town brought about in an era of new reforms. The riot, as an atypical event, expressed conflicts that captured the social and political tensions, which were in a state of flux and were opening up to new possibilities. The metropolitan centre held its grip, but the political complexion and its direction had changed.

The dominant discourse of the Aborigine in the riot was reduced to its most powerful symbolic form, the drunken Aborigine. Although contradictory or competing discourses have the power to disrupt dominant cultural understandings, they do not necessarily 'destroy the force of the operation of the hierarchical principle in culture any more . . . than the fact that "race" is not a valid scientific category . . . undermines its social and symbolic effectuality' (Hall 1996:302). The fact that dominant white discourses compete to produce divergent cultural readings does not mean that determinate, hierarchical social relations cease to dominate. As Hall (1996:302) asserts, the 'fact that a cultural field cannot be stabilised . . . does not prevent the exercise in boundary construction being attempted'. In the media coverage, the Aborigine remained the object of study to be explained, defended, criticised or censured.

Local white discourses about the riot were not the only constructions of the events, nor did they go unchallenged. Indeed, at the height of the controversy, in an article titled 'What if they gave a riot and nobody came', a reporter rejected the claim that the media could have organised the riot (*SMH*, 18 August 1987, p. 18). The *Sydney Morning Herald* developed an empathetic line, which focused on the social and economic inequality and the segregation evident between Aborigines and whites in Brewarrina as evidence of racial discrimination. Following the death of Lloyd Boney, the *Sydney Morning Herald* had published two articles, 'Drinkers know their place in Bre' (8 August 1987, p. 13, discussed earlier) and 'Boney's fight on in Barwon's rubbish, death in custody' (10 August 1987, p. 8), which drew attention to the disadvantaged social existence of Aborigines in the town.

An editorial, 'A riot in Brewarrina', foregrounded the racial problems in Brewarrina and saw the riot as an expression of the problems in the town (*SMH*, 18 August 1987, p. 16). Drawing upon Israeli anthropologist Emmanuel Marx, the editorial argued that the riot was an expression of one of two types of violence. The first type, 'coercive violence', is seen in the violent strategies deployed by terrorists such as the *Irish Republican Army*. The second type is 'appealing violence', which characterises the actions of socially disadvantaged groups that are 'at the end of their tether'. The editorial said that appealing violence is a typical response for social groups like the Indigenous people in Brewarrina, who lived as socially disadvantaged slum dwellers.

The editorial exercised its own form of closure. An Indigenous rioter on the night was quoted as saying, 'All the time white people killing Aborigines. It's been going on for 200 years' (*SMH*, 18 August 1987, p. 16). The statement relays a sense of anger and outrage that may have referred to the death of Lloyd Boney in police custody, but it doubles as a general statement of colonial dispossession. The utterance invokes a legacy of settler colonial violence against Indigenous peoples, the physical vulnerability of those who see themselves, as Aborigines, as potentially sharing the same fate as Lloyd Boney. The spectre of cumulative, ongoing violence renders whites as the agents of an unending violence. Violence is an integral part of the structuring of social relations and, more particularly, the hierarchical relations that constitute Aborigines as political subjects.

That this violence could not be acknowledged in the editorial is significant. Such a depiction of an Aboriginal history is quickly displaced by a more familiar welfare-oriented discourse in the editorial. 'Appealing violence', it appears, functions for oppressed groups, 'as a way of begging the dominant groups to take notice of their inhuman plight'; specifically, the appeal is 'against inadequate and jerrybuilt housing, taps that don't work, sewerage that runs in the streets, the idleness and drinking that come with chronic unemployment' (*SMH*, 18 August 1987, p. 16). Ultimately, the editorial compares the riot to Black American struggles for civil rights in the South some 25 years earlier. The reference to Aboriginal deaths in custody and settler colonial dispossession is reduced to a remedial welfare measure and to a question of civil rights and equality rather than Indigenous rights. The disempowered and dependent Aborigine is restored, but at the cost of a violent colonial history being ignored.

The editor of the *Sydney Morning Herald* sought explanations of the riot from inside the town. The causes derived from the social and economic problems of racial discrimination that existed there. The claims of racial inequality remained general and abstract in their concern for social and economic inequality and discrimination,[11] but the conditions of a political rural/urban divide were more explicit. The metropolitan press represented Brewarrina as a racist town and a backward community. The riot, as the result of prolonged prejudice, racism and backward behaviours, was safely distanced from mainstream society and limited to anachronistic rural places out of step with the rest of society. This was precisely what the town spokesmen rejected. In the representation of the town as racist and redneck, they were depicted as backward, ignorant and irrational in their ways. They reacted against the same kind of homogenising and abstract logic that applied to the Aborigines in the town. Indeed, the white citizens of Brewarrina were given an equivalent inferior status in relation to mainstream society — in the same terms as the Aborigine — as ignorant, backward and irrational.

Clearly, this does not have meaning as a racial discourse, but as a moral and political discourse, which lays part of the blame on the town. The town's citizens are made complicit in the impoverished circumstances of Aborigines, and, indirectly, the riot. They are criticised for not conforming to mainstream norms and for reproducing the attitudes and behaviours of racist policies of the past. The parallels between the cultural constructions of redneck and Aboriginal otherness do not deny the racial overtones attributable to Aborigines. More to the point, the category 'Aborigines', emptied of Indigenous meanings, gains its meaning from moral and political discourses that do the work of constructing otherness. The detail attributed in the categorisation reveals Aborigines as a locus of anxiety subject to intense and oppressive moral scrutiny, both in the past and at present, within such towns and by state regulatory institutions. These are not so much towns differentiated by economic cleavages, but a moral economy in which status is coded in terms of a hierarchy of modes of behaviour. The equating of the Aborigine with irrational behaviour remains powerful as a racially laden stereotype because white identity continues to define itself from what it is not: the Aborigine as cultural other.

The trial riot

The criminal trial, *R v. Bates, Murray and Orcher*, held in Bathurst in March/April 1991 more than three-and-a-half years later (moving from the Magistrate's Court to the District Court), produced the riot as an event in a legal register. This was not the war of categories produced in the media, but individually detailed accounts in the form of personal testimony as evidence. Individual accounts and individual outcomes were presented and contested as evidence in the antagonistic setting of prosecution and defence. The courtroom winnows its own 'truth' through cross-examinations that question and challenge the veracity of the testimony given, with the judge, who presides as arbiter on points of law, deciding what is admissible evidence and what is not. The trial evidence produced the riot in a more personal and visceral register. The testimony came from the police and witnesses in the hotel. There were no Indigenous witnesses. The only Aborigines involved in the court proceedings were the three defendants, who stood mute in the dock throughout the trial.

The police officers' testimony provided the weight of evidence for the prosecution and cumulatively identified the defendants as the perpetrators of violent acts. Police officers, unlike other members of the public, are essentially skilled professionals in evidence and courtroom procedures, given their routine role in criminal inquiry. However, the video of the riot produced no evidence of the alleged criminal acts of the defendants. In addition, the different institutional sites of the trial and the media produced parallel and contradictory stereotypes and narratives (see Chapter 6). In brief, the trial riot did not contain the violence of that night as the product of the relationship between Aborigines and the ABC television crew. In its media treatment, the video images were not 'real' as they were the product of prior incitement by unprincipled and cynical news-seeking journalists. In its contradictory treatment at the trial, in part, the presence of the video was said to restrain the violence. The video images on the footage were not 'real', but the product of the restraining effect on Aboriginal behaviour brought about by the video's surveillance.

The prosecution asserted that the video footage was incomplete and that the Aboriginal violence was committed at times when the video camera was not recording. This matched police testimony. The trial evidence produced contradictory and competing discourses of Aboriginal intentionality and subjectivity. The evidence presented by police and members of the public, in particular, disrupted the stability of hitherto unchallenged dominant cultural understandings of the event by exposing an agonistic relationship between Indigenous people and local whites. The testimony uncovered a more violent exercise in boundary maintenance, where violence is understood as an integral part of the structuring of hierarchical social relations.

In the media accounts of the riot and the trial, up to this point, the explanations of the violence are not drastically disparate. The Aboriginal people in the park remain the sole agents of the violence. The local white community is not a participant, but its roles are relegated to those of passive or biased observers. The template for this distancing and disavowal was set in earlier settler colonial history, where Aboriginal cultural and social incompetence, rather than the actions of the colonisers, accounts for Indigenous dispossession. Violence emerges from a breakdown of social norms or, more pointedly, from the cultural incompetence of Aborigines.

The Indigenous people in the park that night give an entirely different interpretation. They have long maintained that the initial confrontation was between some Aborigines in the park and a group of white people assembled on the Brewarrina Hotel verandah. The claims were repeated in a program about the riot that drew on Indigenous witnesses and was broadcast on the Indigenous, non-mainstream radio station Radio Redfern (in a story titled "'Brewarrina Riot" trial . . . Justice') on 24 May 1991. In this account, the taunts and insults of an armed group of people on the verandah initiated the response from people in the park. The subsequent police action in attempting to forcibly eject the mourners from the park was the catalyst of the melee and retaliation that followed. Provocation and retaliation are the themes that dominated Indigenous representations. Confrontation here is an integral part of the structuring of abusive social relations.

The initial newspaper reports also cited white community involvement. Tony Hewitt, for the *Sydney Morning Herald* (17 August 1987, p. 1), saw the riot from the street:

> The Aborigines shouted and threw bottles at the hotel's white customers, who had gathered on the top floor balcony. One of the customers was armed with a rifle and told the Aborigines he would use it. The Aborigines challenged the customers to come down to the street and the customers hurled back abuse. Each side swore at and threatened the other.

Charles Perkins, an Indigenous spokesman and Commonwealth public servant, picked up this detail and claimed in the *Canberra Times* (18 August 1987, p. 1) that the riot had started after 'the members of a racist charter', who had gathered at the Brewarrina Hotel, began hurling insults at the Aborigines in the park across the road. These details of the confrontation disappeared from mainstream media accounts and explanations of the riot from this point on, but re-emerged as part of the defence counsel's case in the committal hearing. The behaviour of those assembled in the hotel formed a major part of the case for the defence in both the committal hearings and the first trial. The report of the committal hearing in the *Sydney Morning Herald* (29 July 1988, p. 4) claimed:

> The Brewarrina Hotel was turned into a 'fortified' post with police and an armed guard on the verandah after rumours there might be trouble from Aborigines, a barrister claimed yesterday. Men were armed with two shotguns and a small arsenal of rifles more than an hour before last year's riot outside the hotel.

The hotel's licensee denied this. In 1991 evidence from the criminal trial confirmed the presence of white 'customers', said to be family and friends of the licensee, with rifles and shotguns on the balcony of the hotel.[12] The evidence of two police officers, assigned as liaison officers to observe the wake in the park from the hotel balcony, revealed the existence of an estimated 10 to 12 firearms stacked in two separate lots and leaning against the balcony railing (5 April 1991).[13] One police officer stated in evidence that the police removed one rifle from a man after he said, 'I'm going to pick a few of those black bastards off' (5 April 1991). The officers shortly afterwards left the verandah and took no further action (5 April 1991).

A *Sydney Morning Herald* reporter on the street that night gave the most graphic account in evidence of the verbal exchanges of abuse and threats that occurred between both groups before the melee:

Q. Did you hear any words . . . at the point of time you saw the people on the verandah, when was that?

A. When the Aboriginal people left they first left the park that evening, before the damage on the hotel was done.

Q. What did you hear?

A. I heard one particular, 'Nasty fucking niggers, I'm going to kill you'.

Q. Did you hear anything being said by the Aboriginal people?

A. Well, Aboriginal people were telling the people all about them to get fucked or get stuffed . . . (9 April 1991).

The expression 'fucking nigger' is drawn from the archive of western racism, and particularly the southern American states, rather than from local racial idioms. The vehemence of the exchange is perhaps what Perkins alluded to when he claimed that it was the 'members of a racist charter' at the hotel that provoked the riot (*Canberra Times*, 18 August 1987, p. 1). The expression does not have the same currency in Australia as it did in the southern United States as an everyday charter to routinely degrade and humiliate. Such expressions in Brewarrina come from an embattled position rather than a normative one. The use of 'fucking nigger' or any other racially vilifying expression violates existing laws.[14] This transgression puts the perpetrators outside the workings of the law and without regard to consequences. The use of the expression amplifies its violent intent to insult, taunt and provoke.

It is insufficient to suggest that the Indigenous people in themselves were the objects of white anger. The wake was the reason for their presence in the park. It was and remained a unique event negotiated by Indigenous spokesmen and women and the town's political leaders. The wake was unique as a concession to Indigenous sentiment ceded the right to publically mourn and to consume alcohol in a public park. One defendant, Arthur Murray, stated that the racial abuse came from the hotel publican, who said, 'shut up you mob of niggers, you black bastards, I'll blow you away, get out of the park' (*Green Left Weekly*, 8 May 1991, p. 6). Any sense of the wake functioning as an act of contrition on the part of the white community is dispelled in the words, 'fucking niggers' and 'black bastards'.

The trial revealed an antagonistic and violent hierarchy of social relations, where the raw edge of categorical racism expressed itself. The racial abuse gained expression in a social arena in which it had little bearing on the deliberations of the trial. The violent racial expression, the presence of the armed 'customers' at the Brewarrina Hotel, and the violent verbal interchange between the customers and those in the park remained outside the frames of reference of the trial. The deliberation of the jury was confined to the question of the guilt or innocence of the accused. Deliberations on general issues of social injustice and other alleged illegalities were beyond the scope of this criminal trial. Weighing the evidence directed to establishing the guilt or innocence of the accused provided the proper limit of the concern of the judge and jury. Two of the three defendants were found guilty.

Royal Commission and Indigenising crime

The RCIADIC produced another version of the riot in a social register. Although it could make legal findings, the RCIADIC's brief enabled it to move beyond narrow legal parameters to address broader social issues. The RCIADIC was to investigate the circumstances that led to the social pathology of Indigenous people dying in legal custody, and would make recommendations to bring about positive social change. Its commission was to conduct open inquiries into each individual death by drawing on public submissions and, in particular, the expertise of medical, forensic and social science. Scientific opinion and knowledge would shed light on the patterns of normality and pathology and their relationship to the social environment. In particular, the use of social statistics produced perhaps the most significant finding of abnormal conditions existing between Indigenous people and state institutions.

The function of social inquiry assumes the capacity of society to change on the basis of deliberations, findings and recommendations.[15] The social world is subject to laws that can be measured, calculated and understood and which provide the basis for social order and progress. Such technologies of governance are grounded for their functioning in concepts of society and cultural unity and the nationally bounded nature of its institutions. They produce knowledge of social solidarities in human activities that are more than simply the result of individual activity. Yet we are dealing with cultural and historical specificities that emerge from settler colonial governance and the radical historical differences between government and citizens that occur in post-settler colonial settings. The RCIADIC contested societal and cultural unity and the legitimacy or limits of national institutions.

The major findings of the RCIADIC were produced in the detailed evidence of the regular and routine role of police interventions into the lives of Indigenous people, especially in rural towns. The national survey conducted by the RCIADIC found that the detention rate of Aborigines in all offence categories was 3539 per

100,000 (cited in Hogg 1991), a rate 27 times higher than for non-Aborigines. The survey revealed a major statistical deviation from the norm at all levels, and the huge overrepresentation of Indigenous people in custody. The national figures, however, disguise the degree of regional variation, especially in rural areas and the north-west New South Wales towns of Brewarrina, Bourke and Walgett, which have significant Aboriginal populations (see Chapter 3). The RCIADIC figures revealed the extraordinary arrest rates of Indigenous people on petty offences that bring Aborigines into police custody. Such figures also revealed the high-level surveillance and monitoring exercised in these small rural towns — as if communities themselves existed on a form of conditional liberty and were perpetually on parole. The police exercise more discretionary power over public order offences than in the case of serious crime. Swearing and drunkenness are predominantly police-initiated arrests.

Indigenous people and the police in these towns regularly confront each other over the limits of discretionary power and the determinations of public morality. The issue here is not simply one of discretion to determine what affronts public morality, but one of challenging police authority itself. Integral to police authority is its sovereignty over the street. This is often precisely what is at issue: the refusal of Indigenous people to be encapsulated and, instead, the choice to stand outside and challenge the authority of the law. The possibility of these exchanges occurs within a particular social and political context. In preceding decades, fundamental and decisive shifts have occurred in relations between Indigenous people and the local community. The Aborigine is no longer confined to segregated spaces of the reserve and has equal rights and access to public facilities, the school, the hospital, the streets, the hotel and the parks. In the contemporary context, the regulation, monitoring and control of the Indigenous population of the town have become functions of policing. The police have become the public face of the old reserve manager. The concentration of RCIADIC figures in the area of public order offences suggests that the role of the police is more readily deployed to regulate the moral conduct of citizens in public spaces than in pursuing serious crime in such towns. The forms of governance associated with the manager-run reserves are reproduced in public space and principles of surveillance order the streets.

Michel Foucault's modern dystopia associated the art of government with the disciplinary society, which consisted of a series of spaces of enclosure: the school, the prison, the hospital and the factory (see Foucault 1979, 1980, 1984, 1987). Such enclosures regulated social space and time as a means to order human activity and behaviour and traverse state and civil society. The segregation on missions and reserves and the Aboriginal Boys' Home and the Aboriginal Girls' Home are artefacts of this disciplinary society in a settler colonial world. The control of space and the regulation of those who move through such a series of enclosures are attempts to create the sites of social and political domination, within the disciplined and docile body. Such an art of government would seem to be undergoing change. For Foucault, the art of government is much broader than the agents and institutions of the state. The cumulative power of state institutions reproduces the social differences of small rural towns. Yet we merely reproduce a form of ethnocentrism if we characterise such social dystopias and exercise of technologies of power in the image of metropolitan states. In settler colonial spaces, state power as a technology of domination is exercised within a framework of collective unity and political sovereignty (see Foucault 1988:18). The normative and individualising technologies of the self do more to render the Indigenous marginal and culturally or morally deficient and, in doing so, do the work of stratifying social and cultural divides.

The RCIADIC drew attention to the conflictual relations between Aborigines and police in the 1980s. The raw edge of these relations was made apparent in the circumstances that attended Lloyd Boney's death in police custody and the subsequent events. The submissions made by Indigenous people from the region to the RCIADIC recorded, for the first time in a public domain, the antagonism and anger directed towards the police in terms of their understandings of the events surrounding the death of Lloyd Boney (see Chapter 3). Attempts by police to demonstrate how Lloyd Boney died by suicide were considered implausible and were refused by relatives and friends of the deceased (Wootten 1991b). Lloyd Boney's stepfather and the Western Aboriginal Legal Service asserted that he was 'accidentally killed' and the 'faked suicide hanging was staged by police as a cover up' (Wootten 1991b:4). The RCIADIC reports make clear that police force is not seen as neutral, but more often than not is considered the agent of violence, harassment and discrimination.

The contribution to the escalation of violence brought about by the police strategy of forcefully breaking up the funeral wake, comprising men, women and children, was never questioned. At the criminal trial, Senior Officer MacLachlan stated his orders on the night were to 'Charge forward and get them out of the park' (25 March 1991). Under cross-examination, the officer agreed that the police had responded to complaints that Aborigines, mainly young persons, were allegedly throwing missiles at the hotel (25 March 1991). For the officer, the trouble was emanating from the park and to remove the problem meant clearing the park, as if everyone in the park was involved in the trouble (25 March 1991). The individualising strategies of policing practice were replaced by racial typification: the issue became the collective problem of Aborigines drinking in the park. The wake was brought to an abrupt and violent end due to the seemingly aggressive insensitivity shown to public rituals of mourning. Yet the police intervention was in keeping with the role that the police regularly performed in the town in exercising control of the public streets and parks.[16]

It is necessary to look at the habits and routine activities and assumptions of daily life to understand the meanings of the riot. The wake itself was an anomaly, a publicly sanctioned expression of collective identity, a space negotiated with local authorities for Aboriginal activity. It was not a return to tradition, but an expression of Aboriginal autonomy. The implication that it was Aborigines simply drinking in the park rather than mourning a loved one, who had died in police custody, perhaps helps explain Indigenous anger at perceived police harassment, as well as police concerns with clearing the park of those memorialising a death and laying the blame at the feet of these same police officers.

There is a larger point here. The riot provided a platform for debate over the merits and direction of Aboriginal policy. The social situation described here in its complexity reveals something of the tensions in social life at a time when new social possibility was in the process of formation. The Brewarrina riot provides a site where wider social realities can be drawn into focus. Symbolic significance was not so much inhered in the event itself, but testified to the existence of a contested political landscape. The symbolic significance of the riot reflected as much about the emergent changes in state governance as about the events in Brewarrina that night. The racialised images of Indigenous people and the explanations of the riot reveal much about the relations of power, hierarchy and a colonial racist history. However, it was not simply the past manifesting itself in the present. The social crisis asserted in the representations gained much of its significance from the perceived failure of bureaucratic-legal interventions of the welfare state to deal with the 'Aboriginal problem'.

Within six months of the riot a newly elected neoliberal government in New South Wales introduced a program to replace the social logic and structures of the post-war welfare state. The demands of a more conservative polity were met at two levels. The new government committed itself to profound change in existing Indigenous policy in repealing the *Aboriginal Land Rights Act 1983* (NSW) and to rationalise existing government policy by 'mainstreaming' all specialised Indigenous programs (see Chapter 2). It implemented a political program that emphasised a tougher approach to law and order that was intended to put an end to the 'crime wave' especially afflicting rural communities (see Chapter 3). The crisis of identity for many rural communities was being redressed. In the polemical condensations of contemporary debate, the welfare Aborigine was the new antithesis of the neoliberal entrepreneurial subject. In effect, the welfare Aborigine became the symbolic failure of the misguided indulgence of the welfare state and its excesses.

The political expression of antipathy to Indigenous rights fully emerged a decade later. The political force of independent politician Pauline Hanson and the party that formed around her, the One Nation Party, gained significant support after the 1996 federal election (see Kapferer and Morris 2003).[17] Hanson's maiden speech to the Commonwealth Parliament in Canberra on 10 September 1996 condemned the state for subjecting the ordinary population (the taxpayer) to illegitimate hardships because of the government's indulgent treatment of Indigenous people. In Hanson's view, a world of 'fat cats, bureaucrats and do-gooders' had taken advantage of ordinary taxpayers who effectively lost their money to the support of 'Aborigines, multiculturalists and a host of minority groups'.

Chapter 2

Neoliberalism and Indigenous rights in New South Wales

On 9 October 1990 a large number of Indigenous people from all over New South Wales and their supporters demonstrated against amendments to the *Aboriginal Land Rights Act 1983* (NSW) (the Aboriginal Land Rights Act). The amendments eroded Indigenous rights and came only seven years after the Labor government had passed the ground-breaking legislation, which recognised prior ownership and provided compensation. The Aborigines leading the demonstration demanded to meet with the New South Wales Premier, Nick Greiner. When the demand was ignored, it was reported that 'several demonstrators climbed the 2½ metre iron fence at the front of Parliament House and attempted to enter the building' (*SMH*, 10 October 1990, p. 10); the crowd was alleged to have then 'pushed down the fence and 11 demonstrators were arrested'.

The 'violent demonstration' was condemned by the Premier, the Opposition leader, Bob Carr, and the Chairman of the New South Wales Aboriginal Land Council (NSWALC), David Clark. The Premier dismissed the demonstration as a 'ratbag demonstration . . . an irrelevance on the face of the earth' (*SMH*, 10 October 1990, p. 10). Clark, claiming to speak for the overwhelming majority of the Aboriginal people in the state, said that 'there are 40,000 people back home wanting the amendments to go through' (*SMH*, 10 October 1990, p. 10). For Clark, 'the protestors were a sprinkling of minority groups who were misinformed about the amendments'; he stated that 'the amendments are tops and I think it's great and I will not back off' (*Daily Telegraph*, 10 October 1990, p. 10). The Chairman represented one side of a significant split that had developed in the NSWALC over amendments to the legislation. For the Aboriginal protestors, the demonstration was equally directed at the members of a split executive who were accused of betraying them.

For many Indigenous people, the demonstration is remembered for the relaxed rather than violent atmosphere. The collapse of the fence was an unexpected event that surprised the demonstrators rather than a premeditated violent act. Indeed, the photographs taken indicate a relaxed attitude of both police and demonstrators (see Figures 2 and 3). Nevertheless, the media coverage of the Aboriginal protest supported the politician's position, trivialising the protestors as unrepresentative and turning it into a spectacle.

A tabloid newspaper headline, 'Parliament House stormed' (*Daily Telegraph*, 10 October 1990, pp. 4–5), framed the event. The reports focused upon the 'violent protest' and the Premier's description, which dismissed the demonstration as 'ratbag' behaviour. *Daily Telegraph* reporter Peter Grimshaw's two-page spread and special politics reporter Malcolm Farr explicitly supported the Premier's

Figure 2: Men, women and children assembled in orderly protest at the Parliament House fence (Newspix)

Figure 3: Police and demonstrators at the collapsed fence (Newspix)

position of caricaturing opposition to the amendments as an irrelevant farce. For Farr, the 'rampage' was 'good television but sad and
shameful politics'; by contrast, the 'strategy of the government . . . is
generally considered to be one of the most progressive pieces of land
rights legislation in the nation . . . as it made the land councils more
democratic, more accountable and more efficient', and the amendments to the 1983 Act made it the 'most progressive piece of land
rights legislation in the nation' (*Daily Telegraph*, 10 October 1990,
p. 11). The newspaper commentary endorsed the government's own
assessment by paraphrasing the government's press release.

What was striking about the confrontation over the passage of
the bill was the complexity of the political alliances and divisions it
revealed. An unprecedented unity emerged between the dominant
political parties (the coalition, Labor Party and Democrats) during
the passage of the amendments.[1] All political parties supported them,
with the exception of one independent, Richard Jones. The amendments passed through the Upper House unopposed. The unity of
the political parties stood in contrast to the NSWALC, which was
left sharply divided. These political actions conform with a recurring
dilemma associated with the recognition of Indigenous rights in postcolonial liberal democracies — a dilemma that stems from the fact that

government and other political parties are always in an all-powerful position in determining the nature and extent of consultation and the shape of legislation involving Indigenous peoples. Settler colonialism continues as an assumed fact even when legislation seeks to address its consequences. In enacting the legislation, the state affirms its ultimate authority as the guarantor of Indigenous rights and yet exposes something of an ongoing uncertainty and ambivalence surrounding the political status of Indigenous identity in postcolonial states.

The recognition of land rights in New South Wales, like the rest of Australia, came some 200 years after colonial settlement. A sizeable Indigenous population at the time of colonisation did not stop the British colonial authorities declaring the country to be terra nullius — that is, land owned by no-one. The consequences were disastrous for the Indigenous population, whose own institutions received no government acknowledgment. The lack of recognition and legitimacy removed any capacity for Aborigines to negotiate legally the terms of their own existence with the colonial state. The situation reveals the totalising character of the colonial state in Australia, which was able to determine, effectively unchallenged, the social and political conditions of Indigenous existence. This prevailing political and historical legacy in Australia explains much of the lack of political commitment, the limited expectations and outcomes, and, in particular, the conspicuous absence of Indigenous organisational structures and forms of governance recognised by the nation or state.

This chapter focuses on how contemporary political debate on Indigenous land rights in New South Wales came to be shaped in opposition to the government-commissioned Keane Reports.[2] The reports raised expectations among Indigenous people and their supporters and were consequently subject to considerable public attention, but the legislation that eventually resulted was extremely disappointing.[3] Nevertheless, some important gains were achieved in Indigenous political conditions, especially in terms of governance, through the establishment of Aboriginal Land Councils (ALCs). They, too, were later partly undermined by a series of amendments. The changes to the Aboriginal Land Rights Act by the newly elected neoliberal government were likewise presented as the result of commissioned reports: *New Directions in Aboriginal Affairs* (the Zammit Report, Premier's Department 1988) in September 1988; the *NSW*

Government Green Paper: New directions in Aboriginal affairs (the Green Paper, OAA 1989) in February 1989; and *NSW Land Rights Act 1983: Recommendations for Change: Report to the New South Wales Government* (the Perkins Report, Charles Perkins & Associates 1989) in November 1989. Opposition to the changes proposed in the reports sponsored a renewed Aboriginal activism that grew during this period. This was partly due to the ALCs, which had given Indigenous people the resources to mobilise and lobby government. This activism culminated in the massive protest at Parliament House discussed earlier, which occurred while parliament was passing the amendments that were to curtail earlier gains. The surrender to more conservative social and political processes was a retreat from the possibility of arriving at something radically different and it redefined the limits of what was negotiable in the future.

Major structural adjustment and social fragmentation characterised the 1980s. In particular, the experience of social fracture in many communities across Australia became more pervasive in reshaping rural life than at earlier times. Economic decline had a major impact upon both Indigenous and non-Indigenous rural populations. The period was marked by the collapse of small rural centres, the increase in rural migration to urban and regional cities, and the fragmentation and dispersal of working populations previously supported by local industry. Paradoxically, at this time governments, both federal and state, addressed other social inequities concerned with symbolic status and national recognition that had been advocated by the Labor Party in the 1970s. Governments not only instituted efforts to overcome social and economic disadvantage among Aborigines, but also advocated improved rights and recognition, paralleling similar policy recognition of ethnic minorities associated with multiculturalism.[4] As Fraser (2000:107) has rightly argued, 1970s and 1980s politics were directed towards the 'emancipatory promise' of the 'recognition of difference' in terms of gender, sexuality, ethnicity and race. The policies resulted in unprecedented government funding for Aboriginal organisations and land rights legislation, as well as for multiculturalism and encouragement of ethnic minority rights.

The struggle for Indigenous rights initially was an urban-based movement that emerged in south-eastern Australia. The Freedom

Ride in 1965 in rural New South Wales, led by Charles Perkins, inspired a generation of activists, most of them young (see Curthoys 2002; Goodall 1996). Like the 1967 referendum, the Freedom Ride was part of a broader struggle for equal rights. Throughout the 1970s, Redfern in inner-suburban Sydney became a flourishing centre of activism linked firmly to a politics of identity, to a politics of national recognition and reconciliation. This was a politics that sought to make Aborigines partly responsible for governing and managing them-selves. The development of Aboriginal organisations was part of the incorporation of Aborigines into bureaucratic structures that offered avenues of social mobility.

The Aboriginal Medical Service, established in 1971, was perhaps the first alternative organisation to deal with matters of Indigenous health. Staffed by volunteer doctors, nurses and support workers, it set the model for local community health needs (Khoury 1996). A similar alliance between black activists and white lawyers saw the Aboriginal Legal Centre set up in 1971 in Redfern. The Aboriginal Housing Company (1973), the Murawina Child Care Centre (1973) and the Aboriginal Children's Service (1975) each set up programs that catered for the specific needs of Aboriginal people (see Khoury 1996). They provided models of community-based services that spread nationally and forced the pace of change in public institu-tions. Redfern became a centre for Aboriginal artists, writers and performers in theatre, dance, music and film. Cultural innovation emerged with the establishment of the Black Theatre (1968), the Aboriginal Islander Dance Theatre (1976) and Radio Redfern (early 1980s). These institutions were vehicles for the expression of an urban Aboriginal culture, which fused Indigenous and western cultural forms to communicate to broader audiences. Importantly, they provided a conduit for the articulation and creation of specifically Indigenous stories and social issues in the domain of public culture.

Indigenous activism emerged in tandem with urban-based political advocacy of multiculturalism, with migrant groups resisting social and cultural pressures to assimilate that had hitherto characterised public policy. The state set about incorporating disaffected groups into policies, management and service provision. It incorporated migrant and feminist demands, as well as those of sexual minorities, in effect making them comparable to the claims of the Indigenous people it originally dispossessed.[5] Here, the sovereignty of the state, its legitimacy, came to be grounded and articulated through a new universalism that was not invested in assimilation and homogenisation (which came to be criticised). This new universalism resided in the incorporation of difference; it involved a politics of identity that demanded a new kind of state, which recognised and empowered diverse forms of socio-cultural autonomy.

The paradox was that this politics of difference involved a new form of homogenisation, where Indigenous rights became the same as the socio-cultural and political rights of other minorities. Indigenous claims became one difference within a sea of difference. Indigenous claims, however, sought not to have rights *granted* to them, but to have some measure of rights *restored* to them. Indigenous rights were not the same as the rights of multicultural groups, feminists and gay activists. A new kind of politics was emerging around the state, a politics of recognition, of how to be recognised in a contest where state policy extended citizenship rights so as to recognise within public culture the specific social and cultural demands of diverse groups.

The radical aspect of such social liberal reforms was, first, that they claimed equality of social collectivities that went beyond previous individual social and civil rights associated with citizenship. Second, they contested the major force in the institutional construction of modern Australia, the taken-for-granted cultural hegemony of what are now termed Anglo-Celtic values and institutions.[6] Such claims challenged the normative social relations and cultural understandings practised by government institutions as premised on catering for a homogenous field of recipients and a unitary domain of needs. And, lastly, they questioned the assumption of the existence of an all-encompassing historical narrative of origins. Previous policy had focused on individuals and the integration of Indigenous and immigrant groups through the homogenising logic of assimilation. In the new context, reforms that sought greater recognition of Indigenous rights, greater autonomy and self-determination were welcomed as progressive. They reflected broader political aspirations that emerged for a greater diversity of social and institutional relations. Within a context of globalisation, this advocacy of difference and diversity articulated the emergence of a cosmopolitan form of governance, where the role of the state was not to assimilate and homogenise but to manage and foster productive forms of diversity.

As discussed in Chapter 1, such proposed transformations in the identity of the nation produced various forms of backlash and nationalistic anger in those who saw themselves as the marginalised majority population and as the victims of inegalitarian programs that promoted minority interests (see Cowlishaw 1991; Morris 1997; Kapferer and Morris 2006). This was ably set out in Miriam Dixson's (2000) book, *The Imaginary Australian*. Her study captured something of the fragmentation and alienation of 'old identity Australians'. Dixson asserted that a national identity crisis exists among 'old identity Australians', who feel debilitated by self-doubt and disabled by a sense of loss. The 'old identity Australians', the bearers of Anglo-Australian core culture, feel demeaned that their national identity is being discredited by the claims of 'others' to be equally Australian while remaining proudly different. Anglo-Celtic Australia, she argues, was partly discredited by intellectual elites who questioned national identity from the position of Aborigines, migrants and women. Multiculturalism is accused of pushing Anglo-Celtic culture aside, as if it is too provincial and uninteresting, too mainstream and hegemonic. Dixson demonstrates much of the homogenising logic of the 'old tradition', which takes the form of a political equation in which whatever is conceded to ethnic or Indigenous rights ultimately takes away from 'old identity Australians'. This countervailing discourse of loss shaped political opposition to the politics of recognition and Indigenous rights.[7]

The other major force on the political landscape was the transformation of neoliberal ideology into policies and practices of governance, which began in the 1980s and contributed to widespread changes in government in Australia, western Europe and America. The renewed intertwining of neoliberal economics and conservative thought in Anglo-American countries that became the new political and economic orthodoxy significantly changed the contours of state power. Political reform became economic reform. Political decisions and choices were translated into instrumental questions of economic accountability, into maximising the efficient use of resources. Seemingly, the implementation of new social technologies did not involve political choices but rational choices. This application of neoliberal doctrine to Indigenous policy encountered considerable political opposition. Neoliberalism championed the primacy of the individual against the claims of social collectives, and there was a sharp contrast between the imperatives that drove neoliberal policies and the assumptions that underpinned land rights legislation. The repeal and winding back of previous victories in Indigenous rights was the subject of resistance and compromise. The character of these changes in postcolonial Australia reveal not simply incremental reforms, but qualitative shifts in state power that gave rise to new alliances and compromises.

The tension between the recognition of Indigenous rights and neoliberal practices of governance generated political realignments that were to shape Australian politics in the following decades. The social tensions arose not simply from those who opposed the so-called politics of recognition and its perceived alliance with the humanitarian welfare state, but also from the Australian state's own ambivalence towards Indigenous recognition and autonomous forms of governmentality.

Growing criticisms of the welfare state came to inform Indigenous policies. Pat O'Malley (1998) has persuasively argued that Indigenous governance inspired by policies of self-determination was increasingly regarded as problematic.[8] Previously, the social technologies of administration for liberal governance — 'impartiality, formal equality, individual responsibility and accountability' — were often responded to and replaced in Indigenous communities by the qualification of 'sustaining and adapting their own [Indigenous] practices and discourses' (O'Malley 1998:161). Kinship, age, gender and status associated with esoteric knowledge often replaced and qualified the basic forms of administration associated with bureaucratic forms of governance. However, without any sense of paradox, the Department of Aboriginal Affairs increasingly asserted that 'self-determination' was being impeded by the intrusion of Indigenous criteria into forms of governance. In 1988 the Department of Aboriginal Affairs stated that the 'failure to achieve a balance between the demands of cultural imperatives of Aboriginal society and the needs of good administration and proper accountability has been a major cause for the lack of success of self-determination' (cited in O'Malley 1998:161). These concerns point to postcolonial tensions that were increasingly used to problematise self-determination and autonomous forms of governmentality within Indigenous communities. Allegations were made that obligations to kin often overrode the interests of the community at large, and that particular kin groups were monopolising dominant administrative positions in the community to support their own kin above others in employment and the allocation of resources (see MacDonald 2001; Wood 2001) — claims, real and imagined, that could trigger allegations of corruption. Those who held positions of authority could be accused of betraying community interests in their opportunistic use of community funding. In effect, kinship obligations were turned from something socially positive to become part of the problem of why Aborigines could not govern themselves.

The New South Wales Aboriginal Land Rights Act attracted similar criticism and underwent reform amid accusations that Land Councils were corrupt and were misusing funds. Such allegations led to major amendments in May 1986 to strengthen financial controls over ALC funding. The accusations partly reflected the fact that the ALCs had been working without clear guidelines. In 1987 the financial practices of the ALCs were reformed to standardise all financial procedures to concur with the *Accounting and Internal Control Manual for NSW Aboriginal Land Councils* (OAA 1985). The reforms aimed to correct deficiencies in previous legislation, as well as to improve the performance of the ALCs. By contrast, the subsequent reforms of the new government aimed to change existing policy and implement forms of state governance that both repealed and replaced the Aboriginal Land Rights Act. Political opposition to these latter reforms ensured that there was no simple realisation of the new government policy. Instead, a new politics of strategic alliances and compromises emerged in which Indigenous unity unravelled.

In March 1988 the newly elected New South Wales government (a coalition of the Liberal and National parties) became the first in Australia to use major neoliberal policy reforms to wind back existing policies regarding Indigenous recognition. The major assault on Indigenous rights (and multiculturalism) was striking, particularly in the post-settler colonial setting. The reforms were consistent with broader programs of neoliberal reform that sought to minimise and streamline the state. Thompson (2000:89) captures something of the universalising claims of an ideology that 'celebrates the advent of a fully global economy as the embodiment of a market process driven by individualistic calculation of self interest'. Cultural differences dissolve through such market diffusion. Indeed, they are constructed as not just hindering the rational market but as irrational ways of organising society.[9]

The universalistic claim for market regulation naturalises itself as emanating from and tapping into the biological self-survival forces of nature.[10] The economic superiority of western industrialised societies is constructed as coming from the historical, cultural and social reorganisation of this maximising calculative force, which is inherent in each individual. Thus neoliberalism champions a form of egalitarianism that confers on all citizens the same moral status and moral worth. In the context of Indigenous recognition, the importance of specific socio-cultural identifications is rendered secondary and irrational. Government policy, in the name of efficiencies and common sense, seeks to reduce Indigenous collectives to facsimiles of western society to rationalise an inherently irrational social order. The reforms to Indigenous affairs in New South Wales provided a rehearsal for changes on the larger stage of federal politics and native title in the decades to follow. The political contestation over the form of institutional recognition and governance had a major impact on Indigenous communities as it reshaped the horizon of Indigenous political consciousness and aspirations.

Neoliberal policy stridently denies the importance of the struggles for 'recognition of difference' that characterised the 1970s and early 1980s. Indeed, the central tenets of a politics of recognition were heavily criticised. This politics of recognition had increasingly contested institutionalised forms of subordination expressed in the policies, practices and socio-cultural ordering of state institutions. The cultural stigma of colonised peoples was challenged through the representations that sustained racial hierarchies and that framed the institutional sites where such social order was reproduced. A more restricted acknowledgment of a 'politics of difference' emerged within neoliberalism. Difference was reduced to an opposition to discrimination. Discrimination, as expressed through racism and sexism, is an impediment to the efficiency of the market forces because it posits and creates groupings that should give way to the aptitude of individuals. Neoliberal commitment to equal rights ensures that discrimination does not distort economic outcomes, while also promoting the emergence of a more racially and sexually diverse inequality.

Neoliberalism's stand against discrimination is coupled with an adherence to a utopian free capitalist market as the only means in which human advancement can be made. In this respect, neoliberalism has certain parallels with colonialism. Indeed, the form of Eurocentrism avowed here is almost from the Victorian age in valuing individualistic self-interest as the measure and organising logic of all things. Only by making the market-based economies of affluent western societies into a universal organising system could prosperity be placed within the grasp of all. As Nikolas Rose (1999:141) has explained, 'all aspects of *social* behaviour are now reconceptualised along economic lines — as calculative actions undertaken through the universal human faculty of choice' (original emphasis). It is no longer only the regulation of the economy by market principles that neoliberalism demands, but also social and state practices. Addressing historical and cultural injustices in terms of a politics of recognition focused on collective suffering and injustices is rendered irrelevant and a hindrance to rational advancement. The issues are ostensibly no longer about race, ethnicity or Indigenous rights, but about asserting the primacy of the efficiencies of market regulation and competition in social life, which deliver wealth and progress and thus are inherently good. 'True self-determination' is displaced and redefined as coming not from rights of, but from rational improvements to, the socio-economic conditions of Indigenous peoples and by maximising benefits derived from full accountability of expenditures.[11]

The new political order

To understand the changes to land rights legislation, it is essential to grasp the changes in the forms of governance that occurred in the mid-1980s. With the election of a new state government, neoliberal political ideologies were transformed into practices of governance. The neoliberal epoch introduced a new language for apprehending and representing social reality that authorised particular understandings that recategorised and reconceptualised the role of government. To indicate the direction of change, the conservative government described itself as

'NSW Inc.' and the new Premier, Nick Greiner, referred to himself as 'the managing director of New South Wales Inc.' (Laffin 1995:76). In this corporate analogy, the government sought to distance itself from, and challenge important tenets of, the post-war political economy of the welfare state. To grasp the changes in Indigenous rights, we must consider these changes as by no means only a political phenomenon, but one that entails cultural transformation. The shifts dictated by the new forms of governance brought new disciplinary practices that changed the manner of government.

The new government was disinterested in social and cultural diversity, and emphasised individual economic enterprise and the cultural values of competitive individualism. Claims for cultural difference, collective rights and group identity were redefined as the actions of 'pressure groups', with the implication that they corrupted the work of government. Greiner (1984:59) asserted that the social demands on public institutions of women and immigrants and Indigenous 'minority' groups were 'merely private interests in disguise' masked as public interest. If acceded to, government would be reduced to 'merely making deals with powerful interest groups' and presiding over 'gladiatorial contests' that saw 'special interests triumphing over the general interests' (Greiner 1984:59). In effect, collectively shared meanings and histories were translated and rendered as no more than shared self-interest. Land rights and specialist Indigenous programs were redefined as part of the 'Aboriginal industry', and, like any industry, were concerned only with their own material advantage and expansion. Neoliberal reforms redefined how 'interest groups' were to relate to the state.

In this political context, the electoral campaign of the Liberal National Party gained its ideological inspiration and zeal for reform. The government's insistence on the repeal of the 1983 Act differed from earlier opposition to land rights legislation, which was based upon the rejection of treating Aborigines differently from other citizens; instead, the Premier's policy speech appealed to neoliberal principles of economic efficiencies. He baldly stated, 'the Aboriginal Land Rights Act is a gross mismanagement of scarce resources' (7 March 1988, cited NSW Legislative Council, 9 October 1990:7902). In September 1988, within six months of gaining electoral office, the government published *New Directions in Aboriginal Affairs* (Premier's

Department 1988). The Zammit Report, as it became known, stated that the 'government was firmly committed towards significant changes and progressive new directions in Aboriginal Affairs in NSW' (Premier's Department 1988:3). The government set forth four options; two sustained the existing arrangements (A and B) and two sought their abolition (C and D) (Premier's Department 1988:9–10, 58–9). The report stressed that it 'was not intended to reflect any preferred strategies and options for the future' (Premier's Department 1988:1). On 15 April 1988 the Premier abolished the Ministry of Aboriginal Affairs and transferred its functions to the control of the Premier's Department (Premier's Department 1988:28).[12] The transfer foreshadowed a policy of executive governance and direct government intervention in the decision-making processes of the ALCs.

The significant new policy direction was a retreat from the limited forms of 'self-determination' and the specific claims of Indigenous people for redress for their colonial past, which was now deemed to have no direct relevance. Land rights legislation was to be replaced by 'mainstreaming'; that is, the state would cease funding separate services.[13] The government advocated mainstreaming on the grounds of efficiency and dissatisfaction 'with the slow rate of progress to date in improving' the socio-economic living conditions of Aboriginal people in New South Wales (Premier's Department 1988:1).[14] 'Social indicators' in the areas of employment, education, housing, health and criminal justice, drawn from studies in 1986 and early 1987, demonstrated that the gap between the living conditions of Aboriginal people and non-Aboriginal population *had increased* (Premier's Department 1988:16, emphasis added). The 'slow rate of progress' demanded government action.[15]

The radical dimension of the Aboriginal Land Rights Act was that it recognised prior ownership, and it provided compensation to facilitate Indigenous governance and enterprise. Indigenous socio-economic deprivations in housing, health, employment and education were considered to be the responsibility of state and federal governments.[16] The federal government's Department of Aboriginal Affairs and the Aboriginal Development Commission carried out these service functions. The Land Councils, under section 12 of the 1983 Act, administered the acquisition and management of land claims and economic enterprises. An exception was made for housing (s.12 (g)), where local Land Councils could become involved in the 'upgrading and extending of local residential accommodation'. The new 'progressive' policy focused on 'living conditions' and rejected not only the recognition politics that had characterised the earlier legislation, but also the historical claims for justice and redress that framed policies addressed at ending socio-economic deprivation and disadvantage.

Mainstreaming was an opportunistic borrowing from ethnic politics, where it had meant a more active and rigorous pursuit of a multicultural society in Australia and had challenged government policies that continued to reproduce Anglo-Australian values as the core values of dominant institutions in health, education and the law. The major concern was that multicultural policies were being 'ghettoised', under-resourced, separated and rendered an inferior domain. The government expressed a view that multicultural policies helped some migrants to adjust and reflected a higher level of tolerance of cultural difference in Australian society, but the separate services did little to develop a unified multicultural society. Instead, by 'ghettoising' multicultural policy, the dominant institutions were able to remain untouched by the significant changes that post-war immigration had brought to the composition and nature of Australian society. For immigrant groups, a policy of 'mainstreaming' could achieve a major reorganisation of the practices of the major institutions to reflect the diversity of a multicultural society, making multiculturalism the 'mainstream'.[17]

The Zammit Report took up another aspect of mainstreaming as a possible new and important element of major policy reform of Indigenous affairs. Mainstreaming, as it appears in Options C and D, is set out in opposition to the cultural diversity catered for by state institutions. Instead, these options sought the reincorporation of Aboriginal services into existing and *unchanged dominant institutions* of the state. For many, mainstreaming simply gave a new name to the earlier discredited policy of assimilation, but it was not a straightforward replication. The application of mainstreaming restored the classical liberal separation between state and civil society. In particular, the decolonising strategies associated with Indigenous rights cut across the separation between state and civil society. Repealing the Aboriginal Land Rights Act and replacing it with mainstreaming would restore Indigenous rights to their proper place — it would reduce them to particular individual interests legitimately expressed in civil society rather than interest groups supported and promoted by the state. Indigenous Australians, like all citizens, may participate in or form their own voluntary associations in terms of their shared interests, much as they may choose to join a political party, religious denomination or leisure activity. Civil society is seen as expressing the natural individualistic order of social life distinct from the state — it gives expression to relationships between individuals based on their own inclinations and mutual interests. Neoliberal reforms, in this sense, are ahistorical in the application of a political program that requires the erasure of postcolonial histories. Continuing state support for Indigenous rights transgressed this fundamental separation.

Repealing the Aboriginal Land Rights Act

The new government undertook a token 'consultation' approach, in part as a concession to those opposing the repeal of the 1983 Act, but the submissions to the Zammit Report as part of the consultative process were ignored. The next report, the *NSW Government Green Paper: New directions in Aboriginal affairs* (OAA 1989:4), published in February 1989, summarised the 123 submissions as follows:

> A few submissions supported the termination of special services and the complete repeal of the N.S.W. Aboriginal Land Rights Act ... The majority of submissions, however, favoured option A, urging that there should be no significant dismantling of the system established by the Aboriginal Land Rights Act of 1983. Many were strongly critical of any suggestion that the statutory allocation to the N.S.W. Aboriginal Land Council of the equivalent of 7.5 per cent of annual Land Tax collections might be terminated or monies appropriated for other purposes ... Many people also expressed concern that the possible 'mainstreaming' ... seem[s] to signal a return to the 'assimilation' approach of the 1950s ... But some people recognised that there was room for improvement ... Some submissions favoured some combination of Options B and C.

The public submissions overwhelming rejected the government's position, yet the Green Paper reiterated its strong support for the repeal of the Act. In effect, the consultation submissions were ignored, partly because the responses strongly diverged from the government intention to repeal the Act. As the government stated (OAA 1989:1):

> The Government proposes to introduce in the 1989 Budget Session legislation to establish an *Aboriginal Affairs Commission*, appointed and responsible to the Premier for the development, co-ordination and review of State policies and programs for Aboriginal development. The Commission is to be headed by a full-time Commissioner and Chairman, with several part-time Commissioners appointed on a regional basis.

In effect, government control and top-down management were to increase. The existing three-tier structure of administration incorporated Indigenous representation and diverted from conventional models of social liberal governance. Representatives were elected from the Local Aboriginal Land Council (LALC) to the Regional Aboriginal Land Council (RALC) and then to the New South Wales Aboriginal Land Council (NSWALC). Two delegates were elected from each LALC and became members of the RALC Board. The members of the Board then elected a state representative. The 13 members of the NSWALC represented the 13 RALCs, which, in turn, represented the 131 LALCs. The NSWALC was primarily a clearinghouse, which administered land tax revenue and distributed available funds to the RALCs for administrative costs, the purchase of land and economic enterprises. In addition, the NSWALC could make its own claims and purchases (s.26 of the Aboriginal Land Rights Act), as could the RALCs (s.20).

The government proposed to replace the three-tier structure of Indigenous governance with a Commissioner. The Premier would appoint the Commissioner and 'several part-time Commissioners' (OAA 1989:5) and hence the Premier rather than the Indigenous people of New South Wales would determine the composition of the Aboriginal Affairs Commission, the major decision-making body. The proposed Commission would 'absorb and streamline the present

Office of Aboriginal Affairs . . . and the N.S.W. Aboriginal Land Council and the 13 Regional Aboriginal Land Councils, eliminating present unnecessary bureaucratic structures and costs' (OAA 1989:1). What is characteristic of such ideological shifts in the governance of Indigenous affairs is that the pronouncements are made in the politically neutral terms of improving technical efficiencies. Yet the proposed legislation, the Aboriginal Land and Development Act, would radically transform the existing structure of the Land Councils in the state and replace the Aboriginal Land Rights Act. The new Commission itself was to be 'phased out over a period of time' to enable the ultimate mainstreaming of Aboriginal services. A 'sunset clause' of five years governed the existence of the Commission, which 'would cease to exist by 1994 unless Parliament legislates it to continue' (OAA 1989:7). Sally Weaver (1985) has claimed that the strategic use of representative bodies is a common means used by governments to undermine Indigenous claims. For an Indigenous organisation to be representative, it must represent the views of its constituency and be responsive to the views and demands of its constituency (Weaver 1985:114). Such recommendations would end Indigenous representation by separating the representative body from its constituency.

A post-bureaucratic public service

The changes conformed to a broad ideological commitment to neoliberal reforms or 'post-bureaucratic public service' (Laffin 1995). Under the new coalition government, the organisation and structure of government underwent an unprecedented transformation. Laffin (1995) has argued that the major change occurred in the redefining of relations between government departments and the Cabinet. A new stress was placed on 'Cabinet solidarity and corporate purpose', rather than Ministers being 'captured by' the interests and beholden to the support of their departments (Laffin 1995:77). The Minister is the 'departmental head' directly responsible for departmental outcomes and performance. New government policy was geared towards unilateral action rather than consultation (Laffin and Painter 1995:8). Indeed, the propensity for unilateral action is generated by a fundamental rejection of lobby and pressure groups, which are seen to distort public policy because there is no lobby or pressure group that does not represent a vested interest. Such an approach, as Judith Brett (2003:175) indicates, is fundamentally statist, as only people at the top levels of government are empowered and expected to act in the public interest. The Ministers and the Cabinet were given greater powers of control and decision-making and were expected to be more attentive to the details of their portfolio.[18] The result was a significant departure from the professional and independent public service of the Westminster tradition.

The transformation took two forms. The pre-existing Public Service Board was abolished and the Premier's Department was given an expanded and centralised role of monitoring and coordinating policy implementation and the general management of the public service (Laffin 1995:78). The transfer of the former Aboriginal Affairs ministry to the direct control of the Premier complemented such reforms. The Premier's Department centralised control and oversaw policy direction. The departments were run though Ministers, supported by advisers appointed from within and from outside the public service (Laffin 1995:78). Departmental advice could compete with expert advisers and consultants, yet the appointments were likely to reflect views more certain of the merits of government policy than frank or critical assessments. Discretionary power within the Public Service Board declined. As Laffin (1995:75) suggests, the new emphasis on ministerial planning and evaluation of departments and departmental staff further strengthened the Minister's control. In entrepreneurial government, performance evaluation and accountability were the tools of executive governance, which marked a corresponding decline in the discretionary powers of departmental staff. The application of the ethos of executive governance to Indigenous administration in New South Wales, set out in the Green Paper (OAA 1989), extended these top-down principles to Indigenous administration as simply another policy area to be rationalised as part of government reform.

The reforms erased settler colonial history in the name of 'progressive change'. In particular, proposed changes to funding arrangements served to nullify notions of prior ownership and the compensation fund that facilitated Indigenous governance and enterprise. Claims to land ownership, political difference and, presumably, Indigenous identity were to disappear as the investment fund was redirected towards overcoming Indigenous disadvantage. The use of land tax revenue under the 'compensation fund', the other major innovation of the 1983 Act, also underwent change. The compensation fund had provided financial support for Land Councils, initiating investment for development. Subject to a sunset clause, a levy of 7.5 per cent on the state's land tax revenue was to continue for 15 years (1983–98) to sustain ALC funding under the Act.

The Green Paper's major recommendation was to make changes to the investment fund. Initiated in the First Report of the Select Committee Upon Aborigines (NSW Parliament 1980:95), the recommendation for an investment fund did not appear in the Act (see s.28), but was guaranteed under regulation s.24.1–2.[19] The Green Paper (OAA 1989:11) proposed 'that the continued alloca-tion to the Statutory Investment Fund can no longer be justified. It proposes to cease the compulsory diversion of millions of dollars each year but allow the Fund to continue to accumulate interest for the balance of the 15 year period.' The recommendation was to retain current funds for use after 1998, but cease the accumulation of funds from 1989 to 1998.[20] Land tax funding supplied the financial resources for long-term development. Fifty per cent was allocated to administration and to fund land and property purchases. The other 50 per cent was to be placed in a Capital Investment Fund to be used after 1998 as continued funding for Aboriginal projects. Given the proposed administrative changes, the fund was no longer required to support the current structure of Indigenous governance and was to be diverted to 'improve the socio-economic status of Aborigines' (OAA 1989:11). NSWALC 'future funding' was to be redirected to assist existing funding responsibilities of the state and Common-wealth governments in the areas of education, health and housing.

Acceptance of the Green Paper's recommendations entailed a fundamental shift in the nature and use of funding established in the Aboriginal Land Rights Act. The allocation of land tax revenue as compensation had recognised Aborigines' colonial dispossession and acknowledged land rights, primarily through the granting of claimable land (s.36) and the acquisition of land and property (s.38). Further, the establishment of local, regional and state councils to administer funding, the accumulation of land and economic assets had facilitated a form of self-governance. The future fund, the Statutory Investment Fund, was to be diverted to supplement welfare servicing on the basis of the 'urgent needs of Aborigines today' (OAA 1989:11).[21] The changes involved far-reaching transformations of key elements of the Act, specifically in terms of Indigenous self-governance. The structure set up to replace them reduced Indigenous interface with government to an advisory role and by individuals selected by government. Land rights and self-determination were to be replaced by mainstreaming. Indigenous peoples of New South Wales were to be treated the same as other disadvantaged citizens of the state. In this apparent egalitarianism, the claims to land and alternative or limited forms of self-governance were effectively nullified. The proposed amendments erased any reference to Indigenous dispossession and conflated Indigenous identity with other socially disadvantaged groups.

Self-sufficiency, not dependency

The release of the Green Paper engendered increased political activity from both government and the NSWALC as the latter resisted the government's political program. The repeal of the Aboriginal Land Rights Act had been part of the political campaign that swept the government to power. The government wanted the issue to be addressed by public debate rather than negotiations with the established Indigenous body, the NSWALC. Such debate canvassed the issues and sought a reaction from the broader populous rather than Indigenous communities and their representatives. The government's strategy was to appeal to popular public opinion to endorse its policy.

The debate was effectively between different non-Indigenous sections of the population while the minority voice of Indigenous communities was sidelined. In the post-election debate, a strong non-Indigenous voice continued to support Indigenous rights and the NSWALC. The Green Paper received 692 submissions:

24 (3%) of the submissions supported the Government's Green Paper proposals, 643 (92%) rejected the Green Paper proposals, 16 (2%) supported amended Green Paper proposals and 9 (2%)

submissions did not clearly state any position. (Charles Perkins & Associates 1989:13)

The government's recommendations were overwhelmingly rejected, but its position remained unchanged, which illustrated the limited importance the government placed on the consultation process.

Indigenous activism grew during this period, partly because of the Land Council structures, which gave Indigenous people the resources to lobby and potentially negotiate change in New South Wales. The NSWALC produced its own report, *Self Sufficiency, Not Dependency: Briefing papers*, which addressed the matters that were 'available for negotiation' and 'not available for negotiation' (NSWALC 1989:15–16). The NSWALC assumed a novel position for Aborigines in Australia by seeking to negotiate outcomes rather than simply providing advice to government. This was the common situation for Indigenous organisations in the United States or Canada, but not in Australia. Land rights were now a matter of considerable public attention.

Government statements sought to discredit the ALCs in a series of personal attacks on their members and LALCs. Parliament became a platform to conduct many attacks, since parliamentary privilege provided legal immunity. The parliament and media coverage provided the means for the government to discredit the ALCs and the Aboriginal Land Rights Act. The Premier, Nick Greiner, for example, publicly stated in the Legislative Assembly that 'to date 29 people from 10 Land Councils have been charged (for misappropriating funds)' (cited in NSWALC 1989). When he made these claims in 1988, the legal cases had not gone before the courts. The NSWALC responded to the claims and stated that 'no members of any Land Council have been convicted of any criminal offence relating to their Land Council duties' (NSWALC 1989). The most significant attacks alleged inappropriate use of ALC funding. For example, the Chairperson of the NSWALC, Tiga Bayles, was accused by the Premier of feathering 'his own nest by receiving substantial benefits for his own personal gain' (NSWALC 1989).

The amendments and the *Accounting and Internal Control Manual for NSW Aboriginal Land Councils* (OAA 1985), which provided the first working document of the Act,[22] strengthened controls over financial arrangements. The manual clarified and tightened the procedures of accountability and decision-making processes and increased the Minister's powers of intervention. Yet, despite the amendments and the issuing of the manual, which had been instigated by the previous government, the government continued to press 'mismanagement' as the major public issue. The Premier stated that 'Since 1984, almost 50 per cent of the 117 Local Land Councils ceased to be funded because they are under investigation for irregularities in relation to administrative expenditure' (*SMH*, 'Letters', 17 May 1989, p. 16).

The most significant change in political debate was the involvement of an Aboriginal representative body in questioning these claims. This involved a new set of relations between government and Indigenous communities that had not previously existed and opened up hitherto unknown possibilities and potentialities.

The NSWALC *Briefing papers* not only contested but also rejected government claims, often using the government's own documents. With regard to ALCs, at the beginning of the new financial year in 1989, it claimed that '27 of the 36 [hardly 50 per cent] unfunded councils have successfully completed their Investigator's reports and have been *waiting for four months for funding approval from the Office of Aboriginal Affairs in the Premier's Department*' (NSWALC 1989, emphasis added). For the NSWALC, the problem was the slowness of the Premier's Department. It argued that an unsatisfactory report did not necessarily mean gross mismanagement, as was alleged or inferred. The lack of training, skills and experience that had been evident in the early years of the ALCs provided good reasons for a level of 'mismanagement'. An investigator's report could be deemed unsatisfactory because sick pay or holiday leave cards were incomplete, or because the report, set out by a local accountant, did not follow the format required by the Auditor-General.

There were grounds for concern. The first political crisis arising from the Act had occurred amid allegations of the misappropriation of ALC funds. Although some serious misappropriations were alleged, far more allegations concerned provisions for the needs of disadvantaged communities, including assistance with funeral costs and bail sureties, and donations and loans to sporting associations (bus hire, equipment and uniforms) and craft organisations (hall hire, equipment and raw materials), which reflected immediate local priorities and imperatives. The other 'misuse' of funds entailed the payment of unrealistically high salaries, inappropriate granting of wages to elected officers (honorary positions), incorrect payment of sitting fees at meetings, and unauthorised motor vehicle usage and payment of running costs (unofficial usage). Under the Act, the ALCs were to operate as corporate bodies subject to the regulations of the Companies Code (1983). As one RALC staff member said, 'we were expected to be Philadelphia lawyers' fully versed in company law (pers. comm.).[23] In other words, ALCs were incorporated bodies formed under specific corporations legislation and subject to them. Indeed, it would appear that much of the 'misuse' of funds arose from non-compliance with the Companies Code.

The Perkins Report – strategic retreat

The most significant shift in the nature of government involved the relation of business to government. The neoliberal model of governance saw government as the problem rather than a solution. Along with changes to the internal forms of governance of the Public Service Board, there was a corresponding growth in the use of external consultants as providers of advice on policy matters. The government no longer relied upon parliamentary select committees or departmental reports; instead, private sector involvement was favoured as part of policy formulation.[24] Only six months after the release of the Green Paper in 1989, the Premier announced the appointment of Charles Perkins, prominent Aboriginal activist and former head of the federal government's Department of Aboriginal Affairs, as a consultant to advise the state government on its policy changes. The appointment of the respected Perkins was symbolically powerful in terms of Indigenous politics. He had been a major Indigenous advocate *in* government as a forthright spokesperson on Indigenous issues. In his role as consultant *outside* of government he embraced new configurations of power in relation to the state that prefigured new directions in Indigenous politics in the following years.

Unlike the First Report of the Select Committee Upon Aborigines (NSW Parliament 1980), which compiled the original land rights report over 30 months, the Perkins Report, *NSW Land Rights Act 1983: Recommendations for Change: Report to the NSW Government*

(Charles Perkins & Associates 1989), was completed in eight weeks. Consultation involved a series of meetings with Aboriginal and non-Aboriginal organisations and community groups. In the context of the Green Paper, which had been uncompromising in its attempt to remove the Aboriginal Land Rights Act, the Perkins Report was more conciliatory. It rebuked the government's previous approach, stating that 'any unilateral imposition of change on Aborigines from above is counter-productive and doomed to fail. Worthwhile reform can only come about within the context of genuine consensus and informed consent' (Charles Perkins & Associates 1989:3). In addition, the new report, unlike the two previous government reports, operated on the premise that the Act would not be repealed, but amended. The Perkins Report also recommended that 'the government abandon the policy of mainstreaming' (Charles Perkins & Associates 1989:1).

Despite rejecting some aspects of government policy, the report recommended major changes that involved the reorganisation of existing relations between ALCs and the state. The changes proposed the restructuring of ALCs to be directly controlled by the Minister and the NSWALC. The report set about recasting relations between ALCs and the state within the Aboriginal Land Rights Act and proposed that the NSWALC should be under direct control of the Premier's Department. The major recommendation involved stripping powers from the regional Land Councils and the effective removal of all regional control. A centralised, urban-based state council would replace the role of the RALCs and their functions in relation to all the small local Land Councils.

The Perkins Report brought about greater political control of ALCs by government. The amendments to the Act and the *Accounting and Internal Control Manual for NSW Aboriginal Land Councils* (OAA 1985) had already effectively tightened government control of the financial arrangements of the ALCs. The recommendations of the Perkins Report provided a means for the government to exercise direct political control over the administration of all ALCs. The great attraction of the Perkins Report for the government was that it would render the land rights legislation commensurate with other government institutional practices. The relatively radical aspect of the ALC structure, the administrative role of the RALCs, was removed. Representation had been premised upon a decentralised administration directly responsive to the views and demands of the constituency. At one level, the removal of the administrative role served a political function. By ending the administrative role, the government hoped to gain direct political control over all ALCs. Ideologically, such changes conformed to the government's neoliberal commitment to executive governance. At another level, however, the unprecedented unity of the dominant political parties in passing the legislative changes reflected how the Perkins Report articulated a hegemonic coincidence of perspectives about what was rational and necessary.

The report endorsed a more urban-based, hierarchical bureaucratic structure. The radical aspect of the RALC role was not that it replicated Indigenous 'traditional practices', but its capacity to respond to the views and demands of its constituency. The land rights legislation, from its beginnings, involved an attempt to manage difference framed from within the structures and practices of the dominant society. In this context, representative roles are assigned by the state and may be used strategically, as we have seen, to undermine or challenge the legitimacy of state actions. The Aboriginal Land Rights Act did not replicate 'traditional practices', but the decentralised structures for a largely rural constituency conformed more readily to practices engendering Indigenous agency and to people's specific experiences of place.

The Perkins Report recommendations supported changes to the organisational structure of ALCs. The RALCs could be retained, but only as consultative and advisory bodies (Charles Perkins & Associates 1989:14). All their executive functions were taken away and the Aboriginal Affairs Commission was to assume a direct role in processing funding arrangements and recommending land claims and economic assets, and was to assume the additional responsibility of conciliating disputes between and within LALCs. Furthermore, the RALCs were to be stripped of their administrative buildings and commercial assets, which would be controlled by the new commission and used or sold at its discretion (Charles Perkins & Associates 1989:14). The RALCs were to be effectively erased from the administrative structure.

There was something deeply ironic in substituting negotiation by existing Indigenous representative bodies with a prominent Indigenous spokesperson. The report's authority did not rest upon grassroots consultation so much as the authority invested in Charles Perkins & Associates, as a client body selected to provide expert advice to government. Consultation took on a new form, but replicated the limited Indigenous participation in decision-making processes of the past. Perkins, as a prominent Indigenous leader, had a power base independent of government. The political strategy brought into play business–government alliances through a new social technology of governance, the consultant group or company. As the final outcome showed, the Aboriginal consultant company was given greater authority than the recommendations of the NSWALC. The discussion and negotiation of change proceeded on the merits of the Perkins Report.

The NSWALC responded by asserting its own authority. It called a state-wide conference specifically to discuss the Perkins Report. The Conference of Land Councils (the State Conference) was held in Bathurst on 7 and 8 April 1990, and the proceedings were published as *A Response to the Perkins Report* (NSWALC 1990). The conference was attended by 106 of the 117 ALCs (91 per cent) (NSWALC 1990:38). Thirty-one amendments to the Perkins Report were proposed and passed, with the motions debated and voted upon by the elected delegates. All motions and proposals were to be carried forward for consideration of the Premier (NSWALC 1990:1). In its opposition to the precedence given to the Perkins Report, the State Conference delegates voted 278 to 31 in favour of the motion that 'the NSWALC is the elected board of the only truly representative and Indigenous body reflecting Aboriginal opinion of Land Rights in NSW' (NSWALC 1990:19, Motion 13), and held to the view that the changes advocated by the Perkins Report should be considered and debated by the elected representatives of the Indigenous communities they represented. But the government had publicly announced that it broadly accepted the recommendations of the Perkins Report (*SMH*, 14 March 1990, p. 5) prior to the conference, reducing it to a futile political gesture.

The State Conference rejected many of the major recommendations of the Perkins Report. In particular, delegates overwhelmingly rejected the adequacy of the grassroots consultation on which the report was compiled and authorised. Motion 10, which was passed with the support of 293 ALC delegates, with 23 against, stated that 'the Perkins Report is a hastily drawn up document reflecting more the viewpoints of executive staff in the Office of Aboriginal Affairs rather than the Aboriginal people of N.S.W.' (NSWALC 1990:16). The delegates rejected the very premise that meaningful consultation had occurred at the grassroots level.

Similarly, the State Conference delegates strongly rejected the view expressed in the Perkins Report that the LALCs' preferred position was to deal directly with the state body, the NSWALC. According to the Perkins Report (Charles Perkins & Associates 1989:Appendix B:2), the winding back of the roles of the RALCs emerged from the 'consultation' process: 'the representatives of the Local Land Councils were strongly of the view that they should be able to deal directly with the State body and be directly funded by that body, while maintaining Regional Councils with significantly reduced functions'. The State Conference delegates, who included the representatives of the LALCs, vigorously contested this assertion and offered their support, almost unanimously, for the existing structure. Motion 16 stated, 'Be it resolved that the existing Three Tier Land Council structure remain' (NSWALC 1990:22), and was carried 311 votes for, with only seven votes against. The winding down of the RALCs through the transfer of their acquired land and property was also overwhelmingly rejected (Motion 29, with 312 for and seven against).

The recommendations of the Perkins Report provided major advances on the government's attempts to dismantle the Aboriginal Land Rights Act. The State Conference strongly supported the recommendations that maintained the key principles of the Act. The important recommendations accepted were that 'government not repeal the Aborigines Land Rights Act' (NSWALC 1990:1); that government 'maintain the percentage of Land Tax Revenue' and 'the 50 per cent paid into the Investment Fund not be dispersed' (NSWALC 1990:2); that government re-establish the principle that 'each Commissioner shall be elected' rather than appointed by the Minister (NSWALC 1990:5); and that 'the government abandon the policy of mainstreaming' (NSWALC 1990:1). These recommendations of the Perkins Report supported the position of the NSWALC, which the government had ignored.

Removing land rights from the postcolonial landscape

The Aboriginal Land Rights (Amendment) Bill began its passage through the parliament on 4 September 1990, without the endorsement of the NSWALC executive. It did not receive copies of the proposed legislative amendments until 7 September. An NSWALC meeting held on 11 September led to an irreconcilable split, when a simple majority (seven to five) of the 13 executive members voted to accept the amendments.[25] Those who assembled to protest outside parliament on 9 October were protesting not only against the passage of the legislation, but also against the members of the executive who had voted for it. The dissenting members of the executive argued that the haste and secretive manner in which the amendments had been pushed through parliament had left most Aborigines with little idea of the changes.[26]

In the days following the protest, the NSWALC met at an unofficial state-wide meeting of RALCs and ALCs at La Perouse, a south-eastern suburb of Sydney. Twelve RALCs and 79 ALCs attended and voted unanimously against the NSWALC's executive decision to accept the amendments (*SMH*, 11 October 1990). As Neita Scott, Secretary of the NSWALC, stated, 'those seven people — the magnificent seven on council — did not vote in accordance with their own regional councils' beliefs' (*SMH*, 11 October 1990, p. 5).[27] Scott said, 'These amendments turn the Aboriginal Land Council into a bureaucracy. It disenfranchises the Aboriginal people of this State from being part of the decision making process that affects their lives' (*SMH*, 11 October 1990, p. 5).

The mass demonstration that drew Indigenous people from all over the state and their supporters to Parliament House on 9 October 1990 was a final act of defiance that brought to a close a period that had generated high expectations and possibility for the recognition of Indigenous rights in the state. The street demonstration partly expressed the positive utopian promise of democracy that their agency and protest could change the political process. At the same time, the mass rally was a refusal to remain invisible and silent in the face of this significant erosion of previous rights.

The political reform process succeeded in domesticating the operations of Indigenous administrative bodies. The original aims for recognition gained through land claims proved to be extremely meagre. The authority for the provisioning of Aboriginal groups and organisations returned to politicians, bureaucrats, and their legal and political advisers. The short journey of the original legislation to its reform revealed much of the contradictions that lie within postcolonial parliamentary politics. Elected representatives of the dominant society legislate the conditions of Indigenous status and cultural rights. The politics of land rights progressively redefined the limits of what was negotiable and reproduced a legislative framework in the dominant political parties' own image of what was politically reasonable and conceivable. At the same time, the parliamentary road to land rights proved vulnerable to changing political ideologies of governance. These ideological discourses erase the historical specificity of Indigenous claims as their disadvantage minority status becomes interchangeable with any other marginal group. Such appeals to social justice, as Byrd (2011) suggests, paradoxically render them complicit with a settler colonial project in seeking to remove Indigenous land rights and self-governance from the post-settler colonial landscape.

The failure to establish satisfactory land rights legislation across Australia by state governments in the 1980s effectively led to the increased significance given to the enactment of the *Native Title Act 1993* (Cth) through the High Court. Nevertheless, opposition to Indigenous rights continued to set the agenda and frame the ongoing directions of Indigenous politics.[28] The political response and strategies of the post-1996 neoliberal-styled federal government were remarkably similar in their opposition to Indigenous rights in the federal sphere to those strategies conducted in New South Wales in the 1980s. The federal government abolished the elected federal Aboriginal representative body, the Aboriginal and Torres Strait Islander Commission (ATSIC), in May 2004 and pursued a similar strategy. ATSIC was replaced with the National Indigenous Council, which served as an advisory body to the government. The Prime Minister announced that ATSIC should be replaced by 'distinguished Indigenous people' appointed by federal government (Pratt and Bennett 2004–05:16), and 14 part-time commissioners were subsequently appointed to the National Indigenous Council. Neoliberal interventions in Indigenous policy in New South Wales became the model in Australia. Those interventions in New South Wales significantly reshaped and redefined the parameters of debate in the following decades in ways that foreshadowed the federal government's intervention in the Northern Territory, supposedly to combat rampant child abuse. Everywhere the state created a moral crisis around the supposed inability of Aborigines to govern themselves, which required a movement away from a political emphasis on rights and towards an emphasis on practical reconciliation — which came to mean mainstreaming. Again, prominent Aborigines were called upon to legitimise the new direct role of the state in the administration of Indigenous communities.

Neoliberal claims involving cutbacks for the sake of economic efficiency were a way of rationalising the state to make it more productive. The critique of 'interest groups' and the 'Aboriginal industry' was self-serving and selective (the lobbying efforts of industry are never subjected to the same moral critique). In New South Wales neoliberalism removed the political organisational power of Land Councils, which could no longer be relied upon to implement state policies, but used their legitimacy as representative bodies to contest new administrative structures. The neoliberal language of economic rationalism could be used for many purposes — for the political expediency to do away with representative voices, to centralise state power and to move away from dependency on the public service for knowledge by incorporating consultants. In the realm of Indigenous affairs, these experiments in state power took place and occurred first in NSW Inc.

Chapter 3

Firm government: state of siege

Politics in the 1980s underwent a significant shift in the way liberal states governed, what they governed and how they governed. As shown in Chapter 2, a major impetus for this transformation was the shift from neoliberalism as a political ideology to its entrenchment as a form of governance. In a period of major structural change, government policy focused more intensely on programs for governing the socially excluded. Despite the way neoliberal ideology depicts itself as deregulating the state, it is more accurate to assert that it *re-regulates* rather than deregulates the agency of the state, and may be more effectively seen as 'remaking the state as [a] stratification and classification machine' (Wacquant 2012:71). The reclassification of welfare recipients meant that they were to be more punitively governed by a new politics of conduct.

The state's responsibility for the socially excluded, those unemployed and/or in poverty, shifted to policies based upon 'enabling' programs to facilitate individual 'self-actualisation'. Compliance and reformed behaviours were now a condition to receive benefits. Social exclusion could be overcome by enabling social inclusion. The problem of the socially excluded is no longer a structural problem, but a moral and ethical one. In this approach, social exclusion is understood as self-imposed and facilitated by the misguided policies of the welfare state, which engenders conditions of dependency among members of an 'underclass', who lack the motivation to work even when work is available (see Murray 1984). The lack of motivation, rather than capacity or opportunity, and the demands for rights without responsibility were perceived to characterise this 'underclass'. As such, social exclusion is not a problem of society, but a self-imposed one that in turn creates a problem for society, as it prevents or hinders integration and social inclusion.

This chapter develops an account of the relationship between social exclusion and crime as a similar punitive shift that occurred when welfare policy was applied to criminal justice. My focus on government practice shows how the reformulation of the problem of the socially excluded became a moral and ethical issue. While the primary role of market forces was to regulate the economy, the principal goal of government was to regulate and guarantee the security of its citizens, which required the moral reform of society by the force of law. In New South Wales the reintroduction of the *Summary Offences Act 1988* (NSW) and the *Sentencing Act 1989* (NSW) were intended to 'get tough' on crime. The former was directed at giving police greater discretionary powers to deal with public order offences associated with 'street crime'. Public order offences were especially important because they defined anti-social behaviours (e.g. drunkenness, swearing, vandalism) that not only disrupt community values, but also militate against policy reforms based upon social inclusion. In the name of community the law and order campaigns provided a vehicle to reinforce the moral urgency for neoliberal reform of society.[1]

The neoliberal interventions changed the dynamics of the politics of inclusion and exclusion by placing greater emphasis on the individual as the focus of government practice. The interventions intensified rather than reduced the networks of power that already encompassed rural Indigenous communities through increased police actions to 'get tough on street crime'. The shifts in policy effectively led to unprecedented growth in prison populations and had a major impact on the Indigenous population of New South Wales. Neoliberal policies of social inclusion added to 'the weight of the world' for those at the bottom of the socio-economic ladder, their marginal status further exacerbated. The socially vulnerable already lived every day in a 'state of emergency'. In terms of policing and prison reform, the policies followed by Nick Greiner's coalition government followed a model that characterised prisoners 'as a kind of toxic waste' (Simon 1993:259). The prison reforms aimed to control and contain prisoners and rejected 'expensive techniques of discipline' associated with normalisation through re-education and retraining (Simon 1993:259). Containment and isolation of offenders gave new direction to prison reform. The deterrent effect of longer sentences, more austere prison conditions and, for criminals, the prospect of continued connection with prisons was seen as befitting their status as 'toxic waste'. Through empowering police and enacting severe sentencing laws, it was argued that crime would be reduced and order restored.

The significant shift in political rationality had a profound effect on Indigenous Australians. The longstanding marginal employment of Indigenous populations in rural New South Wales had been exacerbated by structural transformations of the economy (see Morris 1989; Gibson 2010). Yet the structural adjustments were rendered more disruptive by the historical shift of neoliberal forms of governance towards more punitive controls. Demands for an ethical subject with habits of self-control and independence, future planning and self-improvement occur in contexts where structural forces readily generate subjectivities of resignation, destructive violence and boredom, as the ethnographies of Cowlishaw (2004) and Gibson (2007, 2010) aptly demonstrate.

The political rhetoric of the Greiner government of a 'moral crisis' of crime shared striking parallels with other Anglo-American countries, although with notable variations. These countries were also afflicted by a moral crisis, described as a 'crisis of authority', and had an urgent need to act if the crisis was to be arrested. State govern-ance required a 'firm hand' to ensure the security and protection of all citizens. As Stuart Hall (1980:5) said about Britain, in 1979 in response to the political ascendency of Margaret Thatcher's government, 'make no mistake about it: under this regime, the market will be free; the people are to be disciplined'. The demands for reform encoded more than concern about increased rates of crime. They reveal the changing contours of state power ushered in through a novel admixing of neoliberal economics and conservative moral thought.

This chapter focuses on the moral imperative that characterised neoliberal politics: campaigns that actively sought to mobilise people through a politics of fear. The political campaigns highlighted crime and demanded the expansion of law and order institutions. Hall (1979:19) observed:

> On law and order, the themes — more policing, tougher sentencing, better family discipline, the rising crime rate as an index of social disintegration, the 'threat to ordinary people going about their private business' from thieves, muggers, etc, the wave of lawlessness and the loss of law abidingness — are perennials of Conservative Party conferences and the sources of many a populist campaign by moral entrepreneur groups and quoting editors.

The 'wave of lawlessness' that was engulfing 'ordinary people' was said to be exacerbated by a more general 'loss of law abidingness', which signalled a deeper social malaise that gave rise to the crisis of authority. Law and order campaigns were complemented by political demands for measures in criminal justice and education to arrest the moral decline. The political exponents of neoliberalism promoted an anti-state free market, but, at the same time, advocated increased state interventions to create a more disciplined and ordered society.

This chapter considers the significance, substance and dynamics of law and order campaigns in New South Wales in the 1980s and analyses the changing configurations of state power that emerged in neoliberal polity. Coalition party politics contended that crime existed without punishment, communities lacked control and schools were deficient in discipline. They demanded a 'return to basics', which insisted on greater school discipline, compulsory flag raising in state schools, mandatory wearing of school uniforms and the reintroduction of corporal punishment under a new Fair Discipline Code (Sherington 1995:175). Criminal justice issues focused on two principal areas: a crackdown on public order offences and tougher sentencing laws. The political rhetoric asserted that the remedy for the crisis of authority required strong leadership demonstrated in legislative action by government. The New South Wales government between 1988 and 1995[2] not only engineered a radical restructuring of the state and economy, but also a return to moral conservatism.

In New South Wales the demands were for more police, more effective policing of the streets, tougher sentencing by the courts and harsher treatment of criminals in prisons. Law and order campaigns frame themselves to reverberate across broad social fields and present themselves as above politics. Crime does pose a real threat to limited or irreplaceable individual and family resources and personal injury and suffering. Through the mobilisation of a biopolitics of fear, the political appeal 'focuses on the defence from potential victimization and harassment' (Zizek 2008:34) as a means to usher in its reform agenda. Despite apparent political neutrality, such appeals to social insecurities revitalise racial and ethnic anxieties. In particular, law and order campaigns appeal to the ethnic anxieties, as well as the social uncertainties, of people. The 'Other' (see Hall 1998) is a source of fear and the target of legitimate moral struggles of good over evil. The consequences of law and order campaigns are striking in their impact upon those deemed ethnically marginal. Michael Tonry (1994:97) argues that in Anglo-American countries 'members of disadvantaged visible minority groups are seven to 16 times likelier than whites to be confined in correctional institutions'.[3] One can only endorse Tonry's (1994:98) point that 'the short term worsening of racial incarceration differences result from foreseeable discriminatory effects of conscious policy decisions'. Nevertheless, the specifics of the law and order campaign are important here. The street crime in rural New South Wales is neither that of the 'black mugger' of urban Britain (see Hall et al. 1978), nor that of the 'black American urban ghetto gangster' or a 'war against drugs' (Anderson 1999; Miller 1996; George 2005) as in the United States. In rural New South Wales, the Aboriginal criminality targeted in populist campaigns related overwhelmingly to public order crimes; that is, drunkenness and swearing, rather than violent crime.

The construction of these 'aberrant minorities' as criminals reveals social histories of marginalisation and discrimination that are nationally distinctive. They reflect specific social histories and social and economic practices ranging from land dispossession to slavery. The assertion here is that increased incarceration of minorities is not simply the result of the implementation of racially inspired laws. Tonry's analysis shows how the effects of law and order campaigns fell disproportionately on the respective 'disadvantaged visible minorities'; the targets were those people who were least integrated socially and culturally and those who enjoyed fewer legitimate economic opportunities (Tonry 1994:99). The structurally marginal become symbolically central in law and order campaigns. The 'return to the basics' framed its appeal in the recovery of a moral order that had been wilfully disregarded by segments of society to the disadvantage of the majority.

Law and order campaigns associated with state interventions in settler postcolonial contexts take on contradictory and complex forms. Interventions to support individual liberty can operate simultaneously to subvert them. Normative interventions of social control and regulation, as evidenced in law and order campaigns, can render Indigenous marginality as a collective cultural or moral deficiency and amplify social exclusion and separation along already existing social divides. The intention of the crackdown on street crime may not have been to victimise Aborigines, but sufficient knowledge existed to recognise that in rural communities such legislation would disproportionately affect Aborigines. Gillian Cowlishaw (2004) has documented how the conditions of social existence for many Indigenous and non-Indigenous people in rural communities nurture and fuel a 'culture of complaint' against society in general, but more especially against law enforcement authorities. Indeed, Indigenous struggles for political rights and, more pointedly, equal rights, such as the Freedom Ride and the Tent Embassy,[4] provide powerful historical examples of how conscious transgressions of existing laws framed struggles against oppression. Violating laws can be viewed as postcolonial acts of resistance or disaffiliation from the state, rather than as law breaking. The disproportionate arrest rates demand their own forms of loyalty in communities perceived to be under siege and may be experienced as evidence of the biased application of the law. The forms of police interventions foster greater loyalties to the communities rather than acceptance of the criminal justice system.

Law and order in New South Wales

The Brewarrina riot was the last of three public 'riots' involving Aborigines and the police in north-western New South Wales (see Chapter 4).[5] Throughout the 1980s the racially divided rural towns of north and central western New South Wales were subject to disturbances that brought about a number of police interventions.

Aborigines in the north-west were defined as the 'problem'. The scale of the problem was exaggerated by a number of dramatic deployments of the newly formed paramilitary, anti-terrorist police squads to the region.[6] The Labor government had formed the Tactical Response Group in 1982 as a specialist riot control squad, and the Special Weapons and Operations Squad was established as an anti-terrorist response group. General duties police also were equipped and trained in the use of specialist riot equipment, shields, batons, helmets and jackets. Throughout the 1980s the Tactical Response Group and Special Weapons and Operations Squad were regularly deployed to deal with actions involving racially divided communities in New South Wales (see Cunneen 1990a). The use of paramilitary style policing, which became identified with the control of Indigenous communities, suggested that 'relations between normal civil policing agencies and certain sections of the public have deteriorated to such an extent so as to necessitate a paramilitary response' (Cunneen 2001:207). The riots, the law and order campaigns, and the announcement of a Royal Commission into Aboriginal Deaths in Police Custody attested to existing regional tensions between Indigenous communities and police.

The 1988 election saw the removal from office of the New South Wales Labor government, which, as discussed in Chapter 2, had introduced the state's first legislation recognising the claims of Indigenous populations. The coalition government campaigned on a platform of repealing land rights legislation and introducing tougher law and order legislation, which gained momentum from rural campaigns against an alleged Aboriginal criminality. Despite relatively small Indigenous communities in New South Wales, they figured significantly in the election campaign. As Ian Armstrong, deputy leader of the New South Wales National Party, stated at a public rally in a large rural city, 'we got to get rid of crime, drugs, hoons and coons' (cited Goodall 1990:26). The racist use of the term 'coon' attracted media attention, but, in rural areas, it was in keeping with a political campaign directed at street crime allegedly generated by an Aboriginal criminality.

The election campaign stressed the need for increased police powers of intervention, regulation and control of public order offences. Specifically, the crisis of authority would be overcome by greater police control of the streets. The political campaign targeted the reintroduction of the *Summary Offences Act 1970* (NSW) (the SOA), repealed by the Labor government in 1979, as indispensable to restoring police authority on the streets.

The New South Wales Police Association supported the political campaign for the reintroduction of the SOA. The crisis on the streets, it said, could be overcome by investing police with greater discretionary powers of arrest over public order offences. The New South Wales Police Association had opposed the repeal of the SOA a decade earlier; full-page advertisements in the major Sydney newspapers said, 'You can still walk on the streets of NSW, but we can no longer guarantee your safety from harassment' (NSW ADB 1982:9). According to a report by the Anti-Discrimination Board, some police stations continued their opposition 'by virtually going on "strike" in relation to street offences'. The Police Commissioner's instruction to police, in Circular No. 87105, 11 September 1987, appears to affirm this; it referred to 'increased public concern about offensive conduct on the streets and to instances in which police allegedly advised members of the community [complaining about such conduct] ... that they [the police] were restricted in what action they could take under existing legislation' (cited in Bonney 1989:29). The repeal of the SOA, the New South Wales Police Association alleged, had made the streets unsafe and contributed to an increase in street crime that the police were powerless to stop.

Law and order campaigns mounted in the 1980s had a particular regional focus that was concentrated in rural towns in central and north-western New South Wales. Public debate in the central and north-western regions led to regional meetings in Dubbo in August 1985 and February 1986, which some 2000 people attended (Cunneen and Robb 1987:5, 6).[7] Similarly, a delegation from Bourke met with the 'State Minister for Aboriginal Affairs, Minister for Police and various representatives from the Police Department, the Commonwealth Department of Aboriginal Affairs and the NSW Anti-Discrimination Board' (Cunneen and Robb 1987:6). The public profile of rural unrest was heightened by sporadic regional disturbances, which reflected the tension and anger that existed in many Indigenous communities and among whites.

The campaigns were centred in Dubbo. The city had been transformed in the previous two decades into a major regional centre as a result of the demographic drift from surrounding regional towns, which had undergone a slow and gradual decline (Cunneen and Robb 1987). Dubbo's growth was directly related to the regional decline and restructuring of the rural economy. The Indigenous population changed from 345 (1971) to an estimated 4000 (1986) (Cunneen and Robb 1987:213). Such population growth, in particular, had involved the movement of Indigenous people from the north-west regional towns of Bourke, Brewarrina and Walgett (Cunneen and Robb 1987:212). The Law and Order Forum, formed in Dubbo, initiated public debate with its first public meeting in August 1985 (Cunneen and Robb 1987:4). As the regional paper, the *Daily Liberal*, reported, those assembled at the meeting expressed 'a deep concern at the decline of law and order throughout the Orana region — a concern shared by many thousands of our fellow citizens' (Cunneen and Robb 1987:4). It was asserted at two regional meetings that Aborigines committed 60 per cent of the crime in Dubbo and the 'new laws' had rendered the police powerless and the courts and magistrates ineffective (Cunneen and Robb 1987:4, 5). The appeals for law and order opposed 'misguided' liberal policies that emboldened Aboriginal lawlessness because the justice system did not provide a deterrent.

The historical link between the role of police, public order offences and Indigenous communities in rural towns is critical to the understanding of the push to reintroduce the powers associated with the SOA. Historically, the control and management of Indigenous communities in the public domain has been through police regulating 'public order'. Such practices were augmented by the *Aborigines Protection (Amendment) Act 1940* (NSW), which carried a number of restrictive laws that applied specifically to Aborigines, in particular the ban on drinking alcohol (see Rowley 1973; Roy 1986; Morris 1989). The history of law enforcement is a history of Indigenous bias in which Aborigines were subject to different treatment before the law. CD Rowley's (1973:356) 1962–64 survey of a number of rural towns in New South Wales (Condobolin, Kempsey, Moree, Nowra, Wilcannia and Walgett) revealed that where distinct Aboriginal populations exist, 'police arrests of and charges against Aborigines will be distinctly higher than those of others as proportions of the respective populations'. As Chris Cunneen and Tom Robb (1987:187–216) point out, more than a decade later, public order offences continued to dominate the number of charges against Aborigines. The anthropologist Arthur Roy (1986:113), working in western New South Wales, gives some insight into the local policing that attended such practices:

> One evening I was drinking in the back bar at the Brewarrina Hotel with a white work mate and a large number of Aboriginal men . . . No-one was drunk, but at 10p.m. the police paddy wagon backed up to the entrance and all the Aboriginal drinkers were ushered into the vehicle, while I and my associate were pushed to one side. The Murris [Aborigines] spent the evening in the lock-up despite our protests.

These practices occurred after the ban on Aborigines drinking alcohol was rescinded in 1963. In Redfern, for example, as Khoury (1996) points out, the routine taking into custody of Aborigines occurred after ten o'clock and operated as a form of police-imposed curfew. As Indigenous spokesman, Chicka Dixon (cited in Khoury 1996:183), said:

> If you're black in [urban] Redfern, Alexandria, Waterloo or Newtown and you're on the street after ten o'clock, brother you're taking a chance. This is the procedure. Along comes the 'hurry up' wagon:
> 'Righto, Rastas, in the back'
> 'But I'm not drunk'
> 'What do you want: Drunk? Or goods in custody?'
> 'I'm drunk!'

The impact of police discretionary powers enabled Aborigines to be singled out unlike other Australians. They were routinely taken into custody, regardless of behaviour. Such practices, ultimately, spurred local Aboriginal organisations into action and were instrumental in the establishment of the Aboriginal Legal Service in Redfern (see Wootten 1974). The unofficial curfews and arrests provide some insight into the inflated figures associated with public order offences and the social tensions that continued to exist between police and Aborigines.

Contrary to the political campaigns of the Law and Order Forum, the statistics showed an increase in police-initiated arrests (the 1978 figure was 43.2 per cent) under the Labor government's *Offences in Public Places Act 1979* (NSW), which had replaced the SOA. The 1980 figures for Bourke and Brewarrina reveal the same trend, with 90 per cent of offensive behaviour charges brought against Aboriginal people. The most significant statistic was that 75 per cent of cases of offensive language involved police-initiated, rather than publically initiated, arrests (NSW ADB 1982:42). As the Anti-Discrimination Board report suggested, contrary to the New South Wales Police Association claims, the figures indicated an increase in police-initiated arrests (NSW ADB 1982:37). Still, the election of the coalition government in 1988 saw the rapid reintroduction of the *Summary Offences Act 1988* (NSW) with increased penalties. Cunneen (1990a:42) describes what followed:

> The introduction of the Summary Offences Act was surrounded with the rhetoric of a 'crackdown' on street crime and hooliganism. The legislation included the reintroduction of specific separate offences of offensive behaviour (s.4 (1)(a)) and offensive language (s.4 (1)(b)). Most importantly the new legislation introduced jail sentences of up to three months for offensive behaviour and language.

The crackdown on street crime had direct implications for Aboriginal communities. A government study, *NSW Summary Offences Act 1988* (Bonney 1989), found that in Bourke, Brewarrina and Walgett the reintroduction of the SOA (1988) saw a 130 per cent increase in arrests for offensive behaviour. The study, conducted by the New South Wales Bureau of Crime Statistics and Research, compared the period from July 1986 to January 1987 with the first six months of the new SOA from July 1988 (Bonney 1989:20–5). The coalition policies produced a major increase in the overall prison population, particularly of Indigenous people.

Punishing crime

During its first term in office, the coalition government placed significant emphasis on reforms to the justice system. The Minister for Corrective Services, Michael Yabsley, quickly asserted control over his department and oversaw major reforms (Zdenkowski 1995:222). Yabsley operated as a highly interventionist Minister who commanded the details of policy and personally implemented them. He stated that he 'would like to be remembered as someone who put *value* back into punishment' (cited in Brown 1991:2, emphasis added). The new government policy showed a direct antipathy to the rehabilitation ethic in prisons and instead championed an ethos of deterrence. As Yabsley (1991:76) said, 'Punishment is synonymous with prison, punishment does have a deterrent value, so too must the prison. Punishment is a lesson.'

The coalition government restored the 'prison as the corner stone of punishment policy' (Zdenkowski 1995:226). These policies were not unique to Australia. Jerome Miller (1996) argues that James Q Wilson's 1975 book, *Thinking about Crime*, was highly influential on American administrations.[8] Wilson 'spurned rehabilitative and preventative programs, [but] ... strongly supported the wide expansion of aggressive law enforcement, stricter laws, harsher sentences and building more prisons' (Miller 1996:139). Neoliberal programs of deterrence, nevertheless, sought to actively fashion new collective representations of the excluded.

The government set in place reforms to legislation, the prisons and the courts that affirmed that punishment ensured greater compliance and respect by criminals for society. For Yabsley (1991:76), 'previous and backward rehabilitation programmes did not work' because they relied upon the 'hogwash of sociological dictum' (Yabsley 1991:75). Such programs, he argued, said too much about the 'needs of the underprivileged' and too little about 'the leeches, those who plunder from our stream of progress' (Yabsley 1991:75). Punishment acquires a sentiment of retributive violence against those who impede 'our' progress. Yabsley advocated that further punitive measures should be applied to prisoners by implementing a regime of austerity. Punishment no longer involved merely the loss of liberty through confinement; existing liberties within the prison were part of the problem. Thus cell property was restricted and henceforth severely curtailed, while existing prisoners' property was confiscated. Cell property was reduced to 'three pairs of underpants and socks, 6 unframed photographs, 2 books and a "limited number of legal documents" . . . property completely banned originally included religious ornaments, thongs, hat/cap, cell curtains, caged budgie or canary, wedding ring, ear studs' (Brown 1991:36). All prisoners' actions and personal effects were placed under the control and discretion of prison authority. Press satirists and cartoonists lampooned the 'daily litany of thong stabbings, budgie attacks, rosary bead floggings and book beatings' (Brown 1991:36). The Premier subsequently intervened to allow wedding rings to be worn (Brown 1991:36).

In keeping with its antipathy to the rehabilitation ethic in prisons, the government cut expenditure to prison programs as part of its major overhaul of the prison system. Major cutbacks occurred in the areas of prison education and rehabilitation.[9] Criminologist David Brown (1991:45) argues that:

> In 1989–90 $3 million of the $18.6 million allocated to staff wages in these areas remained unspent and expenditure for 1990–91 has been cut to $17.7 million. In mid1989 [sic] funding was cut to the Prisoners Aid Association, operating since the beginning of the century, while education, welfare and psychiatric sections in the Department's head office were abolished. Substantial cuts were made in the Equal Opportunity, Occupational Health and Safety, Prisoner Programs and Research Sections.

Expenditure cutbacks in education and rehabilitation were part of a general downgrading of prisoner involvement in education programs. Tape recorders used in educational courses were confiscated, women prisoners were no longer able to practise keyboard skills in their cells, and prisoners preparing for examinations had most of their text books removed from their cells (Brown 1991:46, 47). Rehabilitation through education was of secondary importance in the new prison regime. Instead, the Minister emphasised the value of work in prisons through the expansion of prison industries. These ranged from low-skilled work such as power cord and electric kettle and jug assembly to building furniture. As an extension of market-centred conceptions of neoliberalism, prisons were commod-ified and rehabilitation achieved through the discipline of work. Yabsley (1991:78) explained that:

> A requirement is now imposed on all prisoners to engage in mean-ingful work. This is not a punishment. It provides a double-edged advantage for those in incarceration. It provides an opportunity to earn money while in prison and at the same time offering the acquisition of skills which can advantage the prisoner on release.

Working in prison industries was a 'pragmatic rehabilitative program' that would provide 'self-discipline, meaningful routine and the acquisition of skills necessary to survive in the wider community' (Yabsley 1991:78). Work and participation in a competitive economic world form the motivational force for the development of individual self-interest. The logic of rehabilitation is based upon developing self-interest through discipline achieved in the pursuit of economic self-interest. Without competition, there is no discipline and, hence, exposure to the discipline of the market is the 'real' source of rehabilitation.

The prison reforms were systematic in their adherence to neolib-eral principles. The reforms demanded a redefining of individual behaviour. The withdrawal and cutbacks of the state services were replaced by the expansion of prison industries that approximated practices found in 'wider society'. The social technologies of reha-bilitation that saw prisoners as deprived of educational and vocational opportunities because of their underprivileged socio-economic back-grounds were problematised. Such approaches were seen as pandering to the prisoner's moral weaknesses and dependencies. Individual proclivity, rather than adverse social conditions, was the source of crime. The prisoners' circumstances were a matter of their own conscious, but inadequate, individual decisions, characterised by their own poor choices, insufficient effort or incorrigible conduct. Punish-ment, austerity and work discipline would provide the appropriate rehabilitation measures. The cutbacks in funding and redirection of policy emphasised the fact that prisons were no longer to redress perceived social inequities through education. Prisoners' 'develop-mental programmes' were to be no different to those 'who work in a normal community situation' (Yabsley 1991:76). Prisoners were to develop the self-discipline they lacked through work. The prison provided work for prisoners to gain skills and money to be self-creating, utilising their own personal and financial resources rather than squandering those of the state.

In this respect, the coalition government not only implemented reforms, but reformulated relations between the state and its citizens. This is in part expressed in Yabsley's (1991:75) political hostility to 'hogwash of sociological dictum'. At another level it conforms to the neoliberal critique of the idea of the existence of the 'social' or, more to the point, the social nature of government. As Margaret Thatcher famously stated after the Conservative Party election in 1979, 'There is no such thing as society, only individual men and women'. Neoliberal policy reform remakes the meaning of citizenship through the extension of market-inspired programs. Yabsley's reforms implemented policies that identified individualism, competition and market regulation as the road to social progress.

The prison reforms of the coalition government reflected broad similarities with neoliberal reforms noted elsewhere in Anglo-American democracies.[10] As elsewhere, the restructuring of state expenditures did not reduce aggregate levels of social expenditures as much as alter their priorities. Brown (1991:31) points out, in New South Wales:

Capital expenditure on law and order has more than trebled since 1987–88 with annual increases of 99% in 88–89, 16% in 89–90 and 43.8% in 90–91, reaching $250 million in 1990–91. The 34.5% capital expenditure increase in 1990–91 in the law and order area is the highest of any sector of public expenditure, double that for health and contrasting with education which received a 4.9% cut.

Reduced social welfare provisioning has progressed together with expansion of prison populations and the increase in funding for more prisons. The increase in expenditures is linked indirectly to the political consequences of the 'get tough' law and order policy pursued by the coalition government. Brown (1991:30) records that 'the Research Division of the Correctional Services Department (1990) found an overall increase of 50 days in the average time to serve in custody after the [Sentencing] act, calculating the increase as equivalent to 525 additional sentenced prisoners held on any one day'. A Bureau of Statistics report on the *Sentencing Act 1989* (NSW) found 'the average minimum sentence in Local Courts has risen from six months to one year' (Brown 1991:31). In the higher criminal courts there had been a 25 per cent increase in the average minimum term from eighteen months to two years (Brown 1991:31). The cumulative effect of the new government legislation created another 1400 prisoners in the first half of its term of office — an increased prison population of 35 per cent (Vinson 1991:81). There was no reduction in government expenditures. The social technologies of rehabilitation were replaced by policies of incarceration as the principal technology in the culture of crime control and regulation in criminal justice administration.

The reform of the Sentencing Act was considered an important legislative platform for the implementation of the new policy. Yabsley described it as 'the most important law and order reforms introduced into this parliament in many years' (cited in Zdenkowski 1995:226). 'Truth in sentencing' legislation demanded that the sentence passed by the court stood and that each prisoner should serve 75 per cent of a sentence (Zdenkowski 1995:226). The application of 'truth in sentencing' led to 'a substantial increase in pre-existing sentencing practice' and 'this law has been partly responsible for an explosion in New South Wales's already overcrowded prison system' (Zdenkowski 1995:226). The national increase in the prison population went from 11,436 to 13,600 (18.9 per cent) (Brown 1991:28). In New South Wales, in the same period, the prison population increased by 76.7 per cent (Brown 1991:28). During its period in office, the coalition government's expenditure on correctional services was directed to capital works to build and staff new prisons. The greater prison populations led to a large increase in the correctional services' budget[11] and the new government presided over a massive expansion of the prison system.

Still, the major increase in expenditures represented no 'real improvement in prison services and programs', but was used mainly for the 'containment of prisoners' and 'to keep up with the increase in prison population' (Brown 1991:31–2; see also Zdenkowski 1995). Truth in sentencing affirmed that in this new prison regime punishment must be the lesson. Indeed, during this period, prison program and education, as we have seen, were wound back. During the two terms of the coalition government, the prison population increased from 3950 prisoners in March 1988 to 6354 in April 1994 (Zdenkowski 1995:231–2). As one critic said, the expenditures on new prisons supplied 'more money for human warehouses' (Vinson 1991:84–5).

The re-criminalisation of public offences under the 1988 SOA was part of the cumulative effect of the 'get tough' legislation introduced in the Sentencing Act. The significant increases in Aboriginal imprisonment in New South Wales, recorded in prison census figures, showed its dramatic effects. The census figures are useful because they cover the first years of the coalition government in office. In national terms, the level of Aboriginal imprisonment increased by 25 per cent (Cunneen 1992:352). New South Wales recorded the greatest increase in Australia, with an 80 per cent increase from 369 in 1987 to 664 in 1991 (Cunneen 1992:351). The non-Aboriginal increase was 54 per cent (Cunneen 1992:352). New South Wales also contributed to the imprisonment of Indigenous women, which rose by 167 per cent between 1987 and 1991 (Cunneen 1992:353). Beyond the general increase in the prison population, new penal policy had a major impact upon the New South Wales Aboriginal prison population.[12]

Law and order in north-western New South Wales

The social impacts of the law and order campaigns were not restricted to prison reforms. The deployment of police in the north-western towns increased. The major towns in the North West region of New South Wales (see map, p. xii) — Bourke, Walgett, Wilcannia and Brewarrina — all have significant Aboriginal populations; in Wilcannia and Brewarrina Aborigines formed the majority of the population, 80 per cent and 60 per cent respectively. Despite the evidence that policing was not dealing with dangerous criminal offences or serious property crime, the North West towns had the highest police/ population ratio in New South Wales. In 1982 the figures were Brewarrina, eight police, population 2850; Walgett, 26 police, population 7600; and Bourke, 20 police, population less than 5000 (NSW ADB 1982:12, 239). In 1986 the Bourke police presence was 27 for a shire population of around 4000, giving a police/population ratio of 1:142 (Carrington 1990:5). The RCIADIC report revealed a similar pattern of policing in 1991: 11 police serviced Wilcannia, which had a population of 1000 (800 were Aboriginal) (Wootten 1991a:301). The police/population ratio was 1:77 (Wootten 1991a:301). This compares to a state-wide police/population ratio of 1:432 (Wootten 1991a:5). In the urban, middle-class suburb of Chatswood, by contrast, the ratio was 1:926 (Wootten 1991a:5). Such figures reveal the high level of surveillance and monitoring of populations in these small rural towns. The nature of offences in these towns indicates that the particular concentration of police was a continuation of a historical role of police to control Aborigines' behaviour in public spaces. The trivial offences involved high levels of discretionary power exercised by police.

The increase in imprisonment is significant, given that the Indigenous population was around 1.5 to 2 per cent of the overall population.[13] The rate of imprisonment in New South Wales was 86.2 per 100,000 for non-Indigenous prisoners and 868.5 per 100,000 for Indigenous prisoners (Biles cited in Tonry 1994:108; see also Tonry 2000), with ratio rates of 10:1 (Tonry 1994:108). In this respect, the government policies that increased imprison-ment patterns in New South Wales had a significant impact upon the Indigenous population of New South Wales. In effect, the new penal policy exacerbated the marginal position of Indigenous people. Public order offences, as we have seen, greatly increased the potential for Indigenous people to be taken into custody and, potentially, into prison.

The outburst of racial tension in Brewarrina on 15 August 1987 followed the deaths in quick succession of two Aborigines in police custody in the region at a time when public pressure was mounting for a Royal Commission to investigate Aboriginal deaths in police cells. The decision to proceed with the RCIADIC followed within a week of Lloyd Boney's death. His death is widely understood, as *Time Australia* (24 August 1987, p. 14) stated in its cover story, to have 'clinched the Hawke [Prime Minister] government's deci-sion to give in to the sustained pressure for a national inquiry'. RCIADIC investigations intensified the critical attention given to Aboriginal/police relations in the North West region and elsewhere.

Clarence Alec Nean died in 1982 (Wootten 1991a) from head injuries as a result of a collapse due to alcohol withdrawal while in police custody at Walgett Police Station. Mark Quayle died on 24 June from hanging while in custody at Wilcannia Police Station (Wootten 1991a) and Lloyd Boney died on 6 August 1987 from hanging while in custody at Brewarrina Police Station (Wootten 1991b). This last incident culminated in the riot that erupted at the wake held for Lloyd Boney. Brewarrina was the site of three highly public events involving Aborigines and police in North West towns between 1985 and 1987. The three riots heightened the image of the region as afflicted with Aboriginal lawlessness.

What is perhaps most evident in the region is the way policing became a constitutive process in racialising the towns in the region from the mid-1980s. These towns had a high police presence and the significantly high level of public order offences conformed to a distinctive historical and regional pattern (see NSW ADB 1982; Roy 1986; Cunneen and Robb 1987; Bonney 1989; Cowlishaw 1988, 2004). Policing took a localised form and police surveillance and monitoring intensified.

The law and order campaign fed directly into the local politics of these communities. In the town of Brewarrina, for example, the National Party candidate's campaign slogan was 'Do You Feel Safe in Your Street?' (Goodall 1990:25). The force behind this constant threat to public life was implicitly or explicitly identified as Aboriginal. The particular attention of police to the public order offence of 'drinking in the park' signalled the 'problem' as an Aboriginal one. The Brewarrina Shire Council, for example, made the point in relation to vandalism (Goodall 1990:24):

> The population of the Shire comprises 56% of Aboriginal race and most are concentrated in the townships of Brewar-rina and Goodooga. Unemployment is at a very high level and this probably has a bearing on the extent of vandalism in the town ... The cost of [vandalism in] 1985 was $20,000.

The juxtaposition of Aborigines and vandalism was not coinciden-tal.[14] Aboriginal youth was rendered synonymous with vandalism. The law and order campaign in these rural communities fixated on the Aborigine as a figure of civic and social disorder. The 'you' addressed in the politic slogan was understood to be the ordinary (white) man and his family, who were urged to vote for a National Party politician to make their streets safe from Aborigines, particularly Aboriginal youth.[15]

The image of Aboriginal lawlessness was invoked as a localised sign of rural decline that situated Aborigines as the *source* of the social pathologies of street crime and of alcohol and drug abuse rather than its *outcome*. The work of Heather Goodall and Kerry Carrington on Brewarrina and Wilcannia respectively reveals something of the localised discourses of Aborigines and the rural decline of the North West. In Brewarrina, for example, the Aboriginal presence was constructed as the antithesis of a 'nice country town', the obstacle to economic recovery. Similarly, in Wilcannia, 'the Aborigines' were referred to in terms of a common archive of racial classifications. In the local white opinion, they were 'unruly, disrespectful, smelly, lazy, drunken, bad and so on' (Carrington 1991:167). Aborigines were deemed to be the generic enemy of new prosperity. The proprietor of a Wilcannia motel said (Carrington 1991:167):

> We have found it is increasely [sic] more difficult to run the business due to the behaviour and activities of the aborigines [sic] of the community. I have been informed that the value of the business has dropped considerably and will drop even further. This is because of the aborigines [sic].

In the context of the new service economy, tourism became the source of economic salvation that Aboriginal behaviours threatened. In addition, in the law and order climate the Aborigines 'recently granted citizenship rights are considered the problem. As [a] service station proprietor put it, "I find that since aborigines [sic] received equal rights their previous good behaviour has changed"' (cited in Carrington 1991:166). The general implication echoes unchanged a more explicit racial discourse of an earlier period: 'Aborigines do not know how to cope with liberty and equality' (Carrington 1991:166). In the North West such collective representations gained additional meaning. The process of racialisation displaced the social disruption that had accompanied the demise of the rural economy and highlighted the precarious nature of recovery under the sign of Aboriginal lawlessness.

The policing strategies deployed matched the political culture of the racially separated communities and reinforced the divide in the North West region. The heightened focus of policing in the region was paralleled by an escalation of the police response to Indigenous disturbances. The police strategy to deal with an organised demonstration by the Aboriginal community at the Bourke Court House on 2 September 1986 was to deploy members of the paramilitary Tactical Response Group (TRG) (Cowlishaw 2004; Cunneen and Robb 1987:185). It was also flown into Brewarrina to deal with the Aboriginal riot in August 1987. Twenty TRG officers were deployed in Brewarrina for the following week (Goodall 1990:30). Shortly after the riot in Brewarrina, they were deployed again, in January 1988, for, in the words of the Regional Commander, Inspector Lockton, 'a special campaign to restore Law and Order with particular attention to be paid to people drinking [alcohol] in the park' (Goodall 1990:30). As Goodall (1990:30) described the policing practices, 'The TRG Officers took up their duties with an entirely new style of policing, marching four abreast up and down the footpaths of the main street and shopping centre throughout the day, their batons prominently displayed'.

The use of direct force was politically and symbolically legitimated in terms of the state of emergency surrounding the riots. This extraordinary overreaction was repeated when the paramilitary, anti-terrorist squad was deployed to control a sense of siege seemingly associated with Aboriginal drinking in public parks, which was deemed culturally inappropriate behaviour and proof of the wilful expression of cultural incompetence.

State of siege

> The tradition of the oppressed teaches us that the 'state of emergency' in which we live is not the exception but the rule. (Benjamin 1982:259)

The federal government established the RCIADIC as a national inquiry into the number of Aboriginal deaths in custody in the mid-1980s. The original inquiry listed the deaths of 44 Aborigines, but by 1988 the number of investigations had increased to 105. The Royal Commission found that the major overrepresentation of Aborigines occurred in police custody rather than in prison (Wootten 1991a:21–3). Detention in police custody does not necessarily lead to incarceration. At the completion of the RCIADIC, state and federal Directorates of Public Prosecutions decided that no action should be taken against police officers and prison warders found wanting in the RCIADIC reports. Aboriginal representative bodies were greatly disappointed by the findings of the RCIADIC and the families of those who died in custody expressed deep dismay and much disillusionment at the outcome.

Despite the lack of legal outcomes, the RCIADIC reports did concentrate national attention on the alarming differences in Aboriginal, as opposed to non-Aboriginal, criminalisation and placed a national spotlight on existing Aboriginal/police relations and the criminal justice system in general. What was equally disturbing was the evidence and testimony collected by the RCIADIC, which revealed significant regional variation in levels of criminalisation and varying intensity of policing strategies of control directed towards Aboriginal communities.[16] Collectively, the RCIADIC reports forged a link between the local histories of policing and the plight of many Aboriginal communities in Australia.

The riots in the North West of the 1980s were grounded in the history of social conflicts in these particular places. Specifically, the police strategies in deploying paramilitary-trained police units confirm an historical designation of these Aboriginal communities as potent sites of disorder. Perhaps the most notorious public use of the TRG was in a 1990 raid, Operation Sue, on the Aboriginal community of Redfern, an inner-city community of Sydney with a history of conflict with police. The policing strategy of maximum force by rapid response units was exercised in an early morning raid. Police in full riot gear used sledgehammers to gain entry to targeted Aboriginal households. Eight arrests were made on a number of minor charges (such as goods in possession, possession of an implement for use of drugs, unpaid warrants, breach of bail conditions) (Cunneen 1990b:13). Operation Sue, with 'some 70 police, led by the TRG, [raided] four houses' (Cunneen 1990b:13) and bears some resemblance to the military-style 'sweeps' described by Davis

(1990) on the public housing projects of Los Angeles. Such policing, based on military models of a technologically advanced strike force, seemed grossly disproportionate.

The history of settler colonial domination of the Indigenous population expresses itself as a paradox. At one level, settler colonisers seek to differentiate themselves from the colonised and, at the same time, to commit to a civilising mission organised around Indigenous assimilation. The injunction to homogenise is conducted by special state apparatuses. Settler colonialism takes upon itself the right to determine when the colonised are ready for inclusion. Repetition happens as new policies create distance from previous laws and norms, even while re-enacting the structure of a settler colonial system that is never fully left behind or surmounted. In each of the towns in the North West the elementary settler colonial divisions continue in spatially and socially defined domains: in Walgett, Gingie Reserve or Dewhurst Street (built by the Aborigines Welfare Board as transitional housing in the assimilation period) are designated as Aboriginal; in Brewarrina there is Barwon IV and West Brewarrina, locally known as 'Dodge City'; in Wilcannia, the Mallee; and the formally designated Aboriginal Reserve at the end of town in Bourke. The Aborigines in these communities come before the law as individuals, but are commonly framed in policing strategies as members of a group.

The margins of culture are controlled here not because of a political threat to usurp state sovereignty, but, as is often the case in settler colonies, to regulate and control the perceived cultural disorder and to establish cultural order. Aboriginal disorder feeds and activates a matrix of regulatory agencies that multiply the mechanisms of surveillance and monitoring. The proliferation of these processes encapsulates Aborigines within the dominating gaze of the state. The production of knowledge of cultural or social disorder is met with greater monitoring, surveillance and control through regimes that engage through pedagogical practices as much as they enforce state law. Historically, this was the function of Aboriginal affairs agencies such as the Aborigines Protection Board in New South Wales, which was controlled by state rather than federal legislation (Morris 1989). On these borderlands, Aboriginal communities become abject and other, the subject of more arbitrary or excessive forms of power and the diminution of rights, especially when the exigencies of state power are played out as emergencies.

The exercises in paramilitary policing in the 1980s conjure up images of a spatial grid of power that moves out from its centre to its more vulnerable and attenuated ends on the frontier. The ruptures and crises occur where the state's controlling grasp is most tenuous. State power is considered as extending downwards and outwards from some central point with an ever-diminishing presence. Systematic state order suppresses disorder and forces it to the margins. In spite of this, the state's grasp of such borderlands, in the contemporary period, is not tenuous. Generally, the inhabitants of the North West region are often more dependent on federal and state governments than urban regions (see Cowlishaw 1988). The spatial dimensions of remoteness have been overcome by the parallel development of new information technologies that have provided these communities with access to satellite communication systems and electronic communication, connecting them to national and international grids, and the development of transport facilities has ensured that the geographical distance of these communities from metropolitan centres is considerably reduced. In an 'emergency', as discussed above, the TRG was transported by helicopter and deployed within hours. Furthermore, the state's police presence is relatively more conspicuous and more numerous compared to all other parts of New South Wales.

Despite the self-proclamations of neoliberal ideology that seeks to equate the promotion of the 'self-regulating market' with the withdrawal of the state, the emphasis of neoliberal forms of governance has been to reregulate rather than deregulate the sphere of state agency. As Wacquant (2012:73) has stressed, 'the punitive shifts in welfare and penal policies ... have converged to establish a double regulation' of marginal populations. State reregulation has actively intensified interventions, which have not withered away but have been redirected disproportionately to those defined more generally by the new socio-economic term 'the precariat' — social groups whose lives are affected adversely because of structural unemployment and who are without recourse to steady social welfare provisioning or protective regulations. For advocates of market-oriented policies, precarious employment is the desirable outcome of a flexible labour market. Precarity is an instrument of neoliberal governance, governing through social insecurity (Neilson and Rossiter 2008). This is not a new condition of governance for Indigenous people in settler colonial states. The combination of marginal employment in the regional economy and state attempts to erase Indigenous status by improving Indigenous people through assimilation has meant that precarity has been a condition of most Indigenous people's existence (see Morris 1989). Settler colonial state policy has long cast Indigenous peoples in the role of national outsiders.

Andrew Lattas (1986) and Julie Marcus (1991) have persuasively argued that the strategies and technologies associated with address-ing Aborigines' adverse social conditions exercise their own regimes of power. The discourses that framed the welfare industries' will to power sustained their own complicity in the statistical quanti-fication of disorder. Quantitative difference between Aborigines and non-Aborigines points to the need for continued state inter-vention (Morris 1989:180). Welfare intervention is characterised by the policing of Aboriginal homes, families, marriages and children through the expansion of the mundane bureaucratic machinery of the child welfare, education, health and criminal justice systems. Marcus (1991:129) explains that:

[the] level of supervision and scrutiny, the colonising, dominat-ing gaze which follows Aboriginal Australians around the streets, into their homes, their marriages, their child-bearing and rearing and out again into the schools, the parks and the streets will itself provide the 'detail' . . . to support the dominating interpretation of Aborigines as chaotic and disorderly by nature.

The pervasiveness, its attention to detail and its control of the terms of interpretation is where social marginality is objectified. The demon-strable effect of welfare policing increases rather than decreases the forms of surveillance and regulation associated with administering life, death, education, health, and law and order, which regularly reach into Aboriginal lives in ways most non-Aboriginal people would find undermines the very rights it seeks to preserve.

The ordering of the dominant gaze induces its own forms of frag-mentation and disorder — its own facility to create indeterminacy and a sense of inescapable encapsulation for its subjects. For Marcus

(1991:129), the constitutive power of the gaze creates the conditions of terror, the conditions that sap the will, and the conditions of resentment that engender the ruptures, the riots and the deaths in custody. In its continuing work of ordering the socially disordered, the regulatory agencies achieve a seemingly omniscient reach into the most intimate and private aspects of Aboriginal life. Yet, as I have argued, the intensity of the gaze is not restricted to the will to power of the 'helping professions' in terms of the most intimate and private aspects of Aboriginal life. Welfare regulation and the judicial processes are often opposite sides of the same coin.

The national survey on police custody rates conducted by the RCIADIC produced figures of the overwhelming rate of detention for Aborigines. As Russell Hogg (1991:3) points out, the detention for Aborigines for 'all offence categories was found to be 3539 per 100,000 population compared with 131 for non-Aborigines ...Aborigines were detained 27 times the rate of non-Aborigines for the country as a whole'. Western Australia recorded the highest detention rate of Aborigines, who were detained 47 times more than non-Aborigines (Hogg 1991:3). The survey also found a higher proportion of repeat detentions for Aborigines as opposed to the non-Aboriginal population: 22.5 per cent and 14 per cent respectively (Hogg 1991:3). Between Aboriginal and non-Aboriginal women, the rate of detention was even higher: 'Almost 50% of all female detentions were of Aboriginal women, although they constitute less than 1.5% of the female population in Australia' (Hogg 1991:4). Hogg (1991:5) makes the important point that 'police custody is likely to massively disproportionately affect some groups, as is evidenced in Aboriginal detention rates'. If we reverse the focus from police detention to the Aboriginal community itself, we find a staggering rate and level of police intervention. The annihilating intent of terror regimes legitimated by the state of emergency is absent here. So, too, is the arbitrariness of the exercise of direct force, which produces the terror and holds whole populations in check through the sporadic and random exercise of violence. In the policing of Aboriginal communities, the politics of encapsulating populations operates more in terms of the efficiency and constancy of a seemingly inescapable everyday state of siege.

When we consider the rate of police detentions recorded in the national custody survey, we must consider the intensity of police scrutiny and intervention in Aboriginal lives that finds no comparison among the majority of non-Aboriginal Australians. The introduction of neoliberal policies in New South Wales intensified these interventions and increased the conditions of social insecurity. The regularised and extensive reach of judicial administration into Aboriginal life became more intrusive with the punitive shifts in penal policies. The levels of detention are not borne uniformly by all Aboriginal communities, but massively disproportionately by some. In the North West towns of Bourke, Brewarrina and Walgett, Aborigines were 67 times more likely to be in police custody than non-Aborigines (Wootten 1991a:299). In Wilcannia the rate was a staggering 223 times greater (Wootten 1991a:299) — an arrest rate of an astounding 416 per thousand (Wilson 1988:32). This translates into extraordinary intoxication detention rates: 'an Aboriginal person in Wilcannia in 1986 was 132.7 times more likely to be detained than a non-Aboriginal person anywhere else in Australia' (Wilson 1988:31). In Bourke in 1986, 87 per cent of people arrested on public order offences were Aboriginal (Cunneen 1990a:41), and in Brewarrina in 1986, 84.7 per cent of detentions and receptions for intoxication were for Aborigines (Cunneen and Robb 1987:204). In Bourke and Walgett the figures were even higher, 87.3 and 95.8 per cent respectively (Cunneen and Robb 1987:204). In Wilcannia in the six-month period between November 1987 and May 1988, 415 Aboriginal people and only 14 non-Aboriginal people were detained in the police cells as intoxicated persons (Wilson 1988:32). These interventions regulate and control Aboriginal lives in public space.

Policing in the North West region conforms to the general point that in such circumstances the criminal justice system is *primarily directed at the management of social marginality ... the "disreputable" poor* rather than prosecuting serious crime' (Hogg 1991:5, emphasis added). While the majority of cases involving police detention appear trivial, they also exist 'beneath the threshold of public scrutiny and concern' (Hogg 1991:5). For Hogg (1991:5), the justice system, at this level:

> constitutes a domain of social control that is restricted in its intensity but which exchanges a power of severity for an extensive and regularised reach into the social body, freed from many of

the trappings and protections of the law. What is lost in severity is gained in autonomy.

The question of accountability is tied directly to the wide discretionary powers granted to police and associated with summary offences legislation, especially when applied so disproportionately to specific Aboriginal communities. Within the bounds of small rural communities the reach of such discretionary powers of detention guarantee extensive control. In this, Hogg stresses the regulatory function of policing in the social life of marginal groups in the public sphere.

What I draw from Hogg's argument is that the separation of the law as repressive and prohibitive — as opposed to a positive, productive exercise of power — is overdrawn. The function of policing Aboriginal communities in the North West operates simultaneously as an exercise of legal coercion, but directed towards the regulation of normative behaviours. The regulatory role of policing at the level of summary offences is extended with the use of practices and procedures associated with forms of conditional liberty (e.g. bail conditions, parole and bond conditions, and community service), which extend the reach, facilitate the exercise of continued surveillance and enhance regulatory control of individuals in marginal populations.

An inordinate degree of the importance given to policing petty offences already existed, which suggests that policing strategies in the North West were concerned with defining and regulating what is normal and habitual as opposed to what is deviant. Crime and deviancy are often seen as the consequences of social and economic deprivation in Aboriginal and non-Aboriginal communities, yet comparisons between them continually reveal a level of disparity, especially in the area of street offences, which cannot be adequately explained in such terms. One aspect of the arrests in terms of unseemly behaviour demonstrates this. As Roseanne Bonney (1989:v) has pointed out, the reintroduction of the 1979 Offences in Public Places Act and the SOA (1988) in 1988 produced a common pattern associated with those arrested for offensive language. Brewarrina, Bourke and Walgett accounted for 58 per cent of those charged under the OPP and 64 per cent under the SOA (1988), and, as an element of all arrests for offensive behaviour, 87.8 per cent and 85.4 per cent respectively (Bonney 1989:25).[17] By contrast, the state-wide sample found offensive language rose from 23 per cent to 33 per cent for those arrested under the OPP and SOA (1988) respectively (Bonney 1989:21). The introduction of the new laws intensified the relations that already existed in policing the cultural borderlands of the North West.

The emphasis in policing strategies on 'unseemly words', I argue, is part of a process of defining normalcy, which also acts as a symbolic divide between the Aboriginal and non-Aboriginal communities in the North West. Swearing operates as a currency in an exchange that is both symbolic and conflictual. The asymmetry of the exchange is self-evident. The element of conflict is about who controls and defines the terms of normalcy and the habitual. Swearing is subsumed within the broader focus of police strategies of control of public space. The control of street crime and behaviour in the streets is as much a struggle to control public space as a struggle to regulate cultural space. Swearing in one context may not be designated offensive by one police officer, who has the discretion to make that decision, while in another context it may well be an affront not so much in terms of the public, but to police authority itself and deliberately so.

The postcolonial dimension to such conflictual relations adds to the contemporary situation. The struggle to control social space is also a struggle to control cultural space; social space and cultural space are joined. In the category 'location of offence', Bonney stresses that the bulk of OPP and SOA (1988) offences that took place in these three towns occurred in two locations — the street and inside/outside a hotel: 'these two categories accounted for 78 per cent of locations in the OPP group and 91.2 per cent of the locations under the SOA' (Bonney 1989:21). Many rural towns, like Brewarrina, have a designated 'black pub' for Aborigines. The police are the agents of control over public space. The struggle becomes one over symbolic control of space and casts the police and, by extension, the criminal justice system as the enemy. The demonstrably disproportionate interventions of the police into these communities and the perceived bias of the law effectively nurture Aboriginal grievances against law enforcement. At the local level, the legitimacy of authority is translated into the exercise of control over public spaces. These struggles are understood as policing cultural and political borderlands as much as strictly law and order issues. The situation is heightened in the context of the politics of Indigenous rights. The contestation of space is simultane-ously a contestation of authority and the right to exercise authority over space. In the everyday world of policing the North West, it is police versus Aborigines and Aborigines versus police. Every day is a state of siege.

Chapter 4

Postcolonial fantasy and anxiety
in the North West

Imaginary uncanniness and real threat, it beckons to us and ends
up engulfing us. (Kristeva 1982:4)

One arresting detail that emerged from the national investigation into Aboriginal deaths in police custody, held in Australia
in the late 1980s, was when police expressed the fear of an Aboriginal insurrection. The police reports surfaced as the Australian nation
was preparing to collectively celebrate its bicentenary. While investigating the death of Lloyd Boney, the RCIADIC found unrelated
evidence of the state of siege that haunted those policing the North
West region of New South Wales. These details emerged as an aside,
produced to explain why members of the police Tactical Response
Group (TRG) had been brought to the small rural town of Brewarrina in January 1988. A series of police reports, under the title of
'Bicentenary Celebrations', documented what they said were plans
for an armed Aboriginal uprising planned to coincide with the
bicentennial celebrations. A police constable at Brewarrina filed two
intelligence reports on 16 November 1987 and two further separate
reports submitted on 2 November and 12 December 1987. Commissioner Wootten (1991b:162) commented that the reports revealed
a 'completely unjustified paranoia on the part of local police . . . a
willingness to report completely unsourced gossip and to misinterpret
quite innocent events in amazing ways'.

The constable's report was based on his observation of two Aboriginal men sitting on the bonnet of a car in the bush. The report stated, 'this is a suspicious circumstance as this is almost totally an unused track' (Wootten 1991b:164). The men were 'known aboriginal [sic] activists who, although not vocal in their beliefs, do make it obvious that they are pro-Aboriginal and perhaps anti-police' (Wootten 1991b:164). Being 'pro-Aboriginal' not only made them 'perhaps anti-police', but also made them suspected participants in an Aboriginal conspiracy to disrupt the 1988 bicentenary. The report stated (Wootten 1991b:164):

> It is also believed by Brewarrina police that they may be holding meetings there on a regular basis for an unknown purpose. One possible reason is to organise protests or similar disturbances for the 1988 Bicentenary, which it is believed that there could be trouble in the western part of the state (Brewarrina, Bourke, Walgett).

The conspiracy was further corroborated in another police intelligence report. This unsourced report from Dubbo was headed 'Bicentennial Celebration' and gave further credibility to postcolonial fantasies (Wootten 1991b:162):

> Information . . . received that aborigines [sic] within Bourke, Brewarrina, Walgett and Moree areas have come into possession of a large number of firearms. Informant stated that the firearms were purchased in a crate through M. Mansell by use of government funding. Believed to be hidden for use in 1988.

This report escalated the potential threat by raising the spectre of international terrorism and gun running in the North West. 'M. Mansell' referred to Michael Mansell, who was, at the time, regarded as a controversial Indigenous leader by the media and mainstream politicians because of his strong advocacy for recognition of Indigenous sovereignty. More importantly, Mansell had recently returned from a trip to Libya, regarded at the time as a 'renegade' nation that supported international terrorism (see Ryan 1996:278–82). The police reports raised the spectre by inference of Aboriginal terrorism.

Mansell is a descendent of Tasmania's Indigenous peoples and he came to prominence as an advocate who fought for their rights and recognition. In Australian postcolonial politics, his demands for Indigenous sovereignty brought him into conflict and public confrontation with politicians and the media. It was his 12-day trip to Libya in April 1987 to attend the World Conference against Zionism, Racism and Imperialism and his pursuit of Libyan recognition of Aboriginal sovereignty that had enraged the federal Minister for Aboriginal Affairs, Clyde Holding, and generated massive publicity (Ryan 1996:278–9). As Mansell stated, 'In one day, they [Libya] recognised that the Aboriginal people of Australia are a nation of people. If putting the facts before the world exposes the racism, the oppression and the political madness of the Australian government against Aboriginal people, then that's fine' (*Examiner*, 25 April 1987, cited in Ryan 1996:279).

On his return he announced a second trip to Libya for financial support for Aboriginal programs (Ryan 1996:278). At this point, the federal Minister declared that the submission for land rights in Tasmania would be withdrawn until Mansell renounced his position. Mansell's postcolonial politics denounced colonial aggression, affirmed that Indigenous sovereignty had never been conceded and demanded its full restoration. His position was anathema to the more limited decolonising strategies that had been envisaged in Australia through land rights legislation.

The contents of the police reports that were exposed to public view by the RCIADIC do not simply reflect postcolonial paranoia in the minds of a couple of police officers and their informants, but refracted elements that formed part of a national debate.[1] The police in the North West region had accepted the veracity of the reports in 1987. The reports were taken as credible enough by police intelligence to deploy four TRG officers in Brewarrina in January 1988, which the Royal Commissioner ascertained was 'as a result of the fears concerning the possibility of an armed uprising of Aboriginal people in the Bicentenary year' (Wootten 1991b:165). The incident that raised the constable's suspicions was later explained by the man named in the report, Tombo Winters, at the Royal Commission hearing in Brewarrina. In the courtroom setting, the explanation was quite disarming. Winters revealed that another Aborigine,

Mr Clarke, had gone fishing and his car had broken down (Wootten 1991b:164). Clarke had walked to town for assistance and Winters obliged, only to have his own car run out of petrol. Winters in turn walked back to town to get petrol and then got a lift from another man back to his car before he proceeded to tow Clarke's car back to town (Wootten 1991b:164–5). The whole incident resembled a comedy of errors rather than a conspiracy to terrorise. As Winters quipped in the witness box, 'If every time you help somebody you are going to get this kind of stuff, you'd feel careful about helping people wouldn't you?' (Wootten 1991b:164–5). The infusion of such an excess of meaning into this mundane inconvenience reveals not only something of the conflictual relations that continue to exist in these towns but also something of the contemporary struggles taking place in postcolonial Australia. The bicentennial celebrations passed without incident.

This chapter explores the ways in which the institutional state is coupled with an imaginary state that is driven, in part, by anxiety and the fantasy of menace as much as by the rational procedures for the law. I want to highlight the relations of violence that reproduced an absolute opposition between Aborigines and police, as well as the real and imagined spectres of violence that animated those relations in the 1980s. In the previous chapter I considered the power of government apparatuses and institutional control, but here I focus on the particular couplings of an imaginary state with the workings of the institutional state to reproduce boundaries, both social and imagined, between the people and the state. The social importance of this interplay explains a number of the paradoxes that exist at the heart of the forms of governance of the North West region. There was, for example, an 'overwhelming preoccupation with petty public order offences' (Hogg 1991:3), especially in Aboriginal communities in the North West. The excessive concentration of detentions in the North West region is revealed, as we have seen, in the 1986 statistic that 41 per cent of all Aboriginal detentions in New South Wales were made in the towns of Brewarrina and Walgett (Cunneen and Robb 1987:203). Public order offences predominated. The charge of drunkenness accounted for 76 per cent of arrests (Cunneen and Robb 1987:199). When combined with 'other public order offences, offensive manner, unseemly words, etc., vagrancy, and assault and hinder police, then the public order offences total 96.1 per cent of all charges laid against Aboriginal adults' (Cunneen and Robb 1987:199). The New South Wales Anti-Discrimination Board (NSW ADB 1982) study of street offences revealed that conviction rates in the North West were the highest in the state (Cunneen and Robb 1987:239).

As discussed in the previous chapter, despite very few dangerous criminal offences or serious property crime, the North West towns had the highest police/population ratio in New South Wales throughout the 1980s. Such figures reveal the high level of surveillance and monitoring exercised in small rural towns. The nature of the offences indicates that a particular type of policing is directed at achieving social control over public space. These offences allow for high levels of discretionary power to be exercised by police. Police are required to intervene routinely in social interactions within public space and directly in personal spheres of conduct, behaviour or demeanour. The relatively low status of offences seems completely at odds with the high level of deployment of police, yet the fear expressed by police of an Aboriginal insurrection reveals something of a deeper and more complex picture of interaction between Aborigines and police than statistics allow. The anecdotal evidence in the police intelligence reports suggests that the act of policing is not simply about issues of law and order. The struggle to control community space is more than the containment of those who exist outside normative categories and who must be made to behave through police enforcement. As I have argued, they refuse to be obedient. The interactions were no less than policing cultural and political borderlands, which can account for the emotional energy expended on the struggles for control of public space.

The North West as contested space

In the RCIADIC findings there emerges a social world of ambivalence and ill-defined borders. The individual death reports provide a disturbing picture of the desperate existence of many Australian Aborigines. The asymmetry of power relations is amplified in the prevailing conditions of social life, health, life expectancy and a highly disproportionate rate of criminalisation, which clearly demarcate the social and material conditions of empowerment and disempowerment. Yet testimony in the RCIADIC reports provides a glimpse of something of the equivocation and anxiety that underpins the exercise of power. What emerges is an ambivalent but enduring engagement with alterity. The alterity of Aboriginal social life is not confidently and routinely suppressed and dominated; rather than certitude, there is anxiety and instability in the social demarcation between Aboriginal and white existence. The interplay between the social reality and the moral imagination produces an arena of moral ambivalence and fear. In the imaginative landscape of policing in the North West, the sovereign authority of the state seems vulnerable to challenge.

In particular, the police testimony to the RCIADIC reveals the uncanny experience of those who exercise power, authority and agency, and yet seemingly experience their social world as if they have lost the decisiveness to act. Police seem to inhabit a world that threatens to overwhelm them. The fact that the testimony emerged from an adversarial juridical system must be taken into account. The evidence accumulated in the RCIADIC reports had found expression in the law and order campaigns that dominated the politics of major areas of rural New South Wales in the mid-1980s. In neither the political nor legal arenas are the meanings, norms and behaviours transparent. Social interactions between Aborigines and non-Aborigines lend themselves to multiple interpretations. For the inhabitants of the North West, there existed a more complex social map of spatial and psychic forces.

The politics and proceedings of the RCIADIC provided a major public focus on Aboriginal and non-Aboriginal relations in the 1980s. The RCIADIC was shaped by a commitment to equal rights and the bringing to account of particular institutional forms of discrimination, which began in the 1960s; however, the granting of equal rights and a rejection of racism produced, in part, a more radical contestation of the existing political and social order. Indeed, in the following decade the issues surrounding Indigenous rights, initiated in the High Court decisions in *Mabo v Queensland [No. 2]* (1992) and *Wik Peoples v Queensland* (1996), dominated domestic political agendas of the 1990s. The political incorporation of Indigenous rights, as we have seen, generated a new arena of political debate and contestation. Paradoxically, the legislative change granting equal rights did not resolve the Aboriginal 'problem'. Increasingly, Aboriginal people have come to see themselves as Indigenous subjects in their own right and not simply the objects of assimilation to be acted for or acted upon. Indeed, the latter decades of the twentieth century ushered in a period of indeterminate relations, when all that had previously constituted Aboriginality no longer remained a stable and predictable site of knowledge.

The following is an ethnographic account of some of the disquieting and violent aspects of these relations. In the 1980s the North West appeared as a flashpoint for tensions and conflicts between Aboriginal people and the police and a number of direct confrontations occurred. The narratives of these relations are found in the RCIADIC reports and in the research materials from the Bourke riot (see below) (Cunneen and Robb 1987:182; Cowlishaw 2004, 1994) and the Brewarrina riot trial. The latter riot occurred on the night of the funeral of Lloyd Boney, which was held a week after his death in police custody. As described in Chapter 1, a violent confrontation between Aborigines and police followed when the police moved to break up the wake. Seventeen Aboriginal people were subsequently charged. In the 'Brewarrina 17' trials in Bathurst in 1991, the North West was represented as a violent and unstable world. The riot received national media coverage on television and in the major city and regional newspapers, and the representations were framed in terms of allegedly drunken Aborigines attacking police.

The North West is perhaps better understood as a 'contact zone', as 'social spaces where disparate cultures meet, clash, grapple with each other often in highly asymmetrical relations of domination and subordination' (Pratt 1992:4). It is a contested space because the peculiar conditions of history dominate the life of different peoples with competing interests and claims on the same place. Such contested terrain is not spatially determined by physical geography, but created as part of the Indigenous, historical and cultural geography of the modern settler state formation. For Pratt (1992:7), 'contact zones' emphasise relations between the two groups, not in terms of their separateness 'but in terms of their co-presence, interlocking understandings and practices'. Contact zones exist on the borders and margins of society. Yet it is in these unstable zones that the 'most powerful symbolic repertoires are found' (Stallybrass and White 1995:20). Citing Barbara Babcock (1978), Peter Stallybrass and Allon White (1995:20) assert that 'what is socially peripheral is often symbolically central'. These marginal spaces are where separateness is replaced by co-presence and the raw edges of these symbolic repertoires are played out, often 'out of all proportion to their actual significance' (Stallybrass and White 1995:20).

Policing cultural borderlands

The North West is a cultural borderland, a historically specific one. It is conspicuous for the numerically significant Aboriginal populations that live in the region and their racially and culturally defined distinctiveness. In these particular towns, co-presence is not marginal: it is a central aspect of social existence, but it is achieved at a price. The police intelligence reports provide insight into the depth of the agonistic relations that existed in these towns. The reports were not framed in the realms of fiction or fantasy, but were based upon the statements of police informants and direct police observations. The observations affirmed an expectation of an armed racial uprising in Brewarrina and neighbouring towns. This bicentennial paranoia objectifies in a singular instance something that can be traced to more indeterminate and diverse struggles to maintain the racial dichotomies of self/community and other. The other we encounter here is more often not one of radical difference, but a negative opposite (e.g. drunkenness, street disorder, unemployment, ill health, etc.). Otherness and difference are represented as negativity in terms of hierarchical principles that encode cultural/racial difference, but are unstable and subject to challenge.

The primary concern is with processes of the cultural demarcation and symbolic differentiation associated with boundary phenomena. Stallybrass and White's (1995) attempt to explore 'grotesque of boundary phenomena' along class lines is useful here. For them, the instabilities at the boundary crossovers are where grotesque figures are produced out of the very drive to demarcate boundaries. They give particular focus to two distinct kinds of the production of the grotesque. The first is the simple production of the self/other in relation to the self-defining group. The grotesque is aptly demonstrated with regard to racialised categories. In the period when the Aborigines Protection Board controlled Aborigines in New South Wales, the political exercise of social and cultural boundary demarcation expressed itself through formal policies of discrimination and repression embedded in practices of segregation and exclusion. The construction of the colonised, the inferior natives, did not simply legitimate domination; racial categorisation was part of demarcation and boundary maintenance. Yet while the allegedly diminished capacity and responsibility of the other resulted in the denial of rights, it was not the real source of threat. Rather, the threat of the 'grotesque other' was carried in the fear of pollution and contamination. The spectre of the grotesque other animated the segregation into separate housing on the 'mission' and separate facilities at the local hospital and the front row at the cinema, and it denied access to public facilities like the local school and the swimming pool. In this production of the grotesque, the other is not simply the negation of the self, but a source of contagion, a fear of bodily inundation. The act of exclusion is constitutive of the social identity of the majority.

The second form of the grotesque, Stallybrass and White (1995:192–3) argue, is found in the context of 'hybridisation or inmixing, in which the self and the Other are conceived to be enmeshed in an inconclusive, heterogeneous, dangerously unstable zone'. In this context, a no-man's-land emerges, where pre-existing boundaries become permeable and socially stable zones become unfixed and fractured along internal lines of uncertainty. I deal here with the historical and social conditions, which produce unstable identities. What emerges is the capacity for slippage from one form to another or to simultaneously embody both. 'Hybridity and inmixing' should not be reified here as a necessary principle of uncertainty. What is important is to stress the social and historical context of change and repression as the condition of uncertainty that creates contested space. For Stallybrass and White (1995:194), it is the drive for a singular collectivity that underpins the production of the grotesque. These demands render the 'community' on the cultural borderlands anomalous, not fitting into classificatory systems and rendering the judicial system as a site of cultural contestation.

The construction of political discourse of the law and order campaigns connected with existing social anxieties in positing unity rather than separation as a social ideal. The National Party politicians, who represented all rural communities in the North West, completely rejected recommendations to grant land rights to Aboriginal people in New South Wales, as I have shown in Chapter 2, because they asserted there was no basis for separate land claims or cultural difference. The construction of a racial criminality in the North West region gained momentum in the mid-1980s. It took on the meaning of a particular transgressive threat, which culminated in a law and order campaign run by the conservative political parties for the state election in 1988. This campaign, as discussed in Chapter 3, positioned non-Aborigines as victims of 'Aboriginal criminality'.

The relationship between meaning and events is not bound up in the truth or falsity of the events, but between their symbolic functions and the reactions they engender. The issue of social conflict between Aborigines and non-Aborigines was displaced from the politics of racial condemnation and converted into a social cause for more efficient and effective policing. The threat is not located in themes of contamination, but in disorder born of moral weakness and a loss of control. The dichotomy of self/community and other remains, but the latter has transformed into a transgressive threat: that is, the threat of being subsumed within this criminal form of social order. The other exists within, rather than beyond, the self/community. The 'Aboriginal other' is treated as having the formal rights of the citizen, but is regarded as lacking the requisite sensibility. Aboriginal modernity is reduced to a hollow mimicry of the liberal subject: a copy that menaces the existence of the original. The carefully divided world of the past, where Aborigines and non-Aborigines lived in different social realms, is threatened by the amorphous mix of the present.

The state of siege rests upon an agonistic mode of authority that emerges from the boundaries constructed of self/other. Its discriminatory effects are evident in the policing practices of the North West and in the racial stereotypes of an Aboriginal criminality that remained central to the campaign. But, importantly, it is not simply Aborigines who are condemned by police discourses, but the policies and practices of the state itself, condemned as ill conceived, misinformed, naive and out of touch with the realities of policing the borderlands. In these episodic moments of moral panic, both the centre and the margins are demonised by different groups. But political positions become dichotomised and there is no argument about who the demons are.

On the other side of the social divide, one of the few voices from an Aboriginal perspective on the North West riots is found in an interview with a longstanding Aboriginal resident of Bourke after one of the Bourke riots.[2] The riot began in front of a hotel and led to a confrontation between Aborigines and police on the streets (Cunneen and Robb 1987:182). An estimated 50 to 80 Aborigines, mostly youths, were involved in the melee. Bottles were thrown and some police injured. The catalyst involved the perceived lenient treatment by police of a non-Aboriginal man who had allegedly reversed his car over the head of an injured Aboriginal youth lying on the road the day before. It had been rumoured that 'the driver had only been charged with negligent driving and released' (Cunneen and Robb 1987:181). The substance of the interview makes clear the police are regarded as applying the law in an arbitrary and highly partial manner; this is the common experience of discrimination by local state bodies that many Aborigines share. The experience of sharing the same space as liberal subjects slips away. When asked, 'what you actually saw of the riot', the long-term resident explained (Cunneen and Robb 1987:263):

> I just saw something that has festered over many years and it just came to a head. You see it nearly every day. You see the anger, the frustrations in the people and what happened, it just triggered everything off. It's something that's ... been happening here in Bourke for years ... What annoys me about the whole thing is that people tend to look at Aboriginal people. They point the finger at the Aborigines. It's a problem — it's a black and white problem in this town. What I saw of the riots that night I saw people throwing bottles. I see that nearly every Wednesday night.

There is neither a denial of Aboriginal complicity in this social situation nor of an anger that is reactive and unproductive. But such anger is a perpetual condition of life and not something that can be wished out of existence. Being on the border and being Aboriginal, negotiating a world of opposing ideas and knowledges, Aborigines cannot escape the burden of race: the luxury of not being angry.

What is fundamentally important in the Aboriginal testimony is the assertion of the denial of their rights as liberal subjects. The denial of such rights can be seen in the differential treatment of Aboriginal people before the law, which is made explicit through localised policing practices. In this particular case, the 'lenient treatment' given to the man in custody is contrasted with the treatment given to the Aboriginal people of Bourke who had organised a demonstration on the day of the court case. Those who participated were confronted with a show of force from the paramilitary-trained TRG. Despite the security precautions, it was deemed unsafe for the accused to be led to the courtroom (Cunneen and Robb 1987:265). As the Bourke resident stated, the 'man was kept hidden and the police wouldn't communicate with the people' (Cunneen and Robb 1987:265). By refusing to allow the appearance of the accused, the police actions communicated that the Aboriginal demonstration was potentially violent, but it also communicated a lack of regard for the due process of law. The Aborigine as grotesque other emerges as an imagined possibility in this contested space. According to the Bourke resident (Cunneen and Robb 1987:265):

> All the Aboriginal people wanted to see that man brought across to the court. That's all they wanted to see. But they wouldn't do that. The Aboriginal people were here to see the man being charged. And this is where the anger kept building up all the time. But yet they brought two Aboriginal boys handcuffed with about ten policemen surrounding these two kids. They brought the riot squad from Sydney and mingled with the crowd. But all the people wanted, they weren't going to smash the town up anymore, they wanted to see that man brought over. To see justice being done.

The Aboriginal people had assembled to witness the public expression of justice at the local level. They were placing under critical scrutiny the symbolic status of the law in terms of the equality of all citizens. The precautions taken by police simply reaffirmed for the Bourke resident the historical circumstance that there exists 'one law for the black and one law for the whites' (Cunneen and Robb 1987:265). In effect, Aboriginal people's formal rights are said to exist, but in the absence of any substantive connection to policing practices. Rights remain segregated and racially ordered in their implementation.[3]

Postcolonial subjects

Postcolonialism has created its own subjects on both sides of a racial divide. This section explores the experience and interpretation of the cultural borderlands found in the police evidence of negotiating a world of multiple meaning and opposing ideas and knowledges. In the following analysis of police testimony from the RCIADIC, as well as evidence given at the Brewarrina riot trial, I consider the powerful and yet ambivalent position of police. The police force is the most visible face of state authority and must be willing and able to uphold the law, but, perhaps, more importantly, must seek and win compliance to social order. There emerges in the testimony a strong emphasis on a world of contingency and the application of a contingent jurisprudence. The metaphor of centre/margins is mobilised by police to delegitimise the dictates of the centre as bureaucratically ordered, rule-bound and 'out of touch' with the realities of policing the borders of uncertainty. The experience of police exercising sovereignty over the street is one of confrontation driven by the dictates of seemingly alternate sovereignties. The world of the North West is constituted in terms of fear and provocation, on the one hand, and contempt and derision, on the other. The police call upon the specific conditions in the North West to free it from the dictates of the rules of policing. The contingent conditions require the exercise of more discretionary powers than are usually accepted in policing activities.

The everyday interactions of police and Aborigines can be contrasted with the characterisations that emerge from the politically staged performances of the courts and Royal Commission. A judicial focus by the state apparatuses effectively contains the unanticipated ruptures of riots and Aboriginal deaths in custody. It does this by seeking out specific abuses of power and identifies them as aberrations. The systemic nature of these aberrations is of interest here. By the time the Royal Commission brought down its findings on the death of Lloyd Boney in police custody, the Brewarrina lock-up where he died had been pulled down. The offending structure was removed, as if in an act of cleansing; its erasure from the physical landscape removed the unanticipated aberration at its site. New requirements rule that Aborigines are no longer to be held in custody in Brewarrina for more than two hours before they are driven to the Bourke lock-up and held there. Yet, almost a decade before the RCIADIC reports, the New South Wales Anti-Discrimination Board reported that the conditions in the lock-up 'are clearly unsuitable for any person, let alone one who has committed no legal wrong and is in need of care' (NSW ADB 1982:210). The report here referred specifically to the practice of locking up intoxicated persons, despite the 1979 decriminalisation of public drunkenness. The everyday in which the socially vulnerable are forced to live was not considered exceptional and policing continued to comply with its own rules rather than those of existing legislation.

But erasure has limited efficacy as an act of cleansing. Just as senior administrative authorities may not rigorously enforce their own rules, local police also break the rules. In the continuing attempts to maintain comprehensive control, police find it necessary to 'bend the rules'. There is a continued resort to the exercise of arbitrary power and personal discretion, to the bending of rules and procedures to facilitate control of the population. Thus a subterranean domain of policing is constructed. Under the Offences in Public Places Act and the *Intoxicated Persons Act 1979* (NSW), being drunk in a public place was no longer deemed a criminal offence, but an intoxicated person could be held for eight hours in a 'proclaimed place'. In many small country centres, no civilian-proclaimed place was created and, hence, as in Wilcannia, the police station doubled as a proclaimed place. Thus, despite the decriminalisation of drunkenness, drunk Aborigines continued to be locked up in police cells. In practice, little had changed.

Under the Police Commissioner's instructions (Circular 86/157, August 1986), it was stipulated that such detained persons in police stations 'should be kept to a minimum' and where 'there is no civilian proclaimed place available ... [should] be taken home' (cited in Wilson 1988:32). Yet in late 1986 and through the six-month period following, there appeared no attempt to comply with such instructions. The point is that such a high rate of detention for intoxication was in direct violation of the Police Commissioner's instructions. The situation is further complicated by the apparent conflict between policing practices in the North West and the application of the procedures for the Intoxicated Persons Act. The fact that Wilcannia and other small police stations remained unsupervised overnight meant that intoxicated Aboriginal persons were often detained in excess of the maximum eight-hour detention period. Again, in the case of Wilcannia, the Royal Commission found that in the six-month period between January and June 1987, of the 150 Aboriginal people detained, 109 were held illegally for longer than the prescribed maximum period (Wootten 1991c:51). Evidence from Cunneen and Robb (1987) and the findings of the RCIADIC in New South Wales suggest that such 'discretionary practices' that breached formal rules and procedures were commonplace. What is equally important is that the breaches worked quite pointedly to the disadvantage of Aborigines, who had no avenue of remedy until the RCIADIC.

The Royal Commission reports were highly critical of police actions and conduct in the region. In the case of Mark Quayle, who died in the Wilcannia police cells, the Commissioner was scathing in his assessment. The connection between what he called the 'massive and often illegal locking up of Aboriginal people' and the apparent complacency with which Mark Quayle was removed from hospital care to a police cell was directly linked to illegal but routine policing practices in Wilcannia. The Commissioner found that 'the two officers acted without legal or moral justification' (Wootten 1991c:5) and that the 'shocking and callous disregard' for an Aborigine had resulted in his death: 'The police took Mark to the police station. Except that they did not fingerprint him, they treated him like a prisoner, removing his property and checking whether there were any outstanding warrants, which there were none' (Wootten 1991c:5). These practices, as the Anti-Discrimination Board had revealed in 1982, were routinely applied to Aborigines taken into custody for drunkenness, despite its decriminalisation. In this case, Mark Quayle had not been drinking and had gone to the hospital as a patient to receive treatment, but was, nevertheless, processed as if a criminal. His death was not the result of a rupture of normal practice, but of the accumulation of systematic breaches, which had become part of everyday police practice.

My argument is that police discretion achieves the collective status as a 'given'. The routine processing and practices associated with 'Aboriginal drunkenness' are also acts of social differentiation that reproduce the local social order. 'Bending the rules' allows discretion and discriminating behaviour on the part of police, who socially encode what is locally deemed as necessary and appropriate for Aborigines and other locals. To uniformly apply these rules runs the risk of rendering broader social differentiations meaningless. The Commissioner found a marked discrepancy in the treatment of a drunken and abusive, but prominent and white, citizen and that handed out generally to Aborigines. In one particular case, the Commissioner recorded the procedures revolving around the removal by the police sergeant of a citizen who, drunk and speaking loudly, made abusive accusations in the hotel at closing time aimed at the Aboriginal customers: 'these black cunts have fucked this town', he stated (Wootten 1991c:120). As the police sergeant removed him, he continued his drunken abuse of Aborigines. When taken to the police station, he demanded to ring the Regional Commander. The police officer agreed to the request, which was not followed up by the man. Ultimately, the sergeant used his discretion to contact the man's son, who arrived at the station to calm his father and finally take him home. No police action was taken. This sensible exercise of restraint and discretion, as the Commissioner pointed out, would not have been extended to Aboriginal citizens and demonstrates the hollowness of the formal impartiality of the law (Wootten 1991c:120). Difference is reaffirmed in the capacity to discriminate between civilised behaviours when policing those associated with the self and against the grotesque other. Acts of civility are exercised as a form of discretionary power that affirms the lines of social demarcation and upholds the distinction of the privileged category of 'whiteness'.

Policing the borders of uncertainty in this contested space, the police are more than upholders of the sovereign power of the state; they are mediators across a range of social and institutional domains. The police are called upon as the final arbiter or as the ultimate sanction of authority. The lonely death of Mark Quayle in Wilcannia provides ample evidence of the dynamics of power in this arena of cultural contestation. Mark Quayle died in the early hours of

24 June 1987, alone in a cell at Wilcannia Police Station (Wootten 1991c:1). Earlier that morning, at 2.10 am, he had been brought by relatives to the Wilcannia Hospital after he had woken them to tell them he was starting to go into the 'horrors' (Wootten 1991c:20). He was disoriented and hallucinating because of alcohol withdrawal or what is colloquially called 'being in the dings' or 'the horrors'. For Quayle, 'being in the dings' meant that 'he was shaking' and he kept repeating that 'he was cold, he was seeing things . . . and could not sleep because he was hearing things' (Wootten 1991c:20). The patient could be suffering delirium or some acute psychiatric illness — experiencing schizoid episodes, to use medical discourse. Local Aborigine 'Badger' Bates placed Quayle's symptoms in an Aboriginal frame of reference: 'Aborigines in the area believed in and were afraid of spirits, in particular of *Dinagoollies* or "clever men" who punished wrong doers' (Wootten 1991c:54). This is why he believed Quayle, whom he knew well, 'slept with the light on, because he was afraid of the dark, a fear related to a traditional belief in spirits' (Wootten 1991c:54).

This is not the place for a discussion of a culturally nuanced assessment of Quayle's condition in the medical setting, but one aspect deserves a mention; on the cultural borderlands, being dispossessed and marginalised also means that cultural understandings and social needs are cast aside and ignored. In the working of the institutional space of the hospital, they are simply opaque and erased.

At the hospital, despite the presence of a qualified nurse and a wardsmaid, and telephone conversations between the hospital matron and the medical doctor, Quayle was not placed under observation and was not diagnosed or treated. Three years earlier, in September 1984, friends had brought him to the hospital with the same symptoms and on admission he was treated, 'sedated with a heminevrin regime'[4] (Wootten 1991c:19) and discharged in five days. On this second occasion, confused and wandering about, he disappeared from the hospital. The wardsmaid's response was to comment that he had 'gone walkabouts' (Wootten 1991c:23) and to call the police. 'Walkabout' exists as a national trope often deployed to explain Aboriginal 'unpredictability', the evidence of an unstable interiority. Aborigines have historically been depicted as going walkabout. The failure of the very successful and celebrated Aboriginal tennis player Evonne Goolagong

(Cawley) to win crucial matches was even explained away in terms of her going walkabout. Cultural scripts explained her inconsistency.

The stereotype of Aboriginal identity conditioned the medical staff's response. Quayle's 'unpredictability', not his medical condition, arrested the concern of the medical staff. As the Commissioner pointed out, three concerns dominated: (1) the patient's own safety in as much as he may fall in the river, (2) the absence of a place to confine the patient and (3) the risk to other patients, including two children, due to his unpredictability (Wootten 1991c:36). The image of the unrestrained grotesque is evident in all these concerns. Assessment is made in terms of a calculus of risk based upon Aboriginal unpredictability.

The process of normalisation reveals much of Quayle's progress from a medical setting to a cell, understood in terms of the so-called drunken and disruptive Aborigine (see Carrington 1991). Foucault's characterisation of modern power has made us familiar with such normalising forms of governance. For Foucault, modern forms of regulation operate through a knowledge/power nexus that provides an interpretive strategy and a body of knowledge that renders 'others' knowable and manageable. Yet missing from his account is the pairing of the politics of transparency and the inexorable fear of the unpredictable other. The calculation of risk in processing Mark Quayle is based upon probability, a probability measured in terms of the shadowy grotesque figure of the Aboriginal other, a fantasised construction of the grotesque other.

The death of Mark Quayle provides a localised version of the operation of power through the politics of transparency that not only renders him knowable as a category of being, but provides the course of action needed to manage him. At the Commission hearing, the matron affirmed the pressing concern to call 'the police so that Mark could be kept in a cell overnight to stop him wandering away' and 'patients sleeping in cells happens to lots of other [Aboriginal] boys' (Wootten 1991c:26–7).[5] Unpredictability could be contained in a cell. Defending this practice, the matron stated that 'most people that were uncontrollable in the hospital were under the influence of alcohol and the majority of these people were Aboriginal' (Wootten 1991c:28). Quayle's unpredictability was rendered predictable as an Aborigine in this racial discourse. He was presumed to be affected by alcohol and to be disruptive. Similarly, as the doctor stated, 'he understood that the [Aboriginal] patient was in [police] custody at the time of the telephone call' (Wootten 1991c:34), when he agreed that it would be best if Quayle were placed in a cell. The doctor assumed the sister had all the 'relevant information', but the sister, who had access to the outpatient and inpatient records, 'had not read them' (Wootten 1991c:34–5).[6] The individualising strategies of medical treatment are replaced by Indigenous typification. Quayle, who was in the paddy wagon throughout the matron and doctor's discussions, was removed from the hospital supervision and placed in an unlit cell, where he had no access to the lights. The routine breaches of everyday practices operated across and between state institutions as a norm — not as an aberration. Mark Quayle's confinement in a cell temporarily removed the disorder, but, equally, was a recourse to normative practices that, for a time, would restore order to cultural borderlands.

Yet, as the Commissioner pointed out, such breaches revealed a harder edge than simple complacency and neglect. Contempt and derision surface regularly from behind the veneer of complacency and neglect. This is further revealed in the callous disregard Quayle's family received after his death. The evidence of the police officer who took Quayle into custody is an example of the perverse logic used to explain his death. The fact that Quayle was brought to the hospital for treatment by his relatives became evidence that 'his family didn't want him because they brought him to the hospital and left him' (Wootten 1991c:36). Later, this became police evidence that Quayle's family had 'dumped him' at the hospital, a suggestion the Commissioner described as a 'cruel lie' (Wootten 1991c:37, 49).

In another example of contempt, the conventions associated with dealing with the body of a deceased person were cast aside. This breach is even more telling, given that in the case of wilful or accidental loss of life, the difficult role of informing the next of kin often falls to police. This role is part of their training and part of their public role. In this case, the Royal Commissioner (Wootten 1991c:7) recorded:

In a further revolting display of inhumanity, Constable Coombes stopped an ambulance containing Mark's body in a bag, in the main street of Wilcannia, and called on Mark's brothers to get in, climb along their brother's body to his head and identify him, on the implied, if not expressed, threat that if they did not do so the body would be taken to their mother's house for identification.

As Julie Marcus (1991:129) suggests, at the margins of culture there is no civilisation. In Michael Taussig's (1989:11) terms, this is 'low intensity conflict' affirmed in its 'leading characteristic ... to blur accustomed realities and boundaries and keep them blurred'. The report into Mark Quayle's death illustrates the productions of knowledge practised in the North West that gained currency at the expense of their victims. Indigenous peoples' status as citizen recedes in the face of such abhorrent acts, which afford them neither the empathy nor the dignity that would be extended to other citizens.

Contingent jurisprudence

More extreme evidence shows that the practice of a contingent jurisprudence, shaped by local social circumstance, is widespread in the rural courts. The Royal Commission found evidence of the falsification of evidence and, hence, a violation of criminal justice processes by police officers. The Commission's inquiry into the death of Lloyd Boney supported the coroner's previous findings that the police officers had lied under oath, had fabricated evidence about the events and had unlawfully denied bail to the victim (Wootten 1991b:55–62). The Commission found evidence of police officers lying under oath in other New South Wales cases, namely those of Edward Murray, Bruce Leslie and Lawrence Kearney (Wootten 1991b:55–62). In his final report, Commissioner Wootten found that 'negligence, lack of care and/or breach of instructions' by custodial officers 'played an important role in the circumstances leading to 13 of the 18 deaths' (Wootten 1991a:63–4). Criminal and/or disciplinary action was recommended in relation to seven deaths (Wootten 1991a:83).[7] Thus it is in negligence and in breaches that the sources of these ruptures of proper procedures are found. The Royal Commission sought to regain order, mend the breaches and regain the certainties in order to reaffirm the order of the state. The notion of the state ordering the disorder slips out of view. It is as if the violation of procedures and practices is not part of the potential violence structuring the everyday, but an aberration. For the Commission, these are ruptures and unanticipated events that capture attention and must be rectified.

The police officers whose responsibility it is to police the cultural borderlands have their own theory about the sources of disorder and how to contain them. They assert that a state of siege explains the arbitrariness of order and procedure. Superintendent Harding, the officer in charge of the investigation into the final death investigated by the RCIADIC, made no pretence. David Gundy died in his bedroom as a result of a gunshot wound he received during a pre-dawn police raid on his family home in Marrickville, a suburb of Sydney. The police mistakenly shot and killed Gundy, an innocent man. When asked by the Commissioner if the police had acted reasonably, Harding replied, 'I know why they did these things and to be perfectly frank, I have done them myself and understand the philosophy behind them' (Wootten 1991d:153). When asked whether he was concerned about the actual lawfulness of the raid, he responded by saying, 'In this sterile atmosphere [the Royal Commission hearings] most certainly but out in the field where it's happening, no' (Wootten 1991d:153). For police, no distancing effect exists at the hard edge of policing, where uncertainty is the only constant. In this exchange, there is a falling out within the order of the state. The attention paid to the state's abuses of power is counteracted by the assertion that arbitrariness is needed to control its own state of siege.

The contingency is produced by the tension that exists between what is seen as unavoidable and potentially unmanageable. Yet the management of the risk associated with unknown circumstance, paradoxically, can operate by fixing firm boundaries, by closing ranks, by producing 'all or nothing' categories. Commissioner Wootten (1991a:154) stated:

in my experience as a Royal Commissioner, I have become very conscious of the existence of a 'police culture' ... There is a very great blindness in that culture to the problems of police investigating police, and a very great reluctance to acknowledge the possibility of wrong-doing by police.

The standard procedure of inquiry is for the police to have a central role in investigating police. Wootten criticised other police investigations into Aboriginal deaths in custody for their haste in exonerating fellow police officers. In the report on the death of Lloyd Boney, Wootten (1991b:124) concluded that the inspector who investigated the Brewarrina riot had 'at no stage subjected police conduct to any real scrutiny, or pursued with any enthusiasm any evidence which might have contradicted police'. Indeed, the inspector had only been in town overnight and interviewed one officer before he told the media that 'he had found no suggestion at all of foul play in any sense' (Wootten 1991b:124). This same inspector was sent back to Brewarrina to assist police to investigate and charge Aborigines involved in the melee that followed Boney's funeral (Wootten 1991b:125). The inspector prevailed as a symbol of continuity in his role at the Brewarrina trial, liaising between the Crown Prosecutor and the police witnesses, the principal witnesses in the case against the Aboriginal defendants. The same investigator who exonerated the police officers' conduct promptly began gathering evidence from the same cohort of people for the prosecution of the 'Brewarrina 17'. In this case, as the Royal Commissioner's findings affirmed, the investigator's attention to impartiality had been insufficiently adhered to, which, in turn, reinforced the view among Indigenous people of biases inherent in the application of the law to them.

The major focus of the investigation of 'taking life' that concerned the RCIADIC was the role of the police, police actions and procedures. The members of Lloyd Boney's family accused the police of killing him and, according to the Commissioner, it remained 'a very widespread view amongst Aborigines' despite the findings of a coronial inquiry (Wootten 1991b:1). The Commission's report emphasised Aboriginal anger and suspicion of the police in terms of 'the failure to notify the family [and] give them an opportunity ... to see his body before it was removed from Brewarrina' (Wootten 1991b:17). The major issue for Boney's relatives was the physical impossibility of self-hanging. The attempts of police to explain his death to Boney's relatives failed dismally. The proposition that Boney had 'climbed up the door, put his left arm on the door to prop himself up, then tied the sock around the grille' (Wootten 1991b:97) could not be achieved by two of the relatives on one occasion and by another on a separate occasion (Wootten 1991b:97, 98). Probability was exacerbated by the fact that Lloyd Boney was heavily intoxicated when taken into custody and dragged into the police cells (Wootten 1991b:2).

The evidence of the procedures for policing makes it clear that the formal impartiality of the law routinely gives way to more personalised interactions between police and Aborigines. In the series of incidents preceding his death, Lloyd Boney allegedly resisted arrest and injured the arresting officers before he was subdued. The Royal Commission described the incident as a 'violent struggle' (Wootten 1991b:41). Aboriginal witnesses alleged that after Boney was subdued, the police dragged him 'along the ground roughly for up to 50 yards, and that bystanders had yelled out to stop dragging him like a dog' (Wootten 1991b:40). The coroner at the inquiry into his death stated that the incident had not been forgotten by any of the parties (Wootten 1991b:41). The same police officers who were on duty[8] arrested and detained Lloyd Boney on the afternoon he died. He had absconded from custody when picked upon the night before, but on this afternoon he had submitted quietly.

The Royal Commission reports revealed the potential for policing practices to take on a highly personalised and a deliberately vicious nature. John Quayle, Mark Quayle's brother, alleged that when 'arrested for gesturing at police and saying to police "You're all cunts, why did you lock my brother up?"' (Wootten 1991c:119), he was himself locked in the same cell in which his brother died. The police officer taunted him: 'We're going to lock you in the same cell that your brother took his life. Now, we hope you are not going to do the same thing' (Wootten 1991c:120). Words are meant to wound, to damage, as much as any physical blows in these destructive relationships of power and contestation. Personal knowledge serves to vent and satisfy personal animosities.

Policing on the margins is projected as a world continually negotiated against a background of the destabilisation of social order. Lloyd Boney's contestations of, and, alternatively, conformity to, the sovereign authority of the police saw him categorised as 'unpredictable' (Wootten 1991b:68). The Royal Commissioner concurred, finding the term 'unpredictable' appropriate (Wootten 1991b:68). The report referred to a number of encounters with police in the period immediately prior to his death. On three occasions he reacted violently or ran, and on two occasions he submitted passively. Boney's actions are constructed in terms of the actions of the individual.

On one occasion, when police officers spoke to him while he was involved in an argument with a fellow Aborigine, he allegedly replied in anger, 'it is nothing to do with you cunts, I'll get a fucking gun and shoot both of you' (Wootten 1991c:34). He struggled violently with the police and was arrested, and three months later was convicted of 'causing serious alarm and affront and resisting arrest and [was] fined $80.00 on each count' (Wootten 1991c:34).

The ethics of kinship relations over state law has no place here. The police cannot take the alternative possibilities of the cultural and social world of Aborigines as real. By contrast, in 1982, when Boney was convicted of smashing a glass door at the Royal Hotel, his demeanour was compliant and apologetic as he explained the incident: 'I'm sorry constable, you know I don't do things like that' (Wootten 1991b:34). In 1983, when convicted of break and enter and the theft of a carton of beer, he allegedly stated, 'I took it Sarge. I had to. I'm crook in the gut and I needed it' (Wootten 1991b:32). Boney's own personal characteristics of reasonableness and self-awareness, let alone his experiences, were not registered as significant. Rather, the police considered him unpredictable, erratic and temperamental.

Unpredictability is a discourse of the state that seeks to normalise its subjects. Lloyd Boney's attempts to evade capture are more than acts of individual unpredictability; they act as a form of contestation of sovereignty in an ever-shifting game of cat and mouse. Police sovereignty and the rule of law must insist on being obeyed. No space exists between the exercise of authority and alternate sovereignties, except, perhaps, when constructed in a negative public image of leniency and/or incompetence. Noncompliance, by definition, constructs Lloyd Boney as unpredictable. Indeed, his parole officer considered him a modern-day nomad precisely because he continually evaded the codes, the techniques and procedures of modern state power apparatuses. The parole officer stated, 'Lloyd should never again due to his nomadic life style be placed under the supervision of this Service as it only serves as a useless game of "cat and mouse"' (Wootten 1991b:38).

Lloyd Boney violated not only the sovereign power of authority, but also the forms of conditional liberty, which extend and enhance the power of state apparatuses to administer life. The ultimate state sanction is confinement in a cell. Such a form of closure is not as readily available in the exigencies of everyday policing. Specific biographical evaluations of individuals by those who control the streets are more trusted. They form the basis of a collective knowledge that circulates between station members. The practice of rotating police between stations, which seeks to eliminate such personalised appraisals, is subverted. In the police photograph files at Brewarrina Police Station, under the heading, 'Additional information', Lloyd Boney was described as follows: 'Has been arrested on numerous occasions ... A generally bad egg and should not be trusted. Lives with Gracey who is frequently flogged. Will hit a copper if given the opportunity' (Wootten 1991b:107).

Specific biographical information and evaluation should not affect the formal impartiality of the law. On the cultural borderlands there is no balancing act where violent reactions can be measured against passive compliance, as in the Royal Commission's report. In the police assessment, no hint of equivocation about Boney's character existed. The verdict of his 'unpredictability' found in the report is damning, but too generous. In the interests of policing, the police allow no room for slippage between categories. The lines of demarcation are clearly defined and not blurred. For the police in Brewarrina, Lloyd Boney was considered thoroughly *predictable*. He was a 'bad egg', not to be trusted, the embodiment of Aboriginal violence that pervaded private and public life. A lack of vigilance or restraint may precipitate violence at any time.

The conclusions formed by the Aboriginal community about Lloyd Boney's death cannot be separated from the particular relations, the context of violent confrontations or contestations that formed the social context of Aboriginal/police relations in the 1980s. His relatives put two scenarios forward to explain his death. In the first, put forward by Boney's stepfather and the Western Aboriginal Legal Service, he was 'unintentionally killed ... and, that to cover this up a faked suicidal hanging was staged by police' (Wootten 1991b:4). The second scenario asserted that 'police did intentionally kill Lloyd' as a result of the violent relations that existed between him and the police (Wootten 1991b:5). Both explanations emerge from the agonistic and, often, antagonistic relations that exist between Aborigines and police in the North West. The engagement is an unequal one in which the loss of the 'argument' is visible in the overwhelming representation of Aboriginal people in police custody. The fantasies and anxieties harboured by police of Aboriginal uprisings bear little resemblance to the fear, anger and anxiety that pervades the lives of Aboriginal people; in particular, for many, fear of police and police cells. Death in custody is considered a risk of Aboriginal existence. It is not a risk for any other group in Australia.

The second scenario shows something of the close relationship assumed between personal relations and the escalation of violence. The personalised nature of such contestation is played out in male rituals of violence. As Arthur Hooper, Lloyd Boney's stepfather, put it, 'When Lloyd was drinking and anyone tried to grab him "to go to gaol" he would kick his legs, "struggle no matter how many of them, he's that kind of boy"' (Wootten 1991b:107). The masculine codes of conduct strip the police of their official role and reduce them to the position of 'anyone' to be confronted, no matter the odds. Such masculine codes of conduct are given ritual expression in the video evidence of the riot at the trial, as discussed in Chapter 1. The video reveals a confrontation between an Aboriginal male as he challenges a police officer; the latter is armed with a baton and shield. In abusive and derogatory language, the Aboriginal man demands the police officer put down his shield and baton and fight like a man. The police officer refuses to acknowledge the demand.

For many Aboriginal people, the entry of the police with batons and shields into the park where the wake for Lloyd Boney was being held precipitated the riot. The ABC crew's footage that night begins with an Indigenous man demanding the crew follow him and film the police 'bashing people in the park' (trial video). The film crew members remained where they were as the man proceeded down the street to confront a policeman. This confrontation with the policeman was not indiscriminate, but 'settling the score' for a previous injury suffered that night. The Aboriginal man alleged that he had been hit from behind and fell to the ground after being beaten with a police baton (pers. comm.).[9] The police officer's distinctive dress (he was the only police officer wearing a white shirt and no TRG vest) enabled the Aboriginal man to identify him when he came out of the park into the lit street (pers. comm.). Such violent personal contest resolves personal enmity. To this Indigenous man, this was not a matter to be resolved by the law, but by personal contest between the two men in an open, public fight. The policeman was taunted in a torrent of abuse to drop his baton and shield and fight man to man — to remove himself from the trappings of state authority he was hiding behind. Fighting in this manner was uncommon, but not unprecedented, between Aborigines and police. Personal issues could be resolved unofficially, winner take all. Both police and Aborigines, in these cases, shared common male codes of self-worth in which one's fighting ability was privileged as an important source of one's status and integrity in backing oneself not simply to inflict punishment, but to absorb it as well. The logic of such contests invested status not in who won or lost, but in rising to the challenge.

In understanding the unofficial ground rules, the asymmetry of the power of authority is exercised and sanctioned. A set of ethical codes exists beyond the law in keeping with the asymmetrical relations of power. The unofficial rule was that anyone who hit or injured a police officer was set for a 'flogging' (beating). The initial charging of the 'Brewarrina 17' can be understood as a consequence of the logic of avoiding being taken into custody in such circumstances. The common knowledge of the melee that circulated in the Indigenous community was that two police officers had been taken to hospital. The consequence of this knowledge, for Aborigines, was that no one should be taken into custody. As stated (pers. comm.):[10]

There was a so-called riot . . . police officers got injured . . . we knew that there were police officers in hospital. But we — look, it's hard to explain but it's just a fact of life that in that part of the State . . . I suppose it happens all over the State, but it happens out there on a regular basis, that if you manhandle a police officer or touch him in any form or . . . assault him, you can expect the same to be dealt back to you, you know what I mean? So that's just a common, common practice, that's accepted by both sides, by both parties. So we knew that if we were, had got arrested, if we knew we'd have got arrested that night, what would have happened, they would have escorted us to Dubbo, probably flogged us all the way to Dubbo, because Dubbo is the central base for police operations in the north-west, so we would have been taken to Dubbo and held there for sure. That was our main priority, not to get anyone arrested.

The imaginary state is coupled with the institutional state to reproduce an absolute opposition between Aborigines and police. The 'main priority' is driven by anxiety and the fantasy of menace. This particular group made its way out of town to 'Dodge City', where they spent a sleepless night anticipating police retaliation.

On the Sunday following the melee, as the town bristled with police reinforcements, it was known that arrests were to be made and that they were to be negotiated through an intermediary. The use of an intermediary between the police and the Aboriginal community was a common practice. As stated (pers. comm.):

> Like when — well the police know that, like, in country towns that if they're after someone well eventually, they know they'll catch them eventually because eventually he'll come out. If they want to charge someone, well, the usual process is they'd go and see someone in the community who's, you know, well-known, well-respected, you know what I mean? You know, sort of an elder sort of person, whatever, in that regards anyway, and they come around and they just have a yarn to you and say "Look, come up, get charged", you know what I mean?

A profound paradox resides in such police interventions, which do not secure state authority but consolidate distrust. Loyalty to the Indigenous community is reinforced and belief in the integrity of the criminal justice system is undermined. The relationship between the Indigenous community and police may be connected by circumstance, but it is corroded by distrust and anger.

In Brewarrina the representative of the Aboriginal Land Council in the North West, Tombo Winters, was called to act as a mediator. This desperate guile in negotiation is by those who, ultimately, through experience, know they can neither evade the encompassment of state power nor negate police sovereignty. Tombo Winters was a respected member of the local Indigenous community and the local representative of the newly created New South Wales Aboriginal Land Council (see Chapter 2):

So, like we had our trust in Tombo. We knew like, even though the police, we didn't trust the police — there was no way in the world we trusted anything they said or believed anything they said — but it was only because that Tombo came around, you know, and he reinforced the point that no-one will be arrested, no-one will be locked up, you know what I mean? (pers. comm.)

Deep distrust and anger are directed at the police and there exists a real hatred of perceived abuses of state power. Policing in the North West is not seen as a neutral idiom through which the state's intentions are transmitted. Indigenous people gain concessions through negotiation rather than the formal application of the law. The critical part of this negotiation was that the men were charged, but not arrested or locked up. As it was stressed, 'We didn't want to get locked up, that was the main — that was our main priority and we told that to Tombo and we stressed that on a number of occasions' (pers. comm.).

The members of the 'Brewarrina 17' were initially charged in the courthouse rather than the police station. In a simple procedure, the police sat behind a table and read out the charges to the accused, who promptly left. What is of interest is not so much the expectation of violence, which may or may not eventuate, but the constant state of anticipation of violence. Police and Aborigines understand violence as a condition of existence; only the terms and conditions in which it is meted out were at issue. Both police and Aborigines participated in the anxiety of a fantasy of menace.

The exercise of contingent jurisprudence inverts the authority of the state. The dictates of the margins prevail and must be acted upon. The aberrations or abuses of state power affirm local specificity and the arbitrariness needed to uphold state sovereignty. The refusal of, or noncompliance with, police authority by Aborigines amplifies an adherence to alternate forms of sovereignty, to a muted, uncertain and inscrutable other way of life. It shadows and gives meaning to the astonishing revelation made at the RCIADIC of the spectre of Aboriginal terrorism violently disrupting the bicentenary celebrations. Contingency legitimates the degree of arbitrariness needed to exercise control at the social margins of the state.

The cultural borderlands of the North West in the 1980s, which the nation glimpsed briefly in the RCIADIC reports, emerged from a world where social hierarchies and social distance had been redrawn, rather than suspended, in the wake of political and economic upheavals in previous decades. Hierarchy and difference were reaffirmed through state institutions and through breaches that constituted differential treatment. The reality of a social landscape of the 1980s was one of struggle and tension. Aboriginal people are subject to the constant surveillance of the state, but are equally subject to stereotyping, which renders them predictable. Yet it was no longer a question of the strength of the borders between community/self and other. In these forms of governance, Aborigines were constructed as unpredictable, which legitimised forms of police control in keeping with the kinds of contingencies identified with the marginal world of the North West. In part, the anxiety and tensions emerged in the postcolonial present where the possibility of achieving the forms of closure identified by the segregations of the past no longer existed. The cultural borderlands were no longer stereotypically transparent, nor were they rationally ordered by clear-cut social demarcations, but by a more contested space; haunted by spectres of more intangible, less predictable outcomes.

Chapter 5

Police testimony and the Brewarrina riot trial

Co-authored with Kerry Zubrinich

> Being a court of law ... so far as the findings of guilty or not
> guilty are concerned, this is no place for sympathy or prejudice.
> The fact that police officers ... have been injured ... the fact that
> the three accused are of Aboriginal descent, are all matters to be
> put out of your mind. (11 April)

Judge Nash made this statement during the summing up of the
'Brewarrina 17' riot trial (*R v. Bates, Murray and Orcher*), which
was held at the District Court in Bathurst, New South Wales, in
1991. The statement reiterates his position throughout the trial
that the alleged crimes of the Aboriginal defendants, as citizens of
the state subject to its laws, were on trial — not the issue of race
relations. The composition of the courtroom provided a compelling
but contradictory image to the judge's pronouncement. The only
Aboriginal people in the inner sanctum of the courtroom were the
three accused in the dock. The defence and prosecution lawyers and
their assistants were non-Aboriginal. The press gallery, where fellow
anthropologist Dr Ernst and I sat among reporters and police, were all
non-Aboriginal. The jurors, on the opposite side of the courtroom,
were non-Aboriginal. The judge, bewigged and robed in the ritual
style of the British legal system, was, of course, non-Aboriginal. The
red cedar-panelled bench the judge occupied elevated him directly
in front of and above the accused Aborigines in the dock, beneath

a portrait of Elizabeth II, Queen of England and the symbolic head of Britain and the colonising power of Australia. The only other Aboriginal faces were those of the friends and relatives of the accused in the public gallery. In terms of the symbolism of the courtroom, the positions of authority, and the empowered sites for evaluation and judgment, an Aboriginal presence was confined to the position of objects of the decision-making processes as defendants or passive observers of that process. For my colleagues and myself sitting in the courtroom, the judge's statement had the somewhat hollow ring of an enunciation of principle rather than an observable ethics of conduct in courtroom practice.

Yet the judge was correct in his pronouncements. The justice system operates on the logic that there is no society, only individuals. This legal fiction makes the functioning of the law possible. The court cannot be seen as favouring the interests of particular groups who come before it. Judge Nash simply reaffirmed the seeming paradox that the criminal courts are not an institutional space to deal with social and political injustices. The structural inequalities endured by Indigenous peoples and, presumably, those of social class, evident in the composition of the courtroom, are rendered invisible. Those who occupy the positions in the court are there through a meritocratic system and institutionally produced credentials. The requirements for university entry are beyond the grasp of most people who come before the courts. The historical constitution and evolution of the courts on which authority is exercised, the British legal system, must remain beyond question; to do otherwise would be tantamount to denying its jurisdiction to exercise the law and justice. The quotation from the trial judge (on the previous page) speaks not so much to the specific condition of the law, but more generally to the tensions and contradictory conditions in which Indigenous peoples seek historical redress, social justice and cultural recognition in post-settler colonial societies. The historical and social conditions of their existence are subject to the assent of the legal and political institutions of post-settler colonial societies.

The Brewarrina riot trial provided a perspective on the intersection between Aborigines and the law in the 1980s. There was more on trial than the three Aboriginal men in the dock. The death of Lloyd Boney, along with a growing number of other deaths in police custody, fuelled public sentiments at the time that Aborigines were being mistreated in police cells. In this context, the conditions of apprehension, the trial and the punishment of criminals were often seen as additional burdens placed upon Aborigines because of a racially discriminatory legal system and the racially biased actions of its officials (see Chapter 4). In effect, involvement with the legal system shapes a critique of criminal justice as a perpetuation of settler colonial order rather than the maintenance of legal order. Instances, real and imagined, of discrimination reaffirm that the burdens of the past in terms of the legal system continued in the present. It was not just the three men in the dock who were on trial, but the integrity of the criminal justice system, its officials, police officers, legislators, solicitors and judges, on whose integrity society depends. This issue was palpably evident throughout the trial, prompting Judge Nash, in summing up to the jury, to say that, 'In particular, this is not the case of police versus Aboriginals or Aboriginals versus police. All persons in our courts of law come equally before our courts no matter who they are or what their position in life may be' (11 April).

In the open adversarial contest between the prosecution and the defence, the integrity and validity of the police evidence was questioned by counter-allegations of racially inspired police actions. This chapter explores the narratives in the evidence given by prosecution witnesses at the trial.

The setting of the trial in the regional courthouse in Bathurst presented an imposing building at the heart of the city (see Figure 4). As befits its status as the first inland city and the pathway to the great pastoral wealth of the nineteenth century, Bathurst's public architecture celebrates the triumph of western civilisation in the antipodes.[1] The spatial ordering and architecture of the adjacent park area is replete with historical and cultural meanings. Machattie Park is the symbolic centre of Bathurst's civic design. The courthouse flanks the park on one side, while the Anglican Church flanks the other, and both align with the Carillion, the monument to the Anzacs, Australia's most powerful symbol of nationalism, in the centre of the park. Together they form an axis symbolically balancing religious and secular practice, church and state, an axis of a preserved remnant of a spatial ordering of the late nineteenth century social world of colonial power. The Carillion is central to the other axis formed in the park,

Figure 4: Bathurst District Courthouse

with, at one end, the statue of the explorer George Evans, with his servant, an Aboriginal guide, on one knee, positioned below the explorer and attentive to his command; at the other end of the park is the commemoration of the Boer War contingent from Bathurst, which fought for Empire in South Africa. The park is a symbolic celebration of the achievements of settler colonial civilisation.

The Aboriginal defendants and their families met each day at the park and proceeded through the gates of the courthouse, as did the lawyers, jurors, police witnesses and other interested parties, on their way to the trial. We then proceeded up the steps of the courthouse to join with the defence counsel in the rooms allotted to the three defendants for discussion prior to the day's proceedings. From there, the accused were escorted to the dock. The judge's arrival each day ritually marked the resumption of the trial, when all present would stand as a mark of respect until the judge was seated.

The charge of riotous assembly, which required the prosecution to establish the case that it was the shared intention of the accused Aborigines to attack police on that night, distinguished this trial of three of the 'Brewarrina 17' from a second trial of the remainder of the 'Brewarrina 17'.[2] The Crown had to establish that the three accused had assembled together with the common purpose of aiding each other by force or otherwise to riotously act together to cause a disturbance to the public. In the contemporary period, the charge of riotous assembly had been recently revived to deal with the so-called Mount Panorama 'Bikies riot' (1985) (non-Aboriginal defendants; see Cunneen et al. 1989), the Bourke Bowling Club 'riot' (1985), the Bourke Post Office 'riot' (1986) (Cowlishaw 1994, 2004) and the Brewarrina riot (1987) (all Aboriginal defendants). As Purves (1992), the defence counsel for one of the defendants in the Brewarrina riot trial, pointed out, the lineage of the law of riotous assembly and of what constituted a riot can be traced more readily to its application in nineteenth century English law rather than in Australia (discussed later). The charge of riotous assembly remained the most serious charge, as it carried a maximum sentence of life imprisonment.

The other distinctive feature of the Brewarrina riot trial was that it did not conform to the conventional representations of police exercising authority over Aborigines in public space. The violent images of Aborigines confronting police operated 'against the grain' of a national historical memory (see Chapter 6). Police intervention at the wake of Lloyd Boney, who had died in police custody, sought to clear the park of the Aboriginal participants. Ultimately, the police retreated without making a single arrest or establishing control. The retreat of the police and their inability to assert control went against social and historical expectations. A long settler colonial history speaks of the expectation that Aborigines will passively conform, or, at most, be defiant but defeated. The Brewarrina riot as an event reversed these expectations.

The narratives of the evidence given by prosecution witnesses focus on this by examining some of the discursive themes emerging from the prosecution evidence. The construction of the melee as a riot was, itself, central to the prosecution at this trial, which began on 25 March 1991 and dealt with the charges brought against three Aboriginal defendants. There are a number of understandings in which to embed the events of 15 August 1987. This chapter scrutinises the incident as it emerges in the police accounts and considers aspects of the cultural understandings of 'Australianness' and some of the ramifications for the ordering of state power relations evident within the context of the riot and the courtroom.

Lloyd Boney died in police custody at Brewarrina on 6 August 1987. The riot took place during the evening of the day on which he was buried at Brewarrina. At the time of the funeral no satisfactory

explanation of his death had been given to his relatives. The disturbance began in the park in which Boney's friends and relatives had
gathered for his wake and continued on the adjoining streets. Charges
were laid in March 1989 and the two trials were held at Bathurst
in 1991. In the first trial, discussed here, the three Aboriginal men
pleaded not guilty to all charges. In the following days, the evidence
of the trial was heard and completed, with the final addresses of
Counsel on the ninth day. The judge's lengthy summing up continued
for the next three court days. On Tuesday, 16 April, the jury retired
and returned some six hours later with the verdicts. Arthur Orcher
was found not guilty on all charges. Albert 'Sonny' Bates was found
not guilty of the assault on police officer Vaughan Reid, but guilty
of the charge of riotous assembly and the assault of police officer
Anthony Bordin. Arthur Murray was found guilty of all charges. The
two found guilty were duly sentenced to serve 18 months of imprisonment. The legal process had begun in 1988, but it was six years
later, as a result of successful appeals for a retrial, which occurred in
1994, that Arthur Murray and Albert Bates were granted a permanent
stay of proceedings (see Figure 5).[3]

The evidence of the prosecution witnesses at the trial provides
evidence of how the police viewed the Brewarrina riot, rather than
the perspectives of the Aboriginal people present that evening. The
aim of this analysis is to deal with the specifics of police as agents of
the state and how they frame their actions, but, more so, to attend
to the cultural specificity of their representations of the event as
historically formed ways of knowing and acting. The trial evidence
lent itself to a binary frame of oppositions: identity/difference, white/
black, rational/irrational, civilised/savage. A discursive and repre-
sentational construction of the social event privileged one term as
original, generic and primary and the other as derivative, relational
and secondary. The police evidence gave itself to be read as bound in
the binary logics, echoing colonial modes of thought with their fixed
oppositional identities and embedded rigid hierarchical relations. This
chapter aims to make visible and render problematic the perpetuation
of the taken-for-granted nature of such binary logic. The binary logic
does not simply emerge from a colonial history, but further material-
ises as part of the adversarial legal process itself. Despite the Australian
legal system's adherence to a liberal tradition that extols the virtue of

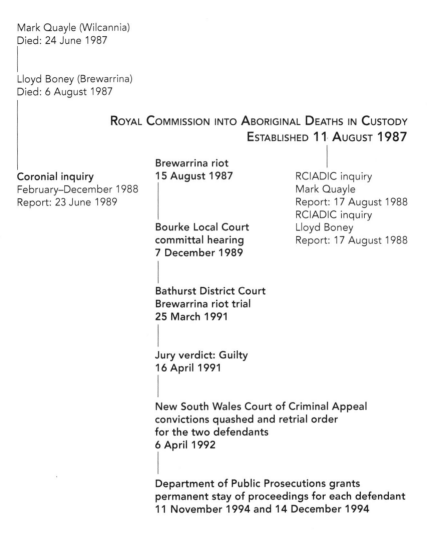

Mark Quayle (Wilcannia)
Died: 24 June 1987

Lloyd Boney (Brewarrina)
Died: 6 August 1987

ROYAL COMMISSION INTO ABORIGINAL DEATHS IN CUSTODY
ESTABLISHED 11 AUGUST 1987

Coronial inquiry
February–December 1988
Report: 23 June 1989

Brewarrina riot
15 August 1987

RCIADIC inquiry
Mark Quayle
Report: 17 August 1988
RCIADIC inquiry
Lloyd Boney
Report: 17 August 1988

Bourke Local Court
committal hearing
7 December 1989

Bathurst District Court
Brewarrina riot trial
25 March 1991

Jury verdict: Guilty
16 April 1991

New South Wales Court of Criminal Appeal
convictions quashed and retrial order
for the two defendants
6 April 1992

Department of Public Prosecutions grants
permanent stay of proceedings for each defendant
11 November 1994 and 14 December 1994

Figure 5: Brewarrina trial chronology

colour and gender blindness, in the formal presentation of the law testimony cannot escape its cultural grounding in everyday practices and beliefs.

A number of problems attend such dichotomous assumptions that privilege a single conception of difference (gender, class or race) as predominant and work in a way to over-determine identities. The proliferation of cultural, gender and racial differences that emerged from analysis of the police testimony revealed a multiplicity that exceeded a simple binary coding. Such a binary coding could not deal with the complexity of Australian cultural politics. Rather than hierarchically ordered social categories organised in terms of fixed boundaries, the evidence encoded inventive elaborations of the meanings of gender and race and competing constructions of the social terrain.

A prosecution account of the riot

This section looks at the riot principally through police evidence in order to develop a narrative drawn from evidence given by prosecution witnesses at the trial. As such, it provides information on how police evidence and the emergence of narratives — a strong story of police courage, for example — provide material for a discursive analysis of the riot and its consequences. But the police handling of the event itself is only part of their role in the trial. Their information gathering and attempts to bring serious charges against the three defendants, as well as their performances on the witness stand, when examined carefully, provide much information about Indigenous and gender relations in Australia. This is not to say there was any improper action on the part of the police involved. It is too easy and analytically suspect to ascribe blame to particular police officers without locating their actions in the specific structures of Australian social life and examining the underlying values of the culture from which they emerge.

The role of the police was central to the construction of the riot itself. This is apparent in the Police Bravery citations awarded to the police involved and a special award to Detective Senior Constable Grant Connelly in 1989. The *Daily Liberal* (20 August 1989, p. 1), reporting on the award ceremony, stated that the police were 'attempting to break up a large group of Aborigines who rioted'; in so doing:

> Police withstood a frenzied attack by a mob armed with lengths of pipe, steel rods and steel posts. During the melee, Senior Constable Terry McGregor broke his leg and fell to the ground in agony. Connelly then disregarded his own safety by using his body as a shield between the rioters and the injured officer. He stod [sic]

over the Senior Constable on the ground and used riot shields to protect them both. The mob repeatedly attacked Connelly with bottles and iron bars but he was able to protect himself and Senior Constable McGregor.

In the newspaper report, the police bravery gains its meaning against the disruptive images of Aboriginal savagery. The police action is said to have helped 'quell the situation'. There is a slippage here between expected outcomes and the event itself. The police intervention did not occur in the manner portrayed, which is in keeping with a binary ordering of events in which everything must be located on one side of the divide of power and powerlessness.

The police officers involved in the action that night were lionised by the state. While Aboriginal actions were to draw punishment, the police received honours from the state. The police report (NSW Police Department 1989:74) to parliament says this of the events of the evening:

> Brewarrina Riot. In August 1987, a riot developed at Brewarrina when hundreds of Aborigines rampaged through the streets. Reinforcements from neighbouring stations, including Dubbo and the Tactical Response Group, were summoned in an attempt to quell the violence. A number of police were injured including Senior Constable T. J. McGregor and Detective Constable 1st Class G. Connelly who received serious injuries. The latter Constable, in recognition of his courageous actions in shielding Constable McGregor from further attack became the first officer to receive the Commissioner's Valour Award. Other police involved received the Commissioner's Commendation.

The honours bestowed confirmed the persuasiveness of police evidence and validated historical images of a retreat made glorious by the actions of the individuals that are widely held in the populist imagination of Australian nationalism. In effect, in the Brewarrina riot as an event the reversal of expectations was simultaneously acknowledged and assimilated and rendered interpretable. What was unsettled and what traversed expectations was an Aboriginality embedded in a long settler colonial history, where Aborigines will passively conform, or, at most, be defiant but defeated. Conformity to expectations is echoed in binary ordering that relies on a temporal logic of a 'prior' Aboriginal Australia withering before the subsequent advance of British colonialism, of primitivism succumbing to civilisation. Such an ordering has proffered a vindication of the moral and political legitimacy of settler colonialism.

According to the police evidence, the aim of the police intervention was to clear the park of Aborigines. The initial reports of individual Aborigines throwing bottles and rocks at a hotel opposite the park was to be addressed by the collective removal of all Aborigines from the park. Individual illegal acts identified as a source of the trouble requiring police intervention quickly reduced Aborigines at the wake to a collective Indigenous category subject to undifferentiated treatment. The fixity and the singular conception of difference worked to override the individuated strategies of policing. Police expectation was that difficulties would arise on the day Lloyd Boney was buried. Rumours about police involvement in his death and a subsequent cover up were current in the Aboriginal community. Additional personnel were brought in to supplement the local police force. By early evening most of the reinforcements had left Brewarrina, although one, Sergeant Reid, was called back from Bourke about 7.30 pm. In the course of the evening police drove past the park at various times and reported to the station that the situation was quiet. Two police liaison officers were stationed in the local hotel to observe the activities in the park. The wake, which included the consumption of alcohol, took place in Memorial Park with the permission of local authorities on the proviso that the park was to be kept tidy. About 9.30 pm one of the police liaison officers who had been watching events from the balcony of the hotel called the station to report that rocks and other material were being thrown at the hotel by a number of young people. Eight police officers equipped with riot shields and batons were sent to the area in two vehicles. The following compilation is a setting out of police evidence in the court, as the officers were led through their evidence.

The prosecution case divided the narrative succession of the evidence of the riot into the testimony of the police from the two police cars. The police evidence came from those in one vehicle, Sergeant MacLachlan, Sergeant Rule, Detective Senior Constable

Connelly and Constable McGregor, and was followed by those in the other car, Constable Bordin, Constable Fernandez, Sergeant Morgan and Sergeant Reid. They explained that police vehicles arrived separately and situated themselves in two locations at the north-eastern and south-eastern boundaries of the park. Initially, the car carrying MacLachlan did not go near the hotel but to a position on Sandon Street, towards Doyle Street, nearly a block from the hotel. The second vehicle parked in Bathurst Street near the hotel. On the arrival of both police vehicles, some of the crowd threw rocks and other material at them. The group led by MacLachlan moved into the park, where, the police said, they saw 40 to 50 men, women and children, some of whom were throwing things and calling abuse at the police. MacLachlan called to the three policemen with him to form a baton and shield line and 'charge forward and get them out of the park'.

At this point the policemen moved forward quickly through the park, banging their shields with their batons and, according to Connelly, yelling repeatedly, 'Get out of the park!' As a result, according to MacLachlan, 'a number of them started to turn and run out of the park'. The police line kept advancing and the people retreated out of the park into Doyle Street, throwing bottles, timber and rocks at them. While there were 'skirmishes' and people continued to throw 'missiles' at the police (and the police responded by using their batons on people), the crowd dispersed down Doyle Street to its intersection with Young Street at the end of the park. After a number of incidents at the intersection, MacLachlan decided that police purposes would be better served if his group joined their colleagues in Bathurst Street, and they retreated down Doyle Street towards the police car. Arriving in Bathurst Street (they travelled in the car they had parked near Doyle Street), they joined the other police.

The second group of policemen had previously entered the park from Bathurst Street after parking their vehicle there. The decision to move the people out of the park in response to rock throwing at the hotel was made, according to MacLachlan (trial evidence, 25–26 March), on the way to the scene. Reid (trial evidence, 3 April), who was in charge of the second group, had similarly ordered the three policemen to form a baton and shield line to pursue four or five people who had been throwing objects at the Brewarrina Hotel and had ran into the park. The police proceeded only 'four or five metres' into the park before '30 or 40 people began throwing bottles, stones and sticks at us'. They retreated to their vehicle in Bathurst Street followed by 10 to 20 people. This group was pushed back into the park by the police line, which came under what Reid described as 'a very intense barrage' of flagon bottles, beer bottles and pieces of wood. After further skirmishes, the police abandoned their vehicle and retreated down Sandon Street. According to Reid, he 'couldn't believe how many bottles were coming through the air. The sky seemed to turn brown. It was absolutely incredible' (3 April). At this time, they joined with MacLachlan's group and formed a line across the Bathurst Street intersection in front of the bank and the hotel.

One incident that occurred shortly after their arrival in Bathurst Street was the fracture of McGregor's leg by an Aboriginal man wielding a star picket fence post. While Connelly (trial evidence, 26 March, 9 April) was shielding the injured constable from the crowd and the missiles being hurled, the siren at the fire station sounded. According to Fernandez (trial evidence, 4 April) the effect of the siren and Rule shouting 'reinforcements, reinforcements' was to confuse 'the mob' and they started to fall back. Under the cover of this ruse, the police seized the initiative and reclaimed their vehicle. The police remained until the ambulance came and McGregor was taken to hospital while his colleagues returned to the station. The police action had not 'quelled the situation' that had escalated considerably since the liaison officer's call. Indeed, as Connelly stated, as he 'got into the back of the police truck, a beer keg was thrown at them, lighted fire buckets, burning logs continued to be thrown at them and bottles and sticks were still being skimmed across the road'. Nevertheless, by 10.15 pm people were going in and out of the Brewarrina Hotel, the publican was supplying alcohol and the crowd from the wake had dispersed completely without further incident.

What is a riot?[4]

As far as the police, the prosecution and the media reporting the event were concerned, the melee that developed in Brewarrina on the night of Lloyd Boney's funeral was a riot. Accordingly, the three defendants at the first trial discussed here were charged with riotous assembly.[5] In order for the charge of riotous assembly to be proven, the Crown had to show that at least three persons had assembled together with the intention of aiding each other against those who may oppose them in their common purpose and that they used sufficient violence to put bystanders in fear. Riotous assembly involved more than a public act of violence by an unruly mob. It involved at least three in a conspiracy to commit violence against those who opposed them (in this case, the police).

The criminal trial is the formal setting for the performance of rituals designed to resolve accusations brought by the government against the persons accused of crime. For the prosecution, the Brewarrina riot trial revolved around making the case that a violent riot took place; for the defence counsels it revolved around contesting or refuting such claims. In preserving the presumption of innocence, the burden of proof always rests with the prosecution. In serious criminal cases, the jury provides the final tribunal for the evidence. The trial ritual proceeds as an open adversarial contest between the prosecution and the defence in presenting the evidence and opposing legal arguments, with a judge acting as the final arbiter of the law. The designation of the event as a 'riot' should not be taken lightly. However, it is doubtful whether within a wider analytical perspective these events would be considered a riot.[6] Although there was a violent altercation with agents of the state confronting a group they considered disorderly, the melee was contained within the streets adjoining Memorial Park. There was no looting (widespread or otherwise) and the duration of the riot was, at the most generous estimate, 40 minutes.

The major debate within the trial was the time span that was allotted to the duration of the so-called riot. From the police accounts, they left the police station at around 9.35 pm to 9.40 pm and their testimony suggests that they were engaged in clearing the park for the next 30 to 40 minutes. The persuasive character of the testimony set out in detail the engagement with the police in terms of their attempts to 'drive them out of the park' and their advance in pursuit of '20 to 25 Aborigines' down Doyle street, before their 'retreat' back to the police car (25 March). One defence counsel objected to the introduction of such evidence, which included 'skirmishes' and 'threats to police', which had no bearing on the Crown case against his client as it related to events that took place at the hotel (25 March). The judge, in response, admitted the testimony; 'although it did not form part of evidence in the trial', it provided 'background material' as 'creating the mood for the night' for the jury (25 March). The major argument of the defence counsel was that the riot was of a much shorter duration. The defence argued that the police had not recorded the time they had left the station and it was hence subject to their own conjecture. By contrast, the ambulance officer who attended the injured police officer gave a very different account of the sequence of events, which suggested that the police testimony was prone to exaggeration.

The ambulance officer attached to the Orana Far West Ambulance Service gave a far more sober account of Brewarrina and the park at the time of the riot. When returning from West Brewarrina, after examining a patient, he travelled slowly up the main street, Bathurst Street, past the park on his way to the hospital. The prosecutor questioned the ambulance officer (9 April):

> Q. When you proceeded up the main street to the hospital . . . did you notice anything there?
> A. Yeah. I noticed the police Land Cruiser parked on my right and I notice some small fires lit in the park on my left.
> Q. Did you see any people?
> A. I didn't see any unusual activity, no.
> Q. Did you stop?
> A. No.

After he arrived at the hospital he received a call to proceed to the Brewarrina Hotel, which he had previously passed. On his way past the police station he was hailed by a policewoman, who got into the ambulance and they travelled to the hotel. When he returned to pick up the injured policeman, there were 'some beer kegs strewn around the intersection and a large amount of broken glass on the roadway' (9 April). He was concerned for his safety, picked up the injured police officer and went straight to the hospital and subsequently returned to the intersection to see if more people were injured (9 April). What was critical for the defence was that the ambulance officer's movements through the area placed a specific timeframe on the duration of the riot. As the defence counsel suggested (9 April):

Q. No unusual activity?

A. I just seen [sic] the Land Cruiser with the back doors open and no other activity, no.

Q. In fact, there was not even a police officer in sight, was there?

A. I didn't see any, no.

Q. You didn't hear anything unusual?

A. No.

Q. You did not drive over any carpet of broken glass, did you?

A. Not at that stage, no.

Q. You did not see any beer kegs on the road, did you?

A. No.

Q. And I suggest to you, Mr L., that was about ten to 10?

A. I believe that to be true, yes.

Q. You went to the hospital. Correct?

A. Yes.

Q. You were called out again, correct?

A. Yes.

Q. I suggest that the call . . . was logged at about 9.56 correct?

A. Yes.

. . .

Q. At all events having then picked up the injured man at the intersection you drove to the hospital?

A. Yes.

Q. And then you returned to the intersection?

A. Yes . . . (I unloaded the patient as quickly as possible and returned to the scene.)

Q. The timetable for the ambulance, I suggest, was this: At 9.50 ten to 10 you drove up Bathurst Street. Correct?

A. No answer.

Q. You returned there shortly after 9.56 to pick up the injured man, is that correct?

A. Yes.

Q. And then you finally returned there about, I suggest, 10.15. Is that correct?

A. Yes.

. . .

Q. But when you returned at 10.15 you saw this broken glass and beer kegs on the road?

A. Yes, that's right.

Q. There was not a single human being, there was not a soul in sight, was there?

A. I didn't see anyone, no.

The ambulance driver's written record of times and his observations stood in direct contrast to the extensively detailed and prolonged conflict outlined in a succession of police evidence. The timeframe of the riot was significantly reduced to no more that 15 to 20 minutes. The time span, along with other missing elements of a riot, was pursued by the defence counsel to sustain an assessment of a conflict more in keeping with a disturbance than a conspiracy to commit violence.

Power relations in the courtroom

The rituals of the courtroom proceed from the prosecution of accused people through the imposition of the authority structures of the legal system and, hence, the authority structures of the Australian state. Yet the veracity of the evidence does not exist outside the cultural scripts that express the values and beliefs of society. The understandings held in the police testimony with regard to the riot resonate in Australian life generally. In examining their actions and the discursive framework used to describe those actions (and the actions of others), this section draws out some of the complexities involved in the reproduction of a system of power relations in Australian society. As chronicled above, the riot started when eight police responded to the call from the hotel about people throwing rocks at the premises. Anticipating trouble, they went with riot gear (or variation thereof) not to the hotel but to the park.[7] One group of police was intent on getting into the park but met resistance. The park had already been established as a location for trouble, with two police liaison officers on the balcony of the hotel monitoring what was happening at the wake. This surveillance (an extension of the gaze usually focused on the Aboriginal community at Brewarrina) was in keeping with the increased police activity in the town during the week preceding Lloyd Boney's funeral.

In police evidence, as suggested earlier, the language to describe the riot provides interesting insight about the perceptions of the night's events. Each police officer, when giving evidence of the fracas, used the language of warfare. There were 'skirmishes', 'missiles' and 'barrages', they 'charged', 'advanced' and 'retreated', and finally, when the fire siren sounded, one of them called 'reinforcements, reinforcements [are coming]' (4 April). The call 'reinforcements' provided a ruse, which, it was said, confused the menacing crowd and allowed the police to take the initiative, regroup and withdraw back to the police station. The events are described in military terms of war. At one level, the military terminology provides the backdrop to chart the grim resolve and heroic actions of individual police who, outnumbered, fought on against the odds. The unequal nature of the conflict and the retreat invokes powerful associations with essentially male imaginings of national identity. The police, it should be remembered, withdrew without making a single arrest and without establishing order or control. The evocation of a 'most glorious failure' is a powerful trope of Australian national and military history. Nevertheless, it was a failure made glorious by the display of manly qualities of courage and endurance that did not fail. Similarly, using the cover of a ruse, the 'reinforcements are coming', saved the grave situation. As Reid (3 April) described the scene in the minutes leading to the fire alarm sounding, 'we were unable to have any impact on them at all. In fact, the crowd just seemed to get bigger and bigger and they seemed to be coming . . . towards us . . . We couldn't advance any further. We couldn't get to the police vehicle. We stood where we were.' Then, through the timely intervention of the fire siren, a spontaneous and ingenious deception, the police made their strategic retreat. The images of war have a readily available national and historical narrative to bring meaning to individuals and their actions. The images frame acts of courage and initiative by individual police that can be readily assimilated into the heroic patterns of a pre-existing masculine nationalist mythology.

For Kapferer (1988) and Lake (1992), the cultural understandings of 'Australian maleness' and subjectivity have been significantly shaped in terms of the military imagery and metaphors of Anzac. Lake

(1992:310) has said, 'proving nationhood was a matter of proving manhood . . . Nations like men had to be tested and proven: and war was the ultimate proving ground of both.' In this, the echoes of national discursive formations resonate beyond the more limited imaginings of the courtroom evidence of the riot. The particular historical and cultural accent on national character and war as a tradition emerged from the coverage of the Gallipoli campaign of World War One and achieved a national focus.[8] The Gallipoli campaign contributed to an emerging nationalist sentiment where sacrifice and failure were co-joined as heroic qualities. These representations of a national culture, formed around a male identity based on loyalty and mateship and against overwhelming odds, operate at a level of abstraction which enables the constructions of imaginary social unities posited in nationalist myth-making.

Commissioner Wootten observed that he was 'very conscious' of the existence of a 'police culture' in which 'there is a very great blindness . . . to the problems of police investigating police, and a very great reluctance to acknowledge the possibility of wrong doing by police'.[9] What is taken here as 'blindness' is translated in the language of mateship as loyalty and solidarity with one's peers that transcend that of the state or the operation of the law. The representations of mateship in the police evidence embody much of the imagery of mateship set against the hostilities of war. The meaning of mateship here is more complex than a simple individualist notion of a special friendship existing between men as individuals. Instead, it encodes what Lohrey (1982:33) has called the 'mateship of the trenches', where men who may or may not have a lot in common nevertheless combine in a common cause and something larger than personal attachment binds them.

The police account of the events of 15 August 1987 also resonates with understandings of war in the way in which maleness is separated from femaleness in the narrative of the riot. As Lake (1992:310) has stated, war is 'the ultimate test of a person's ability to transcend personal self interest, to rise above "feminine" private concerns'. The absence of the female was specifically arranged, for there was a female police officer on duty, but she remained at the station. Interestingly, one of the police giving evidence addressed one answer to the defence counsel (26 March):

Q. There were at least two police officers back at the police station, weren't there?

A. Yes, there were.

Q. Sergeant Lomas and Constable Spooner?

A. Yes, two female police officers, yes.

HIS HONOUR:

Q. Both female police officers?

A. No, Sergeant Lomas is a man; Constable Spooner is a female.

The feminisation of his male colleague may reflect not the perceived attributes of the colleague but that the place for women is away from male action and solidarity. Solidarity for the Australian male has its particular focus in the institution of mateship.

The prerogative of male action and solidarity deployed in the police strategies was paralleled in the actions of the manager of the hotel and other males who gathered there. In evidence, the manager stated he had sent his mother away as he thought there might be trouble. By contrast, according to the evidence of the police liaison officer Sergeant Dorn, the manager's father took up a position on the upstairs verandah, 'with a rifle laying on the balcony rail a short distance way' (5 April). By the time Dorn left, eight more persons were present on the verandah and 'an additional five rifles which were leaning against the balcony rail' (5 April).[10] The actions of the men on the verandah embody ideas of maleness, of mateship and violence, defined as exclusively a male domain of contestations in the public arena and defence of property rights.

Mateship itself is forged in warfare.[11] During the riot the qualities associated with mateship, male courage and loyalty to comrades under fire were all experienced. The most dramatic episode in the narrative is the account of Connelly's protection of McGregor (26 March):

Q. Did you go over to Const McGregor?

A. I walked backwards and started to stand over him with my shield. He had his shield over his leg, over his body trying to protect that.

Q. Was something happening while you were doing that?

A. Bottles were being thrown at the building and on the ground and sticks were being thrown on the ground and slivers of glass cut my nose from when they bounced off the wall and came behind my riot shield and cut my face; and then Const McGregor was yelling out: 'Don't leave me, don't fucking leave me'. I kept on saying: 'I won't leave you, Terry'. I stood over the top of him.

Connelly defended his colleague from the material being thrown until he was placed in an ambulance. For obvious reasons, the images of mateship here rely less upon notions of a lack of discipline to authority and more on the self-effacing and self-enhancing character of mateship. This self-annihilating character of mateship resonates with what Lohrey (1982:33) regards as the distinctive feature of mateship, its basis 'above all [as] a defensive formation against a hostile world'. Mateship may speak of the special conditions of individual friendship, but only against a background in which such unity among men maintains and defines itself in terms of an opposition stance to the world. Warfare is perhaps its most potent symbolic expression.

The prosecution case had to demonstrate a conspiracy by Aborigines, led by the Aboriginal defendants in the dock, to commit public acts of violence against the police. The evidence of one particular police officer was imbued with the logic of the trial in seeking the prosecution of the Aboriginal defendants for riotous assembly. Contrary to the presiding judge's enunciation in his summation that this was not a case of police verses Aborigines or Aborigines verses police, one police officer made clear his view that the riot was not simply a public act of violence by any unruly mob. The Brewarrina riot had proceeded, he said, as a premeditated act of entrapment of the police on the part of the defendants (trial evidence, 5 April). In this policeman's evidence, the discrepancy between the formal equality before the law and the substantive realities of racial stigmatisation and social inequality become evident. The following excerpt is from Sergeant Morgan's testimony (5 April):

Q. And indeed the Aboriginals in that park had stacked the bottles they had drunk neatly did they not?

A. No they didn't, no.

Q. You went into the park later and saw the bottles neatly stacked?

A. Yes, and easily accessible in places where they wouldn't cause any problems.

Q. And easily accessible?

A. Yes where you could get at them very easily.

Q. Or, Sergeant, neatly stacked having been consumed, right?

A. In my opinion, no, because we had been bombarded continually by bottles and I believe they were there for the purpose of weapons against police.

Q. You knew there was drinking in the park. Correct?

A. Correct.

Q. You knew there was a wake going on?

A. During the day, yes.

Q. And later on you knew it continued on?

A. It continued on, yes.

Q. You knew permission had been given for that purpose?

A. I believe so. From the police no permission was given.

Q. But you believe so yes?

A. Yes.

Q. There was discussion at the police station that was the case?

A. It could have been, yes.

Q. When you went in to the park you saw bottles neatly stacked?

A. Which is unusual for Aboriginals when they drink in parks.

Q. Unusual for Aboriginals is it?

A. I have had many experiences where Aboriginals have been drinking in parks they just leave the cartons there and the bottles lying on the ground.

Q. Men, women and children were at the wake?

A. It is out of character for bottles to be stacked like that.

For Morgan, it is not in the nature of Aborigines to be tidy and therefore his conclusion was that the riot must have been a planned event. The degree to which this understanding was developed within police evidence made one defence counsel lament that the defendants were being portrayed as consummate strategists in the same league as 'Charlemagne, Alexander the Great and General Schwarzkopf'.[12] The hyperbole was intended to mock such fanciful constructions, but the ambivalence that lurks in Morgan's construction requires a more complex and less dismissive explanation. The evidence fashioned an explanation of why the events that evening went against the grain in as much as the police failed to assert authority and retreated. What went against expectation was not so much the retreat, but the inability to exercise control in terms of Aboriginal/non-Aboriginal relations. This troubling detail was given explanation in racial constructions of Aboriginal identity. In his evidence, Morgan explained the reversal in terms of Aboriginal cunning that led the police into entrapment through deception. Morgan's evidence reflects ambivalence expressed as contempt born of familiarity, as well as a fear of strangeness.

For Morgan, the Aborigines' civil obedience and disciplined public civility was an act of mimicry. Mimicry, Bhabha (1984:127) suggests, continually transgresses the divide between identity and difference with something recognisably the same but different — as he says, not quite/not white. Mimicry does not reassure but disturbs; it 'is at once resemblance and menace' (Bhabha 1984:127). Imitation, in effect, subverts the identity of what is being represented and the very aim of state authority in policing civil obedience and conformity to patterns of public civility. For Bhabha, the effects of such power produce the form of hybridisation that renders dichotomous forms of representation problematic. The hybrid, as part object, undermines authority because it repeats it differently; as Bhabha (1985:156) says, 'denied knowledges enter upon the dominant discourse and estrange the basis of its authority' and 'the look of surveillance returns as the displacing gaze of the disciplined, where the observer becomes the observed and the partial representation rearticulates the whole notion of identity and alienates it from its essence' (Bhabha 1984:129).

Sameness slips into otherness in a way that has nothing to do with the other, who becomes an unwitting agent of menace. Mimicry is a kind of agency without a subject, which manifests in the fantasy of menace. Morgan attempts to interpret, on the basis of his experience, the menacing purpose of Aborigines. This is a claim to knowledge based upon the familiarity of experience rather than prejudice. For Morgan, the tidy stacks of bottles constituted an arsenal to be used against the police and were part of an elaborate plan of entrapment. For Morgan, each wave of Aborigines moved forward, threw their salvos and retreated to make way for the next wave with military precision. The evidence was clear to him that this had been a planned, orchestrated attack.

There are deeper issues that relate to the specificity of the solicitous form of legal and institutional integration in post-settler colonial societies that lurks here in terms of Aboriginal and police relations. The fantasy of menace reflected the often tense and conflictual relations between Aborigines and police in the North West (see Chapter 4). The particular fantasy of menace exists in misrecognition and exaggeration of menace, but also, as we have seen in the police injuries, in its possibility. As discussed in earlier chapters, the high rate of police intervention in the North West is staggering. An equally high proportion of all detentions are public order offences, which suggests that a perception that many Aborigines vehemently dislike, distrust and are willing to confront police in the North West is often an accurate one (see Cowlishaw 2004). As Commissioner Wootten (1991b:106) commented, 'in Aboriginal culture the image of the police does not stem from a historically benign function. The image derives from their role as armed representatives of dispossessing invaders' and, more directly, as the 'agents of such oppressive instruments' as the Aborigines Protection Board.

The problem of detecting the difference between the civil obedience of Aborigines and its mask, for Morgan, was evidenced in the park. For Morgan, the stacking of the bottles by people at the wake, which fulfilled the order to keep the park tidy, was proof of Aborigines' 'sly civility' and that they held a more sinister and planned intention. In Morgan's evidence, Aborigines become cultural hybrids (Aborigines in south-eastern Australia are not 'real' Aborigines because they are not living traditional lifestyles) whose behavioural conformity masks hidden agendas. Yet his testimony also made visible the slippage between culturally derived preconceptions and individual misdemeanours within the legal process.

Within the courtroom, the narrative developed in police testimony resonated with general Australian meanings and values that framed specific cultural understandings of a riot. The jurors, with the guilty verdicts they delivered, and the judge, as evident in his pre-sentencing remarks, certainly found the police account credible. Although given in narrative form in the courtroom, these aspects of Australianness were initially played out in a violent interchange that reflects aspects of power relations in Australia. What could have been considered a grief-stricken anger of the then inexplicable death of Lloyd Boney is framed as unprovoked and violent. The police response in deciding to enter the park rather than moving the wrong-doers away from the hotel conformed to a view that Aborigines were likely to be subverting public order and was in keeping with routine police practices of maintaining order in rural towns. The defence counsel made the point that the decision to enter the park and remove Aborigines had been made *before* the police vehicles had reached the vicinity of the park rather than *after* assessing the situation at the park. In other words, the police designated the group of Aborigines in the park as a force to be controlled and contained, anticipating that they would be destructive.

In the courtroom the authority of state violence exercised to control that evening in the park was given sanction and those Aborigines found to be responsible for the riot were to be punished. The trial itself constitutes a form of punishment as it has the defendants present in the dock, while statements (as we have seen, sometimes preposterous) are made about not only their actions, but also their intent. The impending trial certainly had bearing on the way that the defendants conducted their daily lives and the pressures that can be exercised with regard to the accused. The trial process of the preceding three-and-a-half years had determined, at the very least, uncertain futures for the three accused. Only two weeks prior to the first trial in Bathurst, slightly less than two years after the committal hearing, the Crown prosecution reduced the charges to seven from the original 15 charges, which had determined for the accused the levels of conditional liberty (e.g. bail conditions, parole and bond conditions) set by the court. As one of the accused stated, '"For me, it has been hell", said [Sonny] Bates. "I've been reporting to the police every week for the last five years, and Arthur's [Murray] in the same position. We've been to jail for crimes we never committed"' (*Green Left Weekly*, 15 April 1992).

The most serious charge, the attempted murder of Constable Terry John McGregor, was dropped, as was the charge against the three accused in relation to Constable Grant Maurice Connelly. In the revision of the charges, Albert James Bates was accused of assault causing actual bodily harm on Constable Anthony John Bordin and against Detective Sergeant Vaughan George Reid. Arthur Edward Murray was further charged with maliciously wounding with intent to do grievous bodily harm to Constable Terry John McGregor and assault occasioning actual bodily harm of Detective Sergeant Vaughan George Reid. All three Aborigines remained accused of riotous assembly. The power of the state to impose custodial sentences in its response to violence reflects the ultimate sanction in which state authority is exercised.

The legal process had begun in the lower courts in 1988 and was not completed until the hearing of a successful appeal in the New South Wales Court of Criminal Appeal (CCA) on 6 April 1992. The fact that the jury found one defendant not guilty of riotous assembly rendered the guilty verdicts in the trial 'unsafe', as the law required all three conspirators.[13] The CCA also set aside the convictions of Bates and Murray for assault due to a 'lack of evidence of identity despite abundant evidence of the police injury and the nature of the offence' (Anthony 2009:12). For the convicted prisoners, the ruling of the CCA provided only the penultimate act in this lengthy legal case. The final phase was completed in November 1994, some two years and eight months after the CCA, when the Department of Public Prosecutions set the hearings for the retrials of Arthur Murray and Albert Bates. On 11 November the district court in Sydney granted Murray a permanent stay of proceedings and on 14 December the court similarly granted Bates a stay of proceedings.

The administration of criminal justice and legal procedures provided pervasive and volatile encounters of conflict in the 1980s. Law and order campaigns, large deployments of police, Aboriginal deaths in custody and disproportionately high arrest rates combined to demonstrate the persistence of major tensions between Indigenous people and other Australians. In particular, the initial implausible explanation of Lloyd Boney's death given by police to relatives in Brewarrina and the failings in simple investigative procedures inflamed mistrust and suspicion. As suggested in the previous chapter, the inspector investigating other police officers in relation to Lloyd Boney socialised with the police officers under investigation rather than retaining a detached approach. In what was described by the Royal Commissioner as an 'extraordinarily insensitive and unwise decision', on the day after the riot, Inspector Peter was appointed to investigate and 'lay charges against those involved' (Wootten 1991b:121). Yet there was no sense that such an appointment may have posed a perceived conflict of interest or compromised the investigation. It did nourish suspicions in the Aboriginal community that as long as police investigated police, Aborigines could neither expect to be treated like other citizens nor should they trust the police. As the Commissioner put it bluntly, 'police are perceived to favour the interests of themselves or the whites' (Wootten 1991b:171). While many Australians continued to see the police as agents of the state performing the task of maintaining law and order and apprehending criminals, as already shown, the police procedures and practices in Brewarrina aggravated existing grievances. Although these breaches in investigative procedures did not automatically suggest that the police conspired to subvert the course of justice, they confirmed for many Aborigines that they would not be treated equally before the law or its agents.

In the case of the Brewarrina riot trial, the courtroom account effectively reproduced the power relations between white Australians and Aborigines. The narrative of the police evidence is certainly not the one 'true' account. While the account given by the police as witnesses was challenged in the courtroom, the defence counsels were ineffective in convincing the jury of the innocence of the defendants. In the courtroom, as Rouland (1994:266) aptly remarked, in 'adducing evidence, each party is concerned more with influencing the third party settling the dispute than with establishing absolute truth'. The police account, as argued in this chapter, resonates most strongly with cultural notions and nationalist metaphors of Australianness. In the Brewarrina riot trial, the images of Australianness put forward by the police are images not only of maleness but also of the law as a white domain. Whiteness was evident in the composition and the very ordering and symbolism of the courtroom. Within the account of the riot given in the police testimony, symbols surrounding Australianness and mateship become lived experiences that resonate with post-settler Australian understandings of themselves.

Chapter 6

Aborigines behaving badly: legal realism and paternalism

Domination ... always has a symbolic dimension, and acts of submission, of obedience, are acts of knowledge and recognition which, as such, implement cognitive structures capable of being applied to all things of the world, and in particular to social structures. (Bourdieu 2000:172)

The Brewarrina riot shows how imagery can be manipulated and recomposed to reinforce older patterns of relations. Besides the aspects already discussed, the riot was a visual event for mass consumption. The flow of dramatic images disrupted prevailing definitions of Indigenous people as the passive bearers of the conditions of their existence. Much of the interpretative work by politicians and the media sought to restore Aborigines to the position of the manipulated objects of others' intentions or as victims of their own inherent weaknesses. My analysis of the media and political discourse shows how the normative power of dominant discourses influences the perceptions of marginalised or subject peoples. Such discourse, by default or design, shaped the way that the riot was understood in terms of ideas, symbols and pre-existing material conditions. Yet, as a visual event, the riot was peopled with bodies, those of Aborigines and the police. It thus becomes interesting to consider the body as a cultural and historical phenomenon and, indeed, to view culture and history as bodily phenomena.

Understanding styles of bodily objectification is important to an exploration of culture and politics.

In this endeavour, I explore Allen Feldman's (1994) perception of history as a 'history of sensory perception' to restore to view a body politics that forms and informs cultural memory. The Brewarrina riot was significant because it was inconsistent with the established cultural scripts and visual imagery of the Aborigine. The national media's violent images of Aborigines confronting state authority ruptured the normative world with shocking effect. The images acted as the breach, so to speak, of a perceptual history of colonisation that is grounded in its legitimation of racism, but, equally, on structured forms of institutional paternalism. Paternalism requires relations of domination. Violence, inequality and dispossession are framed within the normative framework of mutual obligation. The Aborigine, as a generic category, has been framed within the normative category of sensory truth in numerous variants of what Poignant (1993:185) has called 'images of displacement', both historically and culturally. Such disempowering images have operated in tandem with institutional forms of intervention, which together have all but removed Aborigines from control over participation in processes that would facilitate their own social transformations.

Feldman (1994:406) sets out to analyse culturally ordered narrations in combination with 'information technology historically moulded to normative concepts of sensory truth'. His point of departure from more conventional analyses is found in his focus on the power of 'sensory truth' to symbolically eviscerate 'histories of pain' and the 'indigestible depth experience of particular sensory alterities' (Feldman 1994:407). He considers the Rodney King trial in the United States as it crystallised centuries of race relations. Raw footage of the police brutally beating a black man revealed a dimension most Americans did not want to see, let alone experience through the visceral impact of the video footage. The trial and the first jury verdict of not guilty were not only unjust, but an attempt to restore a normative world. The trial was symbolically 'therapeutic' in restoring what Feldman (1994:405) has called 'cultural anaesthesia': the 'banishment of the disconcerting, discordant and anarchic sensory presences'. His concern in developing an understanding of a 'sensory alterity' is to challenge the realism attributed to video evidence in the Rodney King trial. This chapter compares the evidentiary force of the video footage in the Brewarrina riot trial (1991) and the Rodney King trial (1992). It is through a comparative approach to popular representations of racial 'difference' that the relationship between visual, sensorial memory and the production of racialised knowledge in national historical memory must be explored.

The evidentiary effect of video

The visceral effect of the visual image has had a revolutionary impact on society since its progressive emergence in the nineteenth century. What has astonished viewers from its very inception is the unprecedented realism of the photographic process. The camera produces an amazing copying or mimesis between the image and the object it depicts. The ideal of a perfect imitation holds together the variety of images and the various photo-techniques within a homogenous field. Leslie Devereaux makes the point that 'by its very sameness to or identity with what we see with our own eyes', visual images are a form of simulacra (Devereaux and Hillman 1995:329). Objects, people and places leave behind their own images through photographs that have significant value in the recording and preserving of evidence and its dissemination. Nevertheless, the photographic image in its realist register is a representation. Yet, like the video and televisual documentary, the evidentiary force and mimetic power of the photographic image suspends disbelief, seemingly rendering it as simply reality rather than representation. Its early inception framed photography as the ultimate tool of science because of its empirical accuracy. The mimetic qualities of the photograph are also important as a source of social documentary. This leads to its use across an expanding range of scientific, technical, medical and legal assemblages as a source of accurate record, a means of surveillance and a basis of evidence. In its realist register, it is the product rather than its production that is stressed.

John Tagg (1995) has aptly described the photograph as the 'pencil of history', asserting that it is form that is recorded rather than content that is represented. Tagg (1995:289) alerts us to the issues of objectivity that surround the construction of history via photography, and more specifically the privileging of the 'graphic record' as incontestably superior to 'material culture, oral tradition, written records'. The photographic image appears to transcend the frailties of human discourse. The evidentiary force of the image in its immediacy is seemingly unmitigated by intermediaries. There is a reassurance about the past of an event, about people and things that assert a 'truth to presence'. When captured in the photograph, the photograph holds an important place as a reference to the fact that things *really* happened. The power of the image itself does not stand alone but relies for its meaning on its insertion into the 'cross-referenced series of the file and archive' and the acceptance of 'a process of chronological sequence' as a 'system of narration' (Tagg 1995:290). History and photography are given to us as inventions, as devices, as 'machines of meaning' (Tagg 1995:286). For Tagg, it is powerfully phenomenological, but at once ultimately discursive (Petro 1995:ix). In this, he echoes Barthes' (1984:93) oft-quoted statement that 'the photograph is a certain but fugitive testimony' with its intoning of a poststructuralist emphasis on multivocality and ambiguity.

Barthes' assertions may be seen to take on an additional meaning in the context of this chapter, which looks at the evidentiary force of the use of videos in the Brewarrina riot trial and the Rodney King trial. In both trials, the video images provided fugitive testimony. This was aptly demonstrated in the treatment of the riot in the Brewarrina trial and in the riot as a media event, which produced parallel and contradictory stereotypes and narratives. Occurring a year apart, the trials provided a powerful and immediate context for comparison. The Brewarrina riot trial is the inverse of the Rodney King trial in the sense that the video footage was interpreted in opposite ways. In one, the video evidence was endorsed, while in the other the video images were denied. These opposites show the freedom to interpret apparently accurate images, thus demonstrating the limits of veracity of the photographic image. I compare the different styles of bodily objectifications of Aborigines and Black Americans.

Bodies in pain and paternalism

In the Rodney King case, white police were charged with the violent assault of an African-American man. George Holliday's 81-second home video footage shows King being systematically beaten by officers; this video record seemed to provide irrefutable evidence of police brutality. In the images of King being struck 52 times by four Los Angeles policemen, the video seemed to offer irrefutable proof; the prosecutor stated that it was 'the most objective piece of evidence' available that could be seen with 'your own eyes' (Rabinowitz 1994:210). Los Angeles police officers had beaten a black man and thought they would get away with it. The prosecution relied on the 'facts' of the visual evidence. The video images played a critical part in the case for the prosecution. By contrast, lawyers defending the police offered King as a menacing physical threat, which they said a detailed analysis of the video footage would reveal. In the first King trial, the jury duly handed down a not guilty verdict.

For many people the verdict conformed to the historical view that Black Americans require extra-legal violence to be controlled. The use of the video in the trial conformed to the view that Black Americans hold only a veneer of civility, which also requires extra-legal violence to maintain control. It is the popular representation of racial difference that interests me here. My argument is that there is a particular relationship with visual discourse in the production of racialised knowledge as part of a national historical memory. In the United States, Elizabeth Alexander (1994:82) argues, the Rodney King trial was another instalment of 'black bodies in pain for public consumption [which] has been a national public spectacle for centuries'. As Alexander (1994:94, emphasis added) states:

> The whipped male slave, the lynched man . . . all of these are familiar and explicit in the popular imagination. *Black boys and men present a particular kind of physical threat to the white American imagination, a threat that must be contained.* Countless stories of violence are made spectacular to let black people know who is in control . . .

The practices of punishment through violence, and intimidation through public spectacles staged and consumed by white communities, coded Black Americans as subject to a different economy of power. Black Americans were regarded as having what Alexander (1994:84) calls a 'countercitizen relationship to the law'. It is such formations of knowledge and power that continue to code people that interest me here. James Allen's (2000) book *Without Sanctuary: Lynching photography in America* reveals the appetite for the practice of lynching Black Americans as a public visual spectacle in late nineteenth- and early twentieth-century America. A postcard industry grew up around lynchings, whippings and mutilations of Black Americans; a commodification of the public spectacle of the extra-legal violence needed to control the black man. It circulates as a visualised, material event, a portrayal of history and a vernacular history mobilised and disseminated through the artefacts of popular culture. The photograph of the violated black body has served as a visual transcription of race relations and power, a visualised history, which forms part of a collective memory.

The Rodney King video condensed centuries of racial history into an immediate national experience of contemporary race relations. As Alexander (1994:89) says, 'the four police officers of the Los Angeles Police Department specifically embody the state as experienced in the day to day lives' of Black Americans. What happened to King are conditions and possibilities of their own existence in relation to legal and extra-legal violence. In the trial, the very embodied form that state violence took is effectively rewritten for collective reception through the use of the video evidence. According to the lawyers defending the police, King was a physical threat and the police were following standard procedures (Alexander 1994:406). In this trial, 'legal reality is being visually projected in a variety of ways inside the courtroom' (Sherwin 1996:893). The legal realism of the courtroom procedures converges with mass media technologies.

The radical quality of the visual image to preserve and reveal through cropping, framing and enlargement, as Walter Benjamin points out, renders details the eye might not capture and enhances its evidentiary capacity (cited in Taussig 1992:144). In rendering the close-up details, technology works faster than the eye. This is evident in the in-court digital reconstructions by the defence in the Rodney King trial. The videotape was shown 'more than thirty times, projected at various speeds, played forwards and backwards, freeze-frame and fast motion' (Petro 1995:ix). With the aid of visual technology, the defence lawyers successfully authenticated their case by subduing the visceral immediacy of the video. The reduction of the video to fragments, as stills, freeze-frame, fast-motion images, effectively subverted the cumulative temporal force of the video. The defence managed to reduce the duration of the beating and the emotional impact of the cumulative effect of the 52 blows that struck King that night. The temporal flow of the 81 seconds of the video was reduced to frames that undermined its evidentiary force. Indeed, one jury member concluded that it was King who was the author of the video image, 'directing the action' and 'choosing the moment he wanted to be handcuffed' (Feldman 1994:412). What Feldman effectively shows is the inherent ability of the digitised image to be reorganised to achieve facticity. The reconstruction of the documentary evidence of the trial rendered the institutionalised representations to conform to normative portrayals of race.

In addition, the star witness for the defence of the police officers was the 'force expert', Sergeant Charles Duke, who stopped to explain each relevant frame. He showed how it was King who was in control and the officers were simply responding and applying appropriate force to King's escalating violence (Rabinowitz 1994:210). The expert witness could rely on the video frames to show how 'Mr King's leg is cocked' or 'his arm is triggered', necessitating the officer's response (cited Rabinowitz 1994:211). Not only did the defence recontextualise the video, but Sergeant Duke provided a voiceover narrative to frame the interpretation. The defence effectively shifted the evidentiary effect of the video from one confirming police brutality and institutional racism to the operation of standard police procedures. Through a substantial reordering of the affective experience of the video and its affective specificities, a convincing counter narrative was produced.

The not guilty verdict for the policemen involved in Rodney King's bashing saw 'Los Angeles explode in outrage at the injustice of the decision' (Petro 1995:ix). The outcome of the individualisation and atomisation of state violence in the trial was recast as an act of collective political violence. The Rodney King video became a bearer of not just situated acts of violence, but the social memory of a collective of historically situated subjects. The violence of the video reaffirmed the historical and experiential divide between the state (the white police officers) and its particular subjects (Black Americans). On the streets of Los Angeles, the verdict's authentication of the police actions exceeded its courtroom representations and provided a catalyst for an eruption of violent dissent. This histori-cal experience is one of a sensory encompassment of violence as a cultural given. Feldman (1994:406) describes cultural anaesthesia in the courtroom in terms of social processes that 'render the Other's pain inadmissible to public discourse and culture': the sanitising and legitimation of the violence brought upon King's body through the assertions of 'culturally-in-place archetypes' of 'racial difference' is central to Feldman's analysis of cultural anaesthesia as an unvoiced sensory terror.

Nevertheless, the mass circulation of the video can also be seen to rip away the social surface of the normative world of most Americans to reveal with shocking effect a dimension of American life not experienced by most Americans. The visual immediacy of mass tech-nologies circulated violent images that do not fit with the law and the rational violence of the state. As Feldman (1994:408) states:

> the images of King's beating showed the state making pain. The immediate shock of the televised beating originated in unpro-grammed sensory substitution. Even the viewer insulated from race and class could experience the involuntary projection of his or her body to that point of the trajectory marked by swinging police batons as they came down upon the collective retina that was suddenly rendered tactile.

Yet, in the courtroom, the reconstructed video evidence became the 'proof' that the state violence directed at King was in accordance with the protocols of the rationally order violence of the state. The remod-elling of perception was not simply a product of the technology alone. Through the technology, the very nature of the violence was rendered malleable to more historically dominant racial and cultural understandings. The police testimony framed the event as an engage-ment with King's 'bodily alterity'. King's body was frequently alluded to with racialised animalistic characterisations.

The defence testimony illustrates constructions of 'racial difference' and their public currency. Rodney King is represented as 'suspect-as-animal' (Feldman 1994:409). It is King's body that is 'referred to as "bear-like" . . . as "getting on his haunches"', invoking an 'animal imagery' that needed to be 'tamed and caged' (Feldman 1994:409).

Police violence is constructed as a pre-emptive measure necessary to control the 'intrinsic violence known to inhabit King's body' (Feldman 2004:213), and the video footage of the police beating King demonstrates 'the violent passage of King from animality' to 'compliance' (Feldman 1994:410). Black American agency is racially degraded as built upon animal-like strength and mental ineptitude.

Docile bodies and Aborigines behaving badly

The constructions of racial difference and its objectifications in public discourse are of interest here. In the Brewarrina riot and subsequent trial, what is it about the objectification of these marginalised peoples that delegitimates and sanitises the pain of the other within public discourse and culture? The Brewarrina riot video produced different outcomes and different social representations in the mass media from those that circulate in the United States. In Australia, historically, there is a different politics of the body. The social conditions of the subordination of Indigenous peoples have a different historical formation. The images of the Brewarrina riot are distinctive, I argue, in that they neither conform to the collective representations of Aborigines in public culture nor to their place in the archive of a national historical memory. The violent images of Aborigines confronting police disrupt established historical understandings grounded in Indigenous bodily objectifications. The release of the video in the national media ruptured the surfaces of the normative world of most Australians to reveal, with shocking effect, another dimension of society. The normative understanding of an Australian Indigenous body had never been one endowed with agency. The most powerful pre-digested image of Aborigines in Australian history is as passive subjects following 'tradition', or their contemporaneous counterpart, the submissive welfare recipient. The flow of images from the Brewarrina riot presented a spectre of rebellious action and agency and the violent disposition of a more threatening Indigenous modernity. In its media treatment, the violence quickly transformed from an intentional act or an aggrieved response to an act of manipulation by members of a sensationalist press. These were Aborigines behaving badly, but not entirely, it was said, of their own volition. Here in Australia, paternalism and racism take a specific form.

Paternalism works as the benign face of racism and has provided a means to legitimate settler colonial dispossession and domination. I use the term 'paternalism' as shorthand for a system of hierarchical social relations. It involves a social relationship that is hierarchical, as well as entailing conditions of mutual obligation. In Australia paternalism grew out of the necessity to intervene, which morally justified a colonial system of continuing dispossession. Such paternalistic relations define Aborigines' compliance and conformity as a legitimate return for the protection and guidance given them. Paternalism affirms the necessity of intervention in the social relations of these others as a condition of an alleviation of social and individual degradation. It generates a specific set of culturally informed images of racial difference and a different body alterity associated with settler colonialism. In effect, paternalism is a social technology that prefigures the 'sustained denial of any state making capacity of indigenous peoples' (Veracini 2010:105). The perceptual colonisation reflected the Aborigine as passive subject, disseminating and normalising particular sensory dispositions and a more fatalistic sensibility towards mutual relations and obligations. The symbolic dimension of domination requires acts of submission and acts of obedience through assimilation. What is important is that emblematic images have invoked a visual orthodoxy that renders the Aboriginal body a docile body.

What I emphasise is how visual constructs of Aboriginal people ultimately confirm their lack of agency in the modern world and render it natural. They were considered as worthy of ethnographic study as 'our' contemporary ancestors. The work of Spencer and Gillen (1968[1899]), in particular, in their pioneering study, combined a photographic study with film and research (see Mulvaney 1982). As Bernard Smith (1980:24) noted, 'social Darwinism had reduced Aboriginal culture to the lowest rungs of human society, [but] in so doing it placed it in the spotlight of scientific attention'. At this period, the commodification and widespread dissemination of visual images of Aboriginality emerged with the postcard industry from the late 1880s to the early 1900s (Brereton 1981:138). Two major Australian photographers, JW Lindt (see Brereton 1981:138) and Charles Kerry (see Poignant 1993:185), produced photographs for the postcard boom that began in 1890 and lasted until 1910 (Brereton

1981:138).[1] Kurt Brereton (1981:139) calls this the 'Eurofication of Australia', which featured imagery of architectural and engineering landmarks, the pastoral industry, and white Australians at work and play. Aborigines existed in this archive as the exotic other, as salvaged fragments of a 'savage existence . . . speeding towards extinction . . . [and] arranged as a still life [arrested] spectacle' (Brereton 1981:138). The image of the Aborigine as (noble) savage gained its meaning not from what Aborigines were, but what they were not.

The photographs were largely studio portraits. Poignant sees photographs not simply as images of the exotic, but more specifically as 'images of displacement' for public consumption; as she states (Poignant 1993:185):

> These photographs are 'images of displacement'. The Aborigines' removal from the bush to the constructed studio set parallels their actual displacement as the land's owners; and the stripping of the clothes they customarily wore also denies them a place within white settlement. An aura of lethargy and anomie pervades these images, which are visual metaphors for death. With their weapons laid aside and their wildness neutralised by the studio's ambience, the sitters are transformed into specimens . . .

These images reaffirm a social alterity of peoples who lacked agency and a future. Salvaged for posterity, the photographic images depict a way of life doomed to extinction. They also complemented government policy that had created Aboriginal reserves to 'protect the remnant of a [dying] race' (Morris 1989:92). Paternalism affirms the necessity of intervention, but there is no need to recognise any mutual obligation, as the social relationship is considered socially terminal. Popular representations of racial difference, such as those depicted on the postcards, affirmed the necessity of government interventions as benign paternalism. The images of historical displacement and death signified that Aborigines have no agency in the modern world.

The emblematic images of a superseded 'race' mark settler colonial discourses, which have, as their foundation, the denial of Indigenous agency and efficacy. Indigenous passive compliance is seen as not so much a legitimate return for protection and guidance, but an inevitable fate over which the colonisers believed they had no control. Contemporary historians Geoffrey Blainey and John Hirst maintain the most persistent strand of this approach. They express a form of cultural absolutism, the either/or categories that underpin many debates about Aboriginal modernity. Aborigines either exist as 'traditional society' or they are fully subsumed within modernity. For Hirst (2009:63), the 'displacement of one form of life for another was abrupt and complete' and, as a result, Aborigines today are not an 'ancient people, but a modern one'; hence, governments should make determined efforts to 'ensure that Aborigines enjoy the full benefits of European society of which they are part' (Hirst 2009:64). In Hirst's assessment, there is no alternative. The either/or position is supported by Blainey (1993:31), who asserts that the 'Australian version of land rights almost tries to restore this archaic and untenable way of life'. Settler colonial discourse here represents Indigenous dispossession as inevitable and irreversible.

The naturalisation of European colonisation of Aboriginal Australia was legitimated by the originary myth of terra nullius, which in legal terms refers not so much to a land without people, but a land without owners, and, hence, to a 'race' devoid of hierarchy, government, laws and, therefore, rights as Indigenous people.[2] Terra nullius is a charter for colonial dispossession, where Indigenous peoples are again defined in terms of what they lack. The doctrine of terra nullius has not just been a legal justification for the denial of rights, but a primary organising principle of the disparate narratives of settler colonial history in Australia. The history of colonial dispossession chronicles a utopian history of settler progress that renders Aborigines historically obsolete rather than dispossessed. The image of the traditional Aborigine finds a place in a settler colonial nostalgia that substitutes allegory for history. Such allegories fill the historical imagination and encode a historical memory that has constituted the settler mythologies of the nation. The ideological aspects of this nostalgia explain and justify the colonial history of modernity as a fatal environment for an Indigenous people, noble and exotic, but, nevertheless, a people incapable of participating in a secular, progressive society, except, perhaps, as facsimiles of white Australians.

The power inherent in visual modes of discourse is that the image does not argue its ideology, but exemplifies it as if its given meaning is instant and intuitive. The emblematic images present neither an expression of a romantic aesthetic nor of documentary evidence. They are not neutral representations, but emblems that affirm an ongoing obligation to sustain paternalistic social relations where racial and/or cultural inferiority justified Indigenous domination and dispossession. This can be seen in the 1950s image of One Pound Jimmy (see Figure 6), who became the face on a million postage stamps. The photographic image was taken in the 1930s by a young tourism executive looking for spectacular photographs and stories to fill a new Australian tourism magazine, *Walkabout*. Anne-Marie Willis (1993:111) provides an analysis of the nationalist trope that encodes the 1935 photographic image as internal 'other'. The image, she says, is an example of the 'exhausted end point' of the 'traditional Aborigine' as noble savage (Willis 1993:111–12):

> One Pound Jimmy's head was subsequently reproduced on Australian stamps. We can see why — the monumental quality that is produced by the (low) camera angle, facial expression, direction of gaze, and the man's strong sculptural features roughly approximates the crude nationalistic trope of gazing into the future while rooted in the past. But it is not an Aboriginal future for the nation that is being evoked, rather Aboriginality is posited as an ancient foundation over which white culture is laid . . . it functions as a sign rather than as substance of continuity, solidarity and tradition.

The photographic treatment of One Pound Jimmy conforms to the conventions of a romantic aesthetic that featured Aborigines 'partially naked, stiffly posed against a backdrop of nature, holding a traditional artefact (or more in this case), arranged to best display the body and the artefact' (Leslie 1993:85). As suggested earlier, in white-authored tropes the image of the traditional Aborigine as noble savage derives much of its meaning from what it is not. The ethnographically coded Aborigine as hunter/forager represents an outmoded form of existence to which adherence implies an inability to adapt and participate in the modern Australian state. Indeed, it is Aborigines' adaptation to the environment that denied them the possibility of change. Settler colonial

Figure 6: One Pound Jimmy postage stamp (1952)

discourses are not restricted to legal justifications for a denial of rights, but also to visual forms of an already docile body.

One Pound Jimmy (Gwoja Tjungarrayi, a Warlpiri-Anmatyerre man; see Figure 7) also illustrates a form of white nostalgia, sentimentality for a superseded, simple but static way of life — of which the photographic image of him provides a living specimen. He is

Figure 7: Gwoja Tjungarrayi

labelled 'Aborigine' on the stamp. One Pound Jimmy has neither a formal name nor an Indigenous name, but a nickname bestowed upon him by Europeans. What we see is the death of Indigenous social and cultural life, a living dead constituted and reflected upon as historical metaphor. The 'Aborigine' exemplifies a people without history and without a future as the act of dispossession is historically erased and replaced with the production of knowledges about Aboriginal inequality and racism.

In effect, this process did not end in the 1950s. In images contemporaneous with the Brewarrina riot, the displaced image of the Aboriginal subject takes the form of the welfare recipient. Aboriginal existence in modernity is reaffirmed as a problematic condition. The Aboriginal welfare recipient regularly doubles as the object on which the work of redemption by a humane modern state is conducted. In Figure 8 the image is combined with bureaucratically calculated, statistical indices that show the disproportionate inequalities in Aborigines' low standards of housing, health and education, high rates of unemployment and imprisonment, and high infant mortality and relatively early age deaths of adults. The quantitative differences point to the need for continued state intervention to administer Aboriginal life.

The visual image of the Aborigine that accompanies the tabular text positions him as passive and dependent. He is presented in 'modern clothes', but in the bodily posture of begging, of the adult beggar, as the dependent child (*SMH*, 23 May 1985, p. 1). This image has been violently displaced. The original photograph was of an Aboriginal man at a protest rally over Indigenous land rights (see Figure 9). In May 1985 a group of 200 people in Canberra protested against the federal government's intention to legislate a preferred national model of land rights (*SMH*, 17 May 1985, p. 1).[3] The man is bending over a fire warming his hands. The seemingly discordant context is cropped to remove the anarchic sensory presence of the Indigenous protestors exercising social agency. Instead, the image is domesticated within a discursive framework of the displaced and needy Aborigine.

The image of the displaced Aborigine is one of a person who in his/her place is out of place. It repeats a colonial fantasy seeking the reaffirmation of a settler national historical memory. The Indigenous

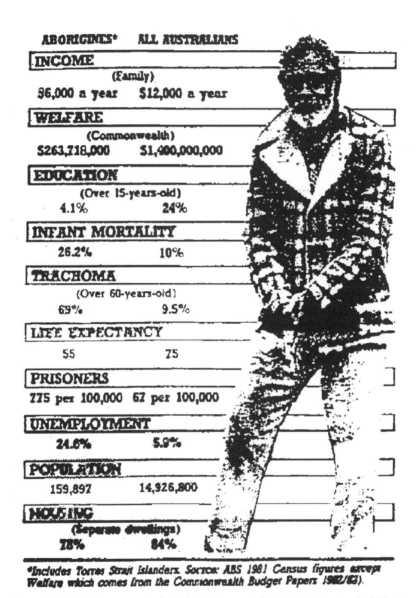

ABORIGINES*	ALL AUSTRALIANS
INCOME	
(Family)	
$6,000 a year	$12,000 a year
WELFARE	
(Commonwealth)	
$263,718,000	$1,900,000,000
EDUCATION	
(Over 15-years-old)	
4.1%	24%
INFANT MORTALITY	
26.2%	10%
TRACHOMA	
(Over 60-years-old)	
69%	9.5%
LIFE EXPECTANCY	
55	75
PRISONERS	
775 per 100,000	67 per 100,000
UNEMPLOYMENT	
24.6%	5.9%
POPULATION	
159,897	14,926,800
HOUSING	
(Separate dwellings)	
78%	84%

*Includes Torres Strait Islanders. Source: ABS 1981 Census figures except Welfare which comes from the Commonwealth Budget Papers 1982/83).

Figure 8: Table that accompanied article, 'It's true . . . Aborigines get a raw deal' (*SMH*, 23 May 1985, p. 1)

Figure 9: Aboriginal man in Canberra for protest rally (Fairfax Photos)

protester, as a self-determining Aboriginal subject, is restored to passivity and dependency at a time when such views were being challenged in the most direct and public way by Indigenous protestors demanding Indigenous land rights. The demonstration was in keeping with an assertive national political profile that had its contemporary precedent in the establishment of the Aboriginal Tent Embassy outside Parliament House.

This representation does more than record social inequality and deprivation. It asserts the failure of Aborigines to become independent entities capable of controlling their own existence. Aborigines are reaffirmed as symbolic failures in modernity. Central to this are the cultural habits associated with notions of employment. It is through employment — regular, disciplined and purposeful activity — that individuals become morally ordered individuals, in direct contrast to the consequences of receiving 'handouts', which is considered as money received for 'doing nothing' or, more recently, as 'sit down money'. Conventional attitudes associated with the idea of work are not simply instrumental values relating to the satisfaction of wants, but are associated with moral values of acting rationally and responsibly. This self-conscious rational individual, an individual with conscious purposes, one who consciously shapes his/her own existence, is juxtaposed against the irregular and undisciplined group behaviour of Aborigines, whose unrestrained desire seeks to satisfy only the most ephemeral and immediate wants. These are bodies that are passive and dependent rather than useful.

In the 1970s and 1980s cracks appeared in the social and ideological architecture of modern Australia. The Tent Embassy was among the first dramatic moves to demand land rights; that is, the assertion of Indigenous rights in defiance of settler colonial laws. By stating that they were an embassy, Aborigines captured their dispossession in a satirical form. Established symbolically on Australia Day, 26 January 1972, the Tent Embassy attracted considerable media attention over a six-month period until the police forcibly removed the tents, making eight arrests, on 20 June 1972. The embassy symbolised a change that captured the struggles for an Aboriginal modernity by self-determining Aboriginal subjects who now competed with and perplexed the image of the passive Aboriginal subject of terra nullius. A more assertive Indigenous politics had begun to emerge. Indigenous discourses of survival and independence turned the colonial gaze back upon itself (Sheridan 1995). Yet it is also clear that the interpretation of the Aboriginal 'problem' has relied for much of its meaning on the continuation of pre-existing paternalistic structures of Indigenous and/or race relations. As discussed, the white-authored media narratives that explained the Brewarrina riot continued to provide the comforting illusion of an Indigenous people as the hapless victims of modernity.

The difficultly in conceptualising the violence of the Brewarrina riot is that it dramatically ruptures pre-existing cultural presuppositions. On the television screens, viewers were confronted with a number of angry, violent confrontations with police. The principal violent exchange in the Brewarrina riot video centres on a confrontation between an unarmed Aboriginal male and a police officer armed with a baton and shield. Abusive and derogatory language directed at the police officer heightened the dramatic effect of the exchange. Minor scuffles between the police and other Aborigines were recorded, while another Aboriginal man broke up potential conflicts by standing between the police and their antagonists. These scenes were recorded against the general background of the melee, with violent sounds of breaking glass, swearing, shouting, violent threats, minor scuffles, bottles being smashed against police cars and hotel windows being systematically broken. These were Aboriginal people directly refusing to yield to police authority, which ultimately resulted in the police returning to their damaged cars and retreating from the scene (see Chapter 1). The visceral immediacy of these violent scenes was initially disavowed as irrelevant to Australia and without precedent; it was displaced and confirmed as exotic and exceptional.

The function of violence categorises people and provides a powerful means to deny justice to those people's rights and protection, and their own claims to victimhood. Social violence transgresses the social contract between citizens and the state as individuals forego taking the law into their own hands and cede a monopoly of violence to state authority. The power of destructive violence and its spectacular nature has the capacity to obfuscate other broader social and economic issues. The arresting nature of violent events often means that the systemic nature of violence, marginalisation and exclusion is displaced and all that is registered is the social disruption. So-called riots and protests turned violent, as discussed in earlier chapters, delegitimate claims of injustice in public discourse. The disordered and undisciplined violent bodies of those involved in the melee become a moral inversion of the idealised disciplined citizen's body, which delegitimates claims to victimhood.

The specifics of this delegitimacy in the Brewarrina riot have a paternalistic frame of reference. The Aboriginal 'rioters' were not responsible for their own angry dispositions, but served as an example of inherent Aboriginal weakness for alcohol and the loss of bodily and mental control that followed. As discussed, the agency for the riot on the evening of the wake was the intoxicated and undisciplined behaviour. Aboriginal behaviour through intoxication was positioned as the source of exceptional violence and the cause of the public disorder. Drunkenness is taken here as a bodily form of compulsive behaviour. Culturally, in Australia, drinking alcohol has never been strongly proscribed; however, the consumption of alcohol in Australia has operated as a differentiating practice separating civilised and ordered behaviour from undisciplined behaviour. Aboriginal drunkenness is often characterised as a compulsive disorder that subverts the civilising process (see Langton 1993). What I have shown is a disempowering paternalism deeply ingrained in these constructions of 'them' that emerges out of the status as settler colonial other, which simultaneously erases the historical act of dispossession.

Legal realism and paternalism

In the institutional setting of the courtroom, the visual image does more than record and preserve. The power of visual images moves beyond their documentary capacity to authenticate and to preserve and reveal, but invokes its own capacity, as it were, to speak as a subject itself: to return the gaze. In the Rodney King trial, the medium's own specific capacities to reveal details the eye cannot capture were exploited. Photography has always demonstrated a capacity, through editing, to frame, crop and enlarge the meaning of the image to convincing effect. In the courtroom setting, the images are more than objects of knowledge. In the Rodney King trial, the slowing, freezing or quickening of the frames sought to reveal something unacknowledged and undetected by the human eye. The images become the subject of meaning and not the object of meaning. In the video's specific capacity to reveal detail, a black body in pain is transformed into an expression of animal-like violence. By contrast, in the Brewarrina riot trial, the fact that the purported criminal violence is absent from the video meant that the Aboriginal defendants became objects to be discursively constructed in courtroom testimony.

The video was critical to the case of the defence solicitors and barristers. Unlike the Rodney King trial, in the Brewarrina riot trial the video footage *showed none of the defendants engaged in the crimes they allegedly committed.* Indeed, one defendant was clearly seen limping and demanding the film crew follow him and start filming the police violence (of which he alleged he was a victim) that was directed towards Aboriginal people in the park. The video shows another defendant clearly trying to defuse potential conflicts rather than escalate them (see Figure 10). The third defendant, who is not seen on the footage, asserted that he was at home at the time, a claim upheld by the jury's not guilty verdict. In this trial, the video evidence seemed to provide proof that the accused were not involved in the violence and could do little to support the police case and that of the prosecution. Indeed, the prosecution had to show that the behaviour of the defendants on the video did not fully record their participation in the riot.

The prosecution case was summed up in a statement by the judge to the jury: 'it does not appear to me that any of the action depicted on that video showed any police officer being injured, and, yet, just about all of them were' (11 April). This was the prosecution's evidence, even if it was not filmed. With one of the accused demanding media scrutiny of police violence and the other breaking up potential conflicts between police and Aborigines, the visual evidence had to be proven to be incomplete and inconclusive. The gaps in the footage were vital, particularly a critical period when the film crew changed its position, which involved running around 'the block' within which all the criminal violence of those accused was allegedly contained. The prosecution had to establish its case despite the video footage. The tape was shown three times. The principal reading for the prosecution was to plot gaps in the footage and to establish the time

Figure 10: Arthur Murray (in white shirt) intervenes to prevent confrontation
(Fairfax Photos)

periods of those gaps. The cameraman's evidence was drawn upon to plot the breaks in the videoing of the event. The filming was stopped only briefly when the video batteries needed to be changed and when the crew changed the vantage point. The detail was not in the footage, in what the eye may have missed, but in detailing the gaps the eye of the video had missed. The unseen gaps in the footage were said by the prosecution to contain a more brutal passage of violence, when the camera was not recording.

The prosecution's emphasis on the gaps was framed by the police testimony that did what the video did not do; that is, it positioned the accused as the perpetrators of the violence. In the police testimony, police had entered the park to disperse the mourners at a wake only to be repulsed by 'a very intense barrage' of bottles, flagons and pieces of wood. After further skirmishes, the police abandoned their vehicle and retreated. In police evidence, the language to describe the riot provides interesting insight about the perceptions of the night's events. Each police officer, when giving evidence of the melee, described it in the language of warfare (see Chapter 5).

In the institutional setting of the courtroom, the social field of meaning was framed by the police testimony. Previous media treatment of an inherent Aboriginal weakness for alcohol that had provided an earlier explanation for the riot was irrelevant to the court. In the courtroom the prosecution had to show agency and the intent on behalf of the accused, which relied on the police evidence to interpret and fill in the gaps in the video. The video images took on a sinister meaning during the trial, which operated in a manner that was against vernacular knowledge of a national historical memory. In the context of the trial, the three accused conspirators had cunningly concealed their violent intentions while under the surveillance of the cameras and unleashed their violent strategies when the camera surveillance was absent. In the courtroom the powerful effects of the video were discursively constructed.

The video evidence, in this case, contradicted the police testimony. There was no visual evidence that the defendants were engaged in violent assaults. In addition, a witness, other than the police, named another Aboriginal man as the perpetrator of the violence. In particular, the video evidence of Arthur Murray's behaviour in intervening and breaking up potential conflicts was at odds with his conviction. As Roderic Pitty (1994:9), a political scientist who attended the trial, asserted, 'The hotel owner clearly described another man known to him striking the policeman where the assault occurred. A journalist saw Murray too far away from the incident to be the attacker.' These major discrepancies led Pitty (1994:9), in his review of the evidence, to state that 'the evidence upon which [the defendants] Arthur Murray and Sonny Bates were convicted is riddled with doubt'.

Two dramatic moments in the sentencing at the first Brewarrina trial saw the accused subvert the proceedings. In the first instance, the sentencing of Murray was put into disarray by a defendant's unexpected outburst directed at the judge. The defendant had joined the two convicted prisoners in the dock for sentencing, having previously pleaded guilty to a lesser offence committed during the melee. He suddenly stood up and shouted, 'Arthur Murray did not break the policeman's leg. I did. That's how much your justice is worth' (3 May 1991).

Sentencing was immediately adjourned and the defendant, accompanied by his solicitor and a police officer, was taken to the court cells to make a statement. Those of us who had witnessed the trial were aware that the hotel owner in earlier evidence had identified this defendant as striking the policeman. The statement put the police evidence into question. The situation was diffused when the police officer returned and stated that the prisoner had retracted his statement, as he had been confused at the time. Sentencing resumed.

In the sentencing that followed, however, a memory more in keeping with a national historical memory returned. The judge asserted that Arthur Murray had been seized by the environment and acted in a 'moment of madness' (3 May 1991). The defendant's body here becomes an infantilised body, lacking reason or control. An exchange between Judge Nash and the defence counsel provoked a more nostalgic sentimentality. The judge explained that as a resident solicitor he had practised law in Bourke and Brewarrina for some 12 years. During the sentencing of the convicted men he stated that the court in Bourke at the time of his residence in the late 1950s and 1960s had sat only once per month and that it had been mainly white people who had come before the court. 'I don't know what happened to change it, but it changed in the 1970s', he stated. Provoked by the defence counsel's assertions of 'white prejudice' and, in particular, the 'concerns of the Aboriginal people regarding police', the judge continued (3 May 1991):

> That is the kind of statement indicating that things could have changed at least since the mid-1960s anyway. We would never have had anything said like that in those days. Things have completely changed. Why? I'd love to know. The housing conditions for Aboriginal people were abominable, but in terms of personal relations, people got on well . . . I have great difficulty following why, if conditions have improved, that race relations have got worse.

Here the Indigenous past is severed from the present and removed from bearing any relationship with the past. When he speaks of increased court sittings in the 1970s and race relations getting worse, he speaks directly to the increased involvement of Aborigines in the court system. The formal equality granted to Aborigines by the state, evidenced in the improved living conditions, in the judge's view, should have removed the sources of anger and conflict. Granted conditions of formal equality, it is Aborigines who are behaving badly, despite their new legal circumstances.

When the judge finished his speech, the defendant Sonny Bates stood up in the dock abruptly, and challenged and rejected the judge's nostalgia with a counter (alternative) memory. Convicted prisoners are not supposed to speak, let alone challenge the judge. In a simple statement of contradiction, he said that this halcyon time was the same time that his father had to carry a 'dog tag', an exemption certificate. The 'dog tag' enabled those who attained it to become honorary whites, and, specifically, was a licence to consume alcohol without fear of being arrested. The holders were freed from the oppressive laws that applied to Aborigines. The judge and the erring defendant evoked two distinct social, as well as legal, positions, and distinct historical memories of paternalistic laws that had curtailed Aboriginal liberty without their consent, because Aborigines had to be protected from doing harm to themselves. Paternalism works to protect people from themselves, but only operates where asymmetrical relations of power exist. The defendant's interjection from the dock was met with a stern rebuke and the threat that another outburst would find the prisoner sent out of the dock and back to the cells.

As the accused had not testified during the trial, the utterances from the dock ended the normative absence of an Aboriginal voice in the courtroom. Their interjections momentarily punctured the normative social and hierarchical relations in the courtroom and offered a counter memory. The judge's 'forgetfulness' was rendered as a form of hierarchical selection that had erased other social experiences unperceivable, inadmissible and subject to sensory closure. In this erasure, we gain a grasp of something of the grounds for the formation of postcolonial social and political Indigenous identities that disrupt and transgress such 'forgetfulness'. In the trial, however, Aboriginal silence, for legal reasons, effectively rendered the accused as abstractions in the courtroom and the objects of post-event narrative framings of the melee's violence in the video. By contrast, the courtroom performances by the police reaffirmed their presence as active subjects whose testimony provided the principal source of memory and explanation that fleshed out the video evidence and gave it meaning and emotional content. The Aborigines appeared as captured, almost as artefacts, in the material substance of the video, and reaffirmed their status as passive objects whose actions could be readily framed and explained by others.

Abbreviations

ABC	Australian Broadcasting Commission
ALC	Aboriginal Land Council
ATSIC	Aboriginal and Torres Strait Islander Commission
AWB	Aborigines Welfare Board
CCA	Court of Criminal Appeal
LALC	Local Aboriginal Land Council
NSW	New South Wales
NSWALC	New South Wales Aboriginal Land Council
OPP	Offences in Public Places Act
RALC	Regional Aboriginal Land Council
RCIADIC	Royal Commission into Aboriginal Deaths in Custody
SMH	*Sydney Morning Herald*
SOA	Summary Offences Act
TRG	Tactical Response Group

Notes

Introduction

1   'Irreversible' takes a number of forms. It exists as an a priori, a given, in which the 'colonial' is erased and 'settler society' is substituted for 'modern Australia' as opposed to 'ancient Australia'. Similarly, colonisation is treated as a fait accompli, an inevitable or necessary transformation of Australia (see Blainey 1993 and Hirst 2009 in Chapter 6).

2   Prime Minister John Howard stated, 'nations make treaties, not parts of nations with each other' (radio interview with Alan Jones, 29 May 2000; cited in Brennan et al. 2004:3).

3   'Aborigine' is a generic term applied to the original inhabitants by the colonial administration in Australia and is in common use. 'Indigenous' has a recent lineage and is used more globally to denote peoples who experienced European colonisation and settlement. I use the terms interchangeably.

4   Although rural workers accounted for only 14 per cent of the total workforce, rural unemployment accounted for 42 per cent of the nation's unemployed (Lawrence 1987:49).

5   The survey was conducted between November 1986 and July 1987. It surveyed 677 Indigenous people from the Western (163), North Western (184), Wiradjuri (115), Far South Coast (167) and Western Metropolitan (48) regions (Ross 1988:24).

6   The North Western region of the state recorded the highest rates of Indigenous unemployment (78 per cent) and the Western region the lowest (73 per cent) (Ross 1988:11).

7   From 1972 the federal Department of Aboriginal Affairs funded Aboriginal Voluntary Resettlement Programs to facilitate the movement of Aboriginal families from small rural towns in the western parts of New South Wales with high rates of unemployment to the regional growth centres of Bathurst, Orange, Wagga Wagga, Albury and Newcastle (Long 2000:111).

8   For example, the statutory native title system has been described as resembling the 'worst aspects of Apartheid' or as a system creating 'living museums' or 'cultural ghettos' (see Ritter 2010:196). The federal coalition government (1996–2007) sought to redefine reconciliation by making a distinction between 'symbolic' and 'practical' reconciliation. The issues of land rights, native title, self-determination and apologies for historical injustices were considered symbolic distractions from the real issues of Indigenous health, housing, education and employment (Howard J 1997).

9   When his government abolished the national Aboriginal representative body, the *Aboriginal and Torres Strait Islander Commission* (ATSIC), John Howard (cited in Gunstone 2006:2) stated:

> We believe very strongly that the experiment in separate representation, elected representation, for indigenous people has been a failure. We will not replace ATSIC with an alternative body. We will appoint a group of distinguished indigenous people to advise the Government on a purely advisory basis in relation to aboriginal (sic) affairs.

Chapter 1

1   Students from The University of Sydney organised the Freedom Ride and travelled around rural New South Wales by bus to challenge and highlight Indigenous segregation in many towns. A year later, in 1966, the Gurindji Pastoral Strike for land, better pay and working conditions in the Northern Territory received major national media attention (see Hardy 1968; Rose D 1991; Anthony 2007).

2   Discriminatory state legislation had been progressively revoked: segregated schooling (1952), non-qualification for social security restrictions on unemployment benefits, maternity allowances, family allowances, sickness benefits (1957), government pensions (1959), and the special legal provisions relating to vagrancy, consorting and the ban on drinking alcohol (1963).

3   The region includes the traditionally held lands of Barkindji, Wongaibon, and Maruwari and Mandananji peoples. The local self-designation is Murrie.

4   Those initially charged in Brewarrina Local Court were remanded to appear at Bourke Local Court on 7 December 1987 (*SMH*, 24 September 1987, p. 4). The committal hearing was held at Bourke Local Court on 25 July 1988, where 17 defendants were committed for trial on a total of 30 charges (*SMH*, 26 July 1988, p. 4). Both trials were held at Bathurst District Court in 1991. The first trial was distinctive because three of the accused were charged with riotous assembly, as well as offences committed against police officers. The second dealt with all the other accused.

5   Research on the newspaper coverage of the riot was collected and collated by Martin Butcher.

6   The *Central Western Daily* report differed in content inasmuch as it recorded that two police officers suffered broken legs in the riot.

7   On national television, the local coroner, Mark Olsen, initiated a parallel debate with his accusation that the ABC television crew started the riot.

8   Goodall's manuscript was later published with a more extended analysis as 'Constructing a riot: Television news and Aborigines' (Goodall 1993). This segment draws on Goodall's unpublished account of the media coverage.

9   In the uncut footage, the video action begins with shots of the darkened park, where movement is discernible; there is yelling, the breaking of glass and the police shouting 'get out of the park'.

10   When the ABC repeated the story on 23 August, the first images were of young men throwing stones at the pub and smashing its windows (Goodall n.d.:10).

11   In another editorial, two weeks later, the position was made more explicit: 'The Brewarrina riot was the result of racial discrimination, the death of Lloyd Boney, primitive living conditions and chronic unemployment among the Aborigines' (*SMH*, 1 September 1987, p. 16).

12 Stated by a witness for the prosecution, cited in the *SMH*, 30 July 1988, p. 5.

13 This fieldwork research in a courtroom setting was carried out by Dr T Ernst, Dr K Zubrinich and myself in 1991 during the trial and the subsequent appeal in the New South Wales Court of Criminal Appeal.

14 The New South Wales *Anti-Discrimination Act 1977* and the federal *Racial Discrimination Act 1975* (Cth).

15 The RCIADIC national report (Johnston 1991) made 339 recommendations.

16 Cunneen (1990b) details a number of raids on Aboriginal communities in Sydney where excessive and dangerous force was applied. The most notorious was by undercover police seeking to arrest a man in Alexandria Park during celebrations for National Aboriginal Day in 1989. Police officers, out of uniform, charged into the midst of some 500 to 1000 people, mostly children, and began discharging their pistols (Cunneen 1990b:10).

17 Pauline Hanson's One Nation Party was antagonistic to Asian immigration, an open policy towards refugees, multiculturalism, government programs that were aimed positively to discriminate in favour of Aborigines, and, in particular, Aboriginal land rights.

Chapter 2

1 The coalition parties, in political opposition, completely rejected the granting of land rights to Aboriginal people in New South Wales. The National Party leader, Leon Punch, opposed the 1983 Act as follows (cited in Wilkie 1985:54):

> The National Party is opposed to the principle of land rights for Aborigines in New South Wales. The party does not acknowledge that Aborigines have a just claim for land based on prior ownership, or tradition, or by way of compensation. No Australian should have the right to acquire land in a manner different to any other Australian.

2 The Keane Reports are the First and Second Reports from the Legislative Assembly Select Committee Upon Aborigines (NSW Parliament 1980, 1981) on the conditions of Aborigines in New South Wales.

3 The legislation undermined the intentions and high expectations generated by the Keane Reports. This applied most clearly to claimable land. The Minister for (Crown) Lands had the power to grant land claims and held the right of veto. Between 1983 and 1990 Aboriginal Land Councils lodged 3406 claims:

15 per cent were granted

35 per cent were under investigation

50 per cent were rejected (State Conference of Land Councils 1990:26).

By 1990 the land granted represented less than 0.05 per cent of the total land area of New South Wales (Chalk 1991:2). Indigenous claims remained a peripheral interest of the state and secondary to non-Aboriginal interests in land.

4 The federal Labor Government officially adopted multiculturalism as policy in 1973.

5 Byrd (2011:xvii) makes the point that the 'cacophony of competing struggles' produced in such liberal multiculturalism 'often coerces struggles for social justice for queers, racial minorities, immigrants into complicity with settler colonialism'.

6 This grouping, recent in its inception, as the major social division within settler Australia existed between Roman Catholic (Celtic) and Protestant (Anglo) populations.

7   I would add that it was not only Anglo-Saxons who expressed this angry sense of loss and marginalisation, but also many individuals from migrant backgrounds, who felt they had also become mainstream. They supported the cultural nationalism of political figures such as John Howard and Pauline Hanson.

8   Many anthropologists working in communities were critical of the notional sense of 'self-management' and 'self-determination' and the gap between bureaucratic controls and funding allocations and guidelines (see von Sturmer 1982; Morris 1989; Tonkinson and Howard 1990).

9   The shift towards assimilation and the rejection of multiculturalism does not always occur with the implementation of market-oriented economics. The historical and political circumstances always play a major role. As in Guatemala (Hale 2006) and Bolivia (Postero 2007), new spaces for political mobilisation for the Indigenous populations occurred and gave rise to multicultural reforms, which both authors refer to as neoliberal multiculturalism.

10   As Mario Blaser (2010:136–8) points out, these descriptions emerge from the core ideas put forward by Friedrich Hayek. According to Hayek, 'the society is the peak of social evolution, its order comes under threat when two moral instincts, altruism and solidarity, are allowed to make their way into state policy' (Blaser 2010:136). For Hayek, while these moral instincts may have been adaptive in earlier stages of social evolution of society, they now threaten the unhindered expression of individual self-interest and a more adaptive market society (Blaser 2010:136).

11   I paraphrase here part of the Premier's press release on the passing of the amendments to the Aborigines Land Rights Act (Zammit (1990) for Nick Greiner, 6 September 1990).

12   The federal coalition government, which came to power in 1996, implemented identical changes. The major policy section of the Aboriginal and Torres Strait Islander Commission (ATSIC) was transferred to the Department of Prime Minister and Cabinet (Howard D 2000:74).

13   The Draft Declaration on the Rights of Indigenous Peoples of the United Nations (1997) has rejected the policy of mainstreaming as inappropriate for Indigenous people.

14   The term 'mainstreaming' appears in Options C and D of the report.

15   The figures used were inconclusive of the government's claims. Figures showed a *decrease* rather than *increase* in the gap between Aboriginal/non-Aboriginal people. Aboriginal infant mortality figures (1987) cited 29 per thousand compared to 9.6 for non-Aborigines (Premier's Department 1988:16), but figures for New South Wales in 1978–79 were estimated at 52 per thousand (NSW Parliament 1981:143). In education, too, the figures used were debatable. In 1987 the retention rate for Aboriginal children in Year 12 was a quarter of that of non-Aboriginal children (10 per cent compared to 41 per cent) (Premier's Department 1988:15). Yet, as recently as 1976, '82% of Aborigines over 15 years of age had no educational qualifications, e.g., school certificate' (NSW Parliament 1981:227). Furthermore, in 1970 only 87 Aboriginal children remained until Year 10, while by 1979 the figure had jumped to 643 (NSW Parliament 1981:223).

16   The 1983 Act followed the federal government's *Aboriginal Land Rights (Northern Territory) Act 1976*.

17   In February 2002 the federal coalition government introduced mainstreaming into government policy. The Minister for Immigration and Multicultural and Indigenous Affairs, Philip Ruddock, announced plans to rationalise urban services to Aborigines by mainstreaming services.

18   Laffin (1995) points out that this was a radical break with New South Wales Public Service Board practice. Historically, the departments of the Public Service Board were run by professional bureaucrats and dominated by professionals (e.g. main roads by engineers and health departments by medical practitioners), and the Public Service Board dominated personnel selections, particularly the appointment of department heads (Laffin 1995:73).

19   It did not appear in the Act until the amendments in 1987.

20   The finances held in the fund were A$50 million (OAA 1989:11).

21   Parallels can be made here with the operations of separate Aboriginal bodies, the National Aboriginal Consultative Committee (1973–77), the National Aboriginal Conference (1977–85) and, finally, ATSIC (1989–2004), which developed at the level of federal government.

22   There was no training of Land Council staff; rather, staff members were expected to learn through experience in the position. The first RALC and LALC representatives were often left to their own devices and often created their own guidelines on the basis of their own priorities or pressing needs.

23   This RALC staff member commented that they were expected to grasp all the relevant sections not only of the Aboriginal Land Rights Act and regulations, but also the *Public Finance and Audit Act 1983* (NSW) and regulations, the *Annual Reports (Statutory Bodies) Act 1984* (NSW) and regulations, and the *Trustee Act 1925* (NSW) and regulations.

24   '[A]cross all NSW Departments (excluding Public Works and Housing), [consultancies] earned . . . $10.7 million in the two years 1989–91 — or 16.2% of total spending by these departments' (Howard M 2005:8).

25   The State Conference had empowered the State Council executive as its representative in discussions with the government.

26   Manuel Ritchie, the Mid North Coast RALC representative, stated, 'the protestors wanted a program of consultation to be conducted before the Act was amended' (*SMH*, 10 October 1990, p. 5). Tombo Winters, representing the North West RALC, echoed the same sentiments: 'the Aboriginal people had not been consulted about the changes' (*SMH*, 10 October 1990, p. 5).

27   Consequently, members of LALCs attempted to remove two RALC representatives for the way they voted.

28   The Queensland Premier called the members of the High Court who recognised the existence of native title 'a pack of historical dills' (cited in McKenna 1997:8). The historian Geoffrey Blainey (1997:21–3) characterised the High Court as the 'black armband tribunal'.

Chapter 3

1   In Britain the need for community policing of public order offences, a politics of anti-social behaviour, was expressed in the 'broken windows' analogy that 'minor crimes if left unchecked will lead communities being engulfed by a rising tide of serious crime' (Bond-Taylor 2005:2).

2   Nick Greiner's coalition (Liberal–National) government was elected in 1988 and was returned for a second term in May 1991. Premier Greiner resigned in June 1992. Under the leadership of Premier John Fahey, the coalition government was defeated in 1995 and replaced by a Labor government.

3   Tonry's study develops a comparative analysis of incarceration rates disaggregated by race in England, Wales, the United States, Canada and Australia.

4   The Tent Embassy was established on the lawns of Parliament House in Canberra in 1972 by Indigenous people in protest at the federal coalition government's refusal to recognise Aboriginal land rights (see Chapter 6).

5   Legal action in these riots established the precedent of charging Aborigines involved in public disturbances with riotous assembly (see Cunneen and Robb 1987; Cowlishaw 2004).

6   Davis (1990) states that technologically advanced military-styled policing was first developed between the Los Angeles Police Department and the military aerospace industry in California.

7   Roy (1986) provides an extensive account of media campaigns by Dubbo and Bourke Shire Councils in support of law and order issues throughout 1985.

8   Miller (1996:140–1) states that Ronald Reagan outlined Wilson's approach in his 1981 anti-crime address to the International Association of Chiefs of Police, and Wilson's views were published widely in right-wing magazines (*Commentary, The Public Interest, Heritage Foundation* and *Policy Review*) and popular conservative magazines (*Fortune, Forbes, The New Republic, The National Review* and *Atlantic*), rather than in peer-reviewed academic and scientific journals (see also Garland 2001:131).

9   Tony Vinson (1991:84) estimated a 20 per cent cut in prison education occurred as the prison system experienced a 35 per cent increase in inmates.

10   Republican administrations in the United States showed the same trends towards hard policies in penal reform. Miller (1996) records that major increases occurred in the Justice Department budgets: as he argues, the figures show 'local funding for justice (police, judicial, prosecutors, public defenders and corrections) rose from about $11.7 billion in 1971 to $66 billion in 1988' (Miller 1996:174) and '$75 billion in 1990' (Miller 1996:2).

11   Brown (1991:31) estimated capital works expenditure increased from $77 million to $108.6 million in 1990, with the construction of new prisons in rural Lithgow ($51 million) and outer metropolitan South Windsor ($51.2 million). The first legislation in New South Wales for private prisons led to a 600-bed private prison being completed at Junee in March 1993 (Zdenkowski 1995:227).

12   Similar comparisons have been made with prison trends elsewhere in relation to marginal populations. Prison increases for black Americans were spectacular, reversing the racial mix for the first time, with 53 per cent black Americans and 46.5 per cent white by 1989 (Tonry 1994:100). Black Americans make up only 12 per cent of the general population. By 1990 Tonry (1994:103) shows the rate of imprisonment in the United States of white American prisoners was 289 per 100,000 and for black American prisoners 1860 per 100,000. The incarceration rates were six or seven times higher than for whites (Tonry 1994:101).

13   The census figures showed the New South Wales population was 5,834,000 and the Indigenous population was 75,020, based on estimates from the 1991 census of population and housing.

14 Public meetings about vandalism were held also in Bourke throughout 1985 (Roy 1986:120–2).

15 The problem was often identified as the cultural incompetence of Aboriginal parents. As one resident stated, 'My opinion is that much of the cause of the problem lies in the lack of parenting by Aboriginal parents, and that a much more welfare-oriented counselling must be done to ensure that they show proper guardianship of their children' (cited Roy 1986:122).

16 They reaffirmed the trends for the North West previously recorded by the NSW ADB (1982), Cunneen and Robb (1987) and Bonney (1989).

17 The NSW ADB (1982:41) report revealed a high incidence of arrests for unseemly words: 56.1 per cent in 1978, and 61.1 per cent in 1980. The state-wide survey revealed a level of 43.2 per cent, which indicates a significant reduction in the incidence of arrests for the general population under the OPP, which was not reflected in Aboriginal communities in the North West.

Chapter 4

1 The federal Foreign Minister, Bill Hayden, declared the Libyan presence in the Pacific a destabilising danger. As he stated, 'There is a very real possibility of Libya, via Vanuatu, becoming a revolution for hire centre and government has hit the "serious problem button" in a hurry' (*Courier Mail,* 2 May 1987, cited in Ryan 1996).

2 This incident occurred in Bourke on the 28 August 1986 (see Cowlishaw 1994, 2004).

3 Cowlishaw (2004) has substantially explored this cultural space of ambiguity and multiple meanings in the North West.

4 Heminevrin is a sedative used in alcohol withdrawal to manage restlessness and agitation.

5 The Commissioner noted some conflict between the matron and the sister in the differing accounts of their conversation that night (see Wootten 1991c:24–9).

6 See Cowlishaw (1990) for a consideration of the media treatment of the role of the medical staff and a different argument.

7 Commissioner Wootten (1991a:83) was the only Commissioner to recommend criminal and disciplinary proceedings, made only for New South Wales and Victoria.

8 For the police, this was not sinister; such practices followed routine procedure for those with prior involvement with a case to follow up the case.

9 This witness of the events wishes to remain anonymous.

10 This person wishes to remain anonymous.

Chapter 5

1 The courthouse (1880) was designed by prominent colonial architect James Barnet and regarded as a major contribution to colonial public architecture (Johnson 1999:195). It is flanked by two identical buildings, Barnet's post office building and telegraph office building (1877) (Johnson 1999:196).

2 The defendants in the first trial faced the following charges: Albert 'Sonny' Bates, charged with riotous assembly, malicious wounding (Constable Anthony John Bordin), assault occasioning actual bodily harm (Detective Sergeant Vaughan George Reid) and malicious injury to property; Arthur Murray was charged

with riotous assembly and assault inflicting grievous bodily harm (Constable TJ McGregor); and Arthur Orcher charged with riotous assembly and malicious injury to property.

3 The appeal to the New South Wales Court of Criminal Appeal was based upon 'Justice Nash's bias to the police role at trial, and against the sentence for not accounting for the death in custody as a mitigating factor' (Anthony 2009:11). The appeal was upheld, with Chief Justice Hunt the most critical of Judge Nash, who, he said, in summing up, gave an 'unhelpful review of the evidence' that 'weighed unfairly against the accused' (Curtin cited in Anthony 2009:11).

4 The descriptions in the trial of 'riot' suggested to us that it was a fracas or melee, a noisy, disorderly, confused and violent disturbance rather than riotous assembly, which implies deliberation and organisation.

5 'Riotous assembly' had been applied variously to an 'election riot in the village of Great Marlow' (1881), 'a crowd ransacking a grocer's shop and dwelling and setting it on fire' (1839), 'bare knuckle prize fights' (1882) and 'a mob attending a theatre for the purpose of interrupting the performance' (1809) (Purves 1992:19). For Purves (1992:19), in 'perhaps the most poignant case . . . an outspoken Methodist minister [who] . . . was on trial for his part in "a great riot, rout, disturbance, tumult an tumultuous assembly": the minister had "urged the torchlight rally of 3000 to fight for their rights", ie, "calling for better wages and working conditions, reform of the Poor law, universal suffrage and a secret ballot at parliamentary elections"'.

6 Commissioner Wootten (1991b:160) used quotations when referring to the incident as a riot and more generally used the word 'disturbance' in his report.

7 Many of the police were only partly attired in riot gear. Subsequently, the *Daily Liberal* (23 August 1987, p. 3) demanded that all police stations in the west be fully equipped with riot gear.

8 On 25 April 1915 Australian and New Zealand troops landed on the shores of Gallipoli, in what is now modern Turkey, beginning Australia's major involvement in World War One. The battles on Gallipoli gave focus and substance to an Australian nationalist imagination and Anzac Day became the most important commemorative ritual of Australian nationalism.

9 Commissioner Wootten (1991b:125–6) observed the following with regard to Lloyd Boney's death:

> The difficulties of police investigating police are numerous and are illustrated by the situation that developed when investigators came to Brewarrina. Far from retaining a remote and detached attitude from the police whose conduct was investigated they socialized with them. Constable Bordin remembered drinking with Inspector Peter, Inspector McGarrigle and Constable Bilton. The fact that he could not remember just what the occasion was — it could have been at a barbeque for the visiting police at the station or it could have been at one of the clubs — shows how normal it seemed that there should be solidarity between investigators and investigated within the police force.

10 Dorn stated that although he did not confiscate the rifles, he told them to put the rifles away as he was leaving.

11 One of Ernst's informants, when commenting on 'Mates, wives and children' (Ernst 1989), specifically told him that he had not given enough of the Australian version of mateship and that it 'all starts in war, where you've really got mates'.

12   The last allusion refers to General H Norman Schwarzkopf, the United States Army Commander-in-Chief of the United States Central Command, who led all coalition forces in the Persian Gulf War in 1990.

13   The CCA judgment 'closed the book on the offence of common law riot in NSW' (Purves 1992:19). Amendments to the *Crimes Act 1900* (NSW) made the charge of riotous assembly redundant and reduced the maximum penalty from life imprisonment to ten years (see Purves 1992:20).

Chapter 6

1   Peterson (1985, 1989) has published an analysis of a sample of 291 postcards in which he has categorised as romantic or realistic (documentary). His classifications neutralise the settler colonial politics involved in such representations.

2   In the 1992 Mabo decision, the Australian High Court ruled that Indigenous Australians could hold native title rights in accordance with British common law.

3   This cropped image had appeared in its original form in the *SMH*, 17 May 1985, p. 1, six days earlier than the displaced image.

Bibliography

Alexander, Elizabeth 1994 '"Can you be BLACK and look at this?": Reading the Rodney King video(s)' in The Black Public Culture Sphere Collective (eds), *The Black Public Sphere*, University of Chicago Press, pp. 81–98.

Allen, James 2000 *Without Sanctuary: Lynching photography in America*, Twin Palms, Santa Fe, NM.

Anderson, Elijah 1999 *Code of the Street*, WW Norton, New York.

Anthony, Thalia 2007 'Criminal justice and transgression on northern Australian cattle stations' in I Macfarlane and M Hannah (eds), *Transgressions: Critical Australian Indigenous histories*, ANU E Press, Acton, ACT, pp. 35–62 (Aboriginal History Series).

—— 2009 'Sentencing Indigenous resisters as if the death in custody never occurred' in M Segrave (ed.), *Australian & New Zealand Critical Criminology Conference 2009: Conference proceedings*, Monash University, Melbourne, pp. 6–17.

Babcock, Barbara 1978 *The Reversible World: Symbolic inversion in art and society*, Cornell University Press, Ithaca, NY.

Barsh, Russel 1988 'Indigenous peoples and the right to self-determination in international law' in B Hocking (ed.), *International Law and Aboriginal Human Rights*, The Law Book Company Limited, North Ryde, NSW.

Barthes, Roland 1984 *Camera Lucida*, Fontana, London.

Benjamin, Walter 1982 *Illuminations*, Fontana, Suffolk.

Bhabha, Homi 1984 'Of mimicry and men', *October* 28:128–33.

—— 1985 'Sly civility', *October* 34:71–80.

Blainey, Geoffrey 1993 'Drawing up a balance sheet of our history', *Quadrant* Jul–Aug:10–15.

—— 1997 'Black futures', *The Bulletin* April:21–3.

Blaser, Mario 2010 *Storytelling, Globalisation from the Chaco and Beyond*, Duke University Press, Durham.

Bond-Taylor, Sue 2005 'Political constructions of the anti-social community: Developing a cultural criminology', paper presented at *Housing Studies Association Autumn Conference*, 8–9 September.

Bonney, Roseanne 1989 *NSW Summary Offences Act 1988*, NSW Bureau of Crime Statistics and Research, Sydney.

Bourdieu, Pierre 1998 *Practical Reason: On the theory of action*, Stanford University Press, CA.

—— 2000 *Pascalian Meditations*, Polity Press, London.

—— and Abdelmalek Sayad 2004 'Colonial rule and cultural sabir', *Ethnography* 5:445–86.

Brennan, Sean, Brenda Gunn and George Williams 2004 *Treaty — What's sovereignty got to do with it?*, Gilbert + Tobin Centre of Public Law, University of New South Wales, Sydney (Issue Paper no. 2).

Brereton, Kurt 1981 'Post cards as intervention' in *Photo-Discourse: Critical thought & practice in photography*, Sydney College of Arts, Sydney, pp. 138–42.

Brett, Judith 2003 *Australian Liberals and the Moral Middle Class*, Cambridge University Press, Cambridge.

Brown, David 1991 'The state of the prisons in NSW under the Greiner government', *Journal for Social Justice Studies* 4:27–60.

Bruyneel, Kevin 2007 *The Third Space of Sovereignty: The postcolonial politics of US–Indigenous relations*, University of Minnesota Press, Minneapolis, MN.

Byrd, Jodi 2011 *The Transit of Empire: Indigenous critiques of colonialism*, University of Minnesota Press, Minneapolis, MN.

Carrington, Kerry 1990 'Aboriginal girls and juvenile justice' in B Morris and G Cowlishaw (eds), *Contemporary Race Relations in Australia: Journal for Social Justice Studies* 3 (special edition):1–17.

—— 1991 'The death of Mark Quayle: Normalising racial horror in country towns and hospitals' in K Carrington and B Morris (eds), *Politics, Prisons and Punishment: Journal for Social Justice Studies* 4 (special edition):161–88.

Chalk, Andrew 1991 'Land rights under New South Wales legislation', *Aboriginal Law Bulletin* 55:1–5.

Charles Perkins & Associates 1989 *NSW Land Rights Act 1983: Recommendations for change: Report to the NSW Government* (Perkins Report), Charles Perkins & Associates, Sydney.

Cowlishaw, Gillian 1988 *Black, White or Brindle: Race in rural Australia*, Cambridge University Press, Sydney.

—— 1990 'Where is racism?' in B Morris and G Cowlishaw (eds), *Contemporary Race Relations in Australia: Journal for Social Justice Studies* 3 (special edition):51–60.

—— 1991 'Inquiring into Aboriginal deaths in custody: The limits of a Royal Commission' in K Carrington and B Morris (eds), *Politics, Prisons and Punishment: Journal for Social Justice Studies* 4 (special edition):101–15.

—— 1994 'Policing the races', *Social Analysis* 36:71–92.

—— 2004 *Blackfellas, Whitefellas and the Hidden Injuries of Race*, Blackwell, Oxford.

Cunneen, Chris 1990a 'Aborigines and law and order regimes' in B Morris and G Cowlishaw (eds), *Contemporary Race Relations in Australia: Journal for Social Justice Studies* 3 (special edition):37–50.

—— 1990b *Aboriginal–Police Relations in Redfern: With special reference to the 'police raid' of 8 February 1990*, report commissioned by the National Inquiry into Racist Violence, Human Rights and Equal Opportunity Commission, Sydney.

—— 1992 'Policing and Aboriginal communities: Is the concept of over-policing useful?' in C Cunneen (ed.), *Aboriginal Perspectives on Criminal Justice*, Sydney University Institute of Criminology, Sydney (Monograph Series no. 1).

—— 2001 *Conflict, Politics and Crime: Aboriginal communities and the police*, Allen & Unwin, Crows Nest, NSW.

—— and Tom Robb 1987 *Criminal Justice in North-west New South Wales*, NSW Bureau of Crime Statistics and Research, Sydney.

—— Mark Findlay, Rob Lynch and Vernon Tupper 1989 *The Dynamics of Collective Conflict: Riots at the Bathurst bike races*, Law Book Company, Sydney.

Curthoys, Ann 2002 *Freedom Ride: A freedom rider remembers*, Allen & Unwin, Crows Nest, NSW.

Davis, Mike 1990 *City of Quartz*, Random House, London.

Devereaux, Leslie 1995 'Cultures, Disciplines, Cinemas' in L Devereaux and R Hillman (eds), *Fields of Vision: Essays in film studies, visual anthropology, and photography*, University of California Press, Berkeley, CA, pp. 329–39.

Dixson, Miriam 2000 *The Imaginary Australian: Anglo-Celts and identity*, University of New South Wales, Sydney.

Ernst, Thomas 1989 'Mates, wives and children: an explanation of concepts of relatedness in Australian culture' in J Marcus (ed.), *Writing Australian Culture: Social Analysis* 17 (special edition):110–18.

Farmer, Paul 2005 *Pathologies of Power: Health, human rights and the new war on the poor*, University of California, Berkeley.

Feldman, Allen 1994 'On cultural anesthesia: From Desert Storm to Rodney King', *American Ethnologist* 21(2):404–18.

—— 2004 'Memory theatres, virtual witnessing, and the trauma-aesthetic', *Biography* 27(1):163–202.

Foucault, Michel 1979 'Governmentality', *Ideology and Consciousness* 6:5–21.

—— 1980 *Power/Knowledge*, edited by C Gordon, Harvester Press, Sussex.

—— 1984 *The History of Sexuality*, Penguin, Harmondsworth.

—— 1987 *Discipline and Punish*, Penguin, Harmondsworth.

—— 1988 'Technologies of the self' in L Martin, H Gutman and P Hutton (eds), *Technologies of the Self: A seminar with Michel Foucault*, University of Massachusetts, Amherst.

Fraser, Nancy 2000 'Rethinking recognition', *New Left Review* 3(May, June):107–20.

—— and Linda Gordon 1994 'A genealogy of dependence: Tracing a keyword of the U.S. welfare state', *Signs* 19(2):309–36.

Garland, David 2001 *The Culture of Control: Crime and social order in contemporary society*, University of Chicago Press.

George, Nelson 2005 *Hip Hop America*, Penguin, Harmondsworth.

Gibson, Lorraine 2007 Articulating culture(s): Being black in Wilcannia, unpublished doctoral thesis, Macquarie University, Sydney.

—— 2010 'Making a life: Getting ahead and getting a living in Aboriginal New South Wales', *Oceania* 80:143–60.

Goodall, Heather 1990 'Policing in whose interests?', *Journal for Social Justice Studies* 3:19–34.

—— 1993 'Constructing a riot: Television news and Aborigines', *Media Information Australia* 68:70–7.

—— 1996 *From Invasion to Embassy: Land in Aboriginal politics in NSW from 1770 to 1972*, Black Books and Allen & Unwin, Sydney.

—— n.d. Constructing a 'riot': Television news and Aborigines, unpublished manuscript.

Greiner, Nick 1984 'Restoring the public interest', *Quadrant* May:59–63.

Gunstone, Andrew 2006 'The Howard government's approach to the policy of indigenous self-determination', *MAI Review* 1, <www.review.mai.ac.nz/index.php/MR/article/view/3/3> accessed 15 May 2013.

Hale, Charles 2006 *More than Indian: Racial ambivalence and neoliberal multiculturalism in Guatemala*, School of American Research Press, Santa Fe, NM.

Hall, Stuart 1979 'The great moving Right show', *Marxism Today* January:14–20.

—— 1980 *Drifting into a Law and Order Society*, Cobden Trust, London.

—— 1996 'For Allon White: Metaphors of transformation' in *Critical Dialogues in Cultural Studies*, D Morley and K Chen (eds), Routledge, London, pp.287–305.

—— 1998 'The spectacle of the other' in S Hall (ed.), *Representation: Cultural representations and signifying practices*, Sage Publications, London, pp.225–74.

—— Charles Critcher, Tony Jefferson, John Clarke and Brian Roberts 1978 *Policing the Crisis: Mugging the state and law and order*, MacMillan Press, London.

Hardy, Frank 1968 *The Unlucky Australians*, Nelson, Melbourne.

Hirst, John 2009 *Sense and Non-sense in Australian History*, Black Inc. Agenda, Melbourne.

Hogg, Russell 1991 'Policing and penality' in K Carrington and B Morris (eds), *Politics, Prisons and Punishment: Journal for Social Justice Studies* 4 (special edition):1–26.

Howard, Deirdre 2000 Re-centring whiteness: 'Practical' politics, moral conservatism, and the marginalisation of Indigenous rights in contemporary Australian society, unpublished doctoral thesis, University of Newcastle, NSW.

Howard, John 1997 'Australian Reconciliation Convention 1997: Opening address to the Australian Reconciliation Convention — Melbourne', Australasian Legal Information Institute: Indigenous Law Resources, <www.austlii.edu.au/au/other/IndigLRes/car/1997/4/pmspoken.html> accessed 15 May 2013.

Howard, Michael 2005 'Income and "expenditure": The big accounting–consulting firms and their pathways of promotion within the political and bureaucratic system', paper presented at Australian Political Studies Conference, Otago University, Dunedin, 27–30 September.

Johnson, Chris 1999 *Shaping Sydney: Public architecture and civic decorum*, Hale & Iremonger, Sydney.

Johnston, Elliott 1991 *Royal Commission into Aboriginal Deaths in Custody: National report volume 5*, Australian Government Publishing Service, Canberra, <www.austlii.edu.au/au/other/IndigLRes/rciadic/national/vol5/> accessed 19 April 2013.

Kapferer, Bruce 1988 *Legends of People: Myths of state*, Smithsonian Institution Press, Washington.

—— 2010 'In the event: Toward an anthropology of generic movements', *Social Analysis* 54(3):1–27.

—— and Barry Morris 2003 'The Australian society of the state: Egalitarian ideologies and new directions in exclusionary practice', *Social Analysis* 47(3):80–107.

—— and Barry Morris 2006 'Nationalism and neo-populism in Australia: Hansonism and the politics of the new Right in Australia' in A Gingrich and M Banks (eds), *Neo-nationalism in Europe and Beyond: perspectives from social anthropology*, Berghahn Books, Oxford, pp. 248–68.

Khoury, Peter 1996 Contested rationalities: Aboriginal organisations and the Australian state, unpublished doctoral thesis, University of New South Wales, Sydney.

Kristeva, Julia 1982 *The Powers of Horror: An essay on abjection*, Columbia University Press, New York.

Laffin, Martin 1995 'The public service' in M Laffin and M Painter (eds), *Reform and Reversal: Lessons from the coalition government in New South Wales, 1988–1995*, MacMillan Education, Melbourne, pp. 73–90.

—— and Martin Painter 1995 'Introduction' in M Laffin and M Painter (eds), *Reform and Reversal: Lessons from the coalition government in New South Wales, 1988–1995*, MacMillan Education, Melbourne, pp.1–21.

Lake, Marilyn 1992 'Mission impossible: How men gave birth to the Australian nation — nationalism, gender and other seminal acts', *Gender and History* 4(3):305–22.

Langton, Marcia 1993 'Rum, seduction and death: "Aboriginality" and alcohol', *Oceania* 63:195–206.

Lattas, Andrew 1986 'The aesthetics of terror and the personification of power: Public executions and cultural construction of class relations in colonial New South Wales, 1788–1830', *Social Analysis* 19:3–21.

Lawrence, Geoffrey 1987 *Capitalism and the Countryside: The rural crisis in Australia*, Pluto Press, Sydney.

—— 1996 *Social Change in Rural Australia*, Rural Social and Economic Research Centre, Central Queensland University, Rockhampton, Qld.

Leslie, Norman 1993 'Black and white: Photographic imagery and Aboriginality', *Australian Journal of Communication* 20(2):79–96.

Lohrey, Amanda 1982 'Gallipoli: Male innocence as a marketable commodity', *Island Magazine* 9–10:29–34.

Long, Jeremy 2000 'The Commonwealth Government and Aboriginal housing, 1968–81' in P Read (ed.), *Settlement: A history of Australian Indigenous housing,* Aboriginal Studies Press, Canberra, pp. 103–17.

Lyons, Gregory 1984 'Aboriginal Legal Services' in P Hanks and B Keon-Cohen (eds), *Aborigines and the Law,* Allen & Unwin, Sydney, pp.137–59.

MacDonald, Gaynor 2001 'Does "culture" have "history"? Thinking about continuity and change in central New South Wales', *Aboriginal History* 25:176–99.

McKenna, Mark 1997 *Different Perspectives on Black Armband History,* Australian Parliamentary Library, Canberra (Research Paper 5, 1997–1998).

Marcus, Julie 1991 'The detail of the law', *Journal of Social Justice Studies* 4: 117–32.

Miller, Jerome 1996 *Search and Destroy: African-American males in the criminal justice system,* Cambridge University Press, New York.

Morris, Barry 1989 *Domesticating Resistance: The Dhan-Gadi Aborigines and the State,* Berg, Oxford.

—— 1997 'Racism, egalitarianism and Aborigines' in G Cowlishaw and B Morris (eds), *Race Matters,* Aboriginal Studies Press, Canberra, pp. 161–76.

—— 2001 'Policing racial fantasy in the Far West', *Oceania* 71(3):242–62.

Muirhead, James 1989 *Australian Royal Commission into Aboriginal Deaths in Custody 1989: Interim report,* Government Printer, Sydney.

Mulvaney, John 1982 'Introduction: Walter Baldwin Spencer' in *The Aboriginal Photographs of Baldwin Spencer,* edited and annotated by G Walker, John Currey, O'Neil Publishers, South Yarra, Vic.

Murray, Charles 1984 *Losing Ground: American social policy 1950–1980,* Basic Books, New York.

Neilson, Brett and Ned Rossiter 2008 'Precarity as a political concept, or, Fordism as exception', *Theory, Culture and Society* 25:51–72.

NSW ADB (New South Wales Anti-Discrimination Board) 1982 *Report on the Study of Street Offences by Aborigines,* Government Printers, Sydney.

NSW Parliament (Legislative Assembly, Select Committee Upon Aborigines) 1980 *First Report from the Select Committee of the Legislative Assembly Upon Aborigines*, Government Printer, Sydney.

NSW Parliament (Legislative Assembly, Select Committee Upon Aborigines) 1981 *Second Report from the Select Committee of the Legislative Assembly Upon Aborigines*, Government Printers, Sydney.

NSW Police Department 1989 *Report of the Police Department for the Year Ended 30th June 1988*, Government Printer, NSW.

NSWALC (New South Wales Aboriginal Land Council) 1989 *Self Sufficiency, Not Dependency: Briefing papers*, The Council, Liverpool, NSW.

—— 1990 *A Response to the Perkins Report, by the NSW Aboriginal Land Councils, State Wide Conference — 7/8 April 1990*, NSWALC, Sydney.

O'Malley, Pat 1998 'Indigenous governance' in M Dean and B Hindess (eds), *Governing Australia: Studies in contemporary rationalities of governance*, Cambridge University Press, Cambridge, pp. 156–72.

OAA (Office of Aboriginal Affairs) 1985 *Accounting and Internal Control Manual for NSW Aboriginal Land Councils*, D West, Government Printer, Sydney.

—— 1989 *NSW Government Green Paper: New directions in Aboriginal affairs*, D West, Government Printer, Sydney.

One Nation (MCMXCI) 1991 directed by Christine Sammers, Australian Broadcasting Corporation, TV Documentary Department.

Pearson, Noel 2000 *Our Right to Take Responsibility*, Noel Pearson and Associates, Cairns, Qld.

Peterson, Nicolas 1985 'The popular image' in I Donaldson and T Donaldson (eds), *Seeing the First Australians*, Allen & Unwin, Sydney, pp. 164–80.

—— 1989 'A colonial image: Penetrating the reality of the message', *Australian Aboriginal Studies* 1989/2:59–62.

Petro, Patrice (ed.) 1995 *Fugitive Images: From photography to video*, Indiana University Press, Bloomington.

Pitty, Roderic 1994 'Brewarrina riot: The hidden history', *Aboriginal Law Bulletin* 3(70):9–11.

Poignant, Roslyn 1993 'The photographic witness?', *Continuum* 6(2): 178–206.

Postero, Nancy 2007 *Now We Are Citizens: Indigenous politics in postmulticultural Bolivia*, Stanford University Press, Stanford, CA.

Pratt, Mary L 1992 *Imperial Eyes: Travel writing and transculturation*, Routledge, London.

Pratt, Angela and Scott Bennett 2004–05 'The end of ATSIC and the future administration of Indigenous affairs', *Current Issues Brief* 4.

Premier's Department 1988 *New Directions in Aboriginal Affairs* (Zammit Report), D West, NSW Government Printer, Sydney (discussion paper).

Purves, W (Billy) 1992 'On common law riots in New South Wales, 1985–1992', *Bar News: The Journal of the NSW Bar Association* spring/summer:19–23.

Rabinowitz, Paula 1994 *They Must Be Represented: The politics of documentary*, Verso, London.

Ritter, David 2010 'The ideological foundations of arguments about native title', *Australian Journal of Political Science* 45(2):191–207.

Rose, Deborah Bird 1991 *Hidden Histories: Black stories from Victoria River Downs, Humbert River and Wave Hill Stations*, Aboriginal Studies Press, Canberra.

Rose, Nikolas 1999 *Powers of Freedom*, Cambridge University Press, Cambridge.

Ross, Russell T 1988 *The Labour Market Position of Aboriginal People in Non-metropolitan New South Wales*, Social Welfare Research Centre, University of New South Wales, Sydney (Discussion Paper no. 1).

Rouland, Norbert 1994 *Legal Anthropology*, translated by Philippe G Planel, Athlone Press, London.

Rowley, Charles Dunford 1973 *Outcasts in White Australia*, Penguin, Ringwood, Vic.

Roy, Arthur 1986 Aborigines in capitalist society: A focus on north west New South Wales, 1824–1985, unpublished doctoral thesis, Somerset University, England.

Ryan, Lyndall 1996 *The Tasmanian Aborigines*, Allen & Unwin, Sydney.

Sheridan, Susan 1995 *Along the Faultlines: Sex, race, and nation in Australian women's writing, 1880s–1930s*, Allen & Unwin, Sydney.

Sherington, Geoffrey 1995 'Education policy' in M Laffin and M Painter (eds), *Reform and Reversal: Lessons from the coalition government in New South Wales, 1988–1995*, MacMillan Education, Melbourne, pp.171–204.

Sherwin, Richard 1996 'Introduction: Picturing justice: Images of law & lawyers in the visual media', *University of San Francisco Law Review* 30(4):891–901.

Simon, Jonathan 1993 *Poor Discipline: Parole and the social control of the underclass, 1800–1900*, University of Chicago Press.

Smith, Bernard 1980 *The Spectre of Truganini*, Boyer Lectures, Australian Broadcasting Commission, Sydney.

Spencer, Baldwin and Francis J Gillen 1968[1899] *The Native Tribes of Central Australia*, Dover Publications, New York.

Stallybrass, Peter and Allon White 1995 *The Poetics and Politics of Transgression*, Cornell University Press, Ithaca, NY.

State Conference of Land Councils 1990 *A Response to the Perkins Report by NSW Aboriginal Land Councils, State Wide Conference, Bathurst — 7/8 April 1990*, NSWALC, Sydney.

Sutton, Peter 2009 *The Politics of Suffering: Indigenous Australia and the end of the liberal consensus*, Melbourne University Press.

Tagg, John 1995 'The pencil of history' in P Petro (ed.), *Fugitive Images: From photography to video*, Indiana University Press, Bloomington, pp. 285–303.

Taussig, Michael 1989 'Terror as usual', *Social Text* 23:3–20.

—— 1992 *The Nervous System*, Routledge, London.

Thompson, Grahame 2000 'Economic globalisation?' in D Held (ed.), *A Globalising World?: Culture, economics, politics*, Routledge, London, pp. 85–126.

Tonkinson, Robert and Michael Howard (eds) 1990 *Going it Alone?: Prospects for Aboriginal autonomy*, Aboriginal Studies Press, Canberra.

Tonry, Michael 1994 'Racial disproportion in US prisons', *British Journal of Criminology* 34:97–115.

—— (ed.) 2000 *The Handbook of Crime and Punishment*, Oxford University Press, Oxford.

United Nations 1997 'Indigenous people: Challenges facing the international community', United Nations Department of Public Information, <www.un.org/rights/50/people.htm> accessed 16 May 2013.

Veracini, Lorenzo 2010 *Settler Colonialism: A theoretical overview*, Palgrave Macmillan, Basingstoke.

Vinson, Tony 1991 'Prison reform: Backwards or forward thirty years', *Journal for Social Justice Studies* 4:81–6.

von Sturmer, John 1982 'Aborigines in the uranium industry: Towards self-management in the Alligator River region?' in R Berndt (ed.), *Aboriginal Sites, Rights and Resource Development*, University of Western Australia Press, Perth, pp. 69–116.

Wacquant, Loïc 2012 'Three steps to a historical anthropology of actually existing neoliberalism', *Social Anthropology* 20(1):66–79.

Weaver, Sally 1985 'Political representivity and indigenous minorities in Canada and Australia' in N Dyck (ed.), *Indigenous People and the Nation State*, ISER, St Johns, pp. 113–50.

Wilkie, Meredith 1985 *Aboriginal Land Rights in NSW*, Alternative Publishing Cooperative Limited in association with Black Books, Chippendale, NSW.

Willis, Anne-Marie 1993 *Illusions of Identity*, Hale & Iremonger, Sydney.

Wilson, Eric 1988 *Aspects of Aboriginal Interaction with Criminal Justice System in Wilcannia and the Far West Region*, submission to Royal Commission into Aboriginal Deaths in Custody, Western Aboriginal Legal Service.

Wilson, James Q 1975 *Thinking about Crime*, Basic Books, New York.

Wolfe, Patrick 1999 *Settler Colonialism and the Transformation of Anthropology*, Cassell, London.

Wong, Allison 2008 *Build Communities, Not Prisons: The effects of the over-representation of Indigenous people in the criminal justice system*, UTS Communications, Sydney.

Wood, Marilyn 2001 'Journey to "Forked Mountain"', *Aboriginal History* 25:200–15.

Wootten, John Halden (Hal) 1974 'Aboriginal Legal Services' in G Nettheim (ed), *Aborigines, Human Rights and the Law*, Australia and NZ Book Co., Sydney, pp.59–67.

Wootten, Hal 1991a *Regional Report of the Inquiry in New South Wales, Victoria and Tasmania* (Royal Commission Into Aboriginal Deaths In Custody), Australian Government Publishing Service, Canberra.

—— 1991b *Report of the Inquiry into the Death of Lloyd James Boney* (Royal Commission Into Aboriginal Deaths In Custody), Australian Government Publishing Service, Canberra.

—— 1991c *Report of the Inquiry into the Death of Mark Anthony Quayle* (Royal Commission Into Aboriginal Deaths In Custody), Australian Government Publishing Service, Canberra.

—— 1991d *Report of the Inquiry into the Death of David John Gundy* (Royal Commission Into Aboriginal Deaths In Custody), Australian Government Publishing Service, Canberra.

Yabsley, Michael 1991 'Prison reform: Backwards or forward thirty years', *Journal for Social Justice Studies* 4:73–80.

Zammit, Paul 1990 'NSW government reaches historic agreement with the NSW Land Council', Premier of New South Wales, 6 September (media release).

Zdenkowski, George 1995 'Punishment policy and politics' in M Laffin and M Painter (eds), *Reform and Reversal: Lessons from the coalition government in New South Wales, 1988–1995*, MacMillan Education, Melbourne, pp.220–36.

Zizek, Slavoj 2008 *Violence: Six sideways reflections*, Profile Books, London.

Index